Behavior Modification

Principles and Clinical Applications

Behavior Modification

Principles and Clinical Applications

BY 7 AUTHORS

EDITED BY

W. Stewart Agras, M.D.

*Professor and Chairman, Department of Psychiatry,
University of Mississippi School of Medicine,
Jackson*

LITTLE, BROWN AND COMPANY
BOSTON

Library of Congress catalog card No. 78-189720

ISBN 0-316-02030

4276-18G1-M06/72

Published in Great Britain
by Churchill/Livingstone, Edinburgh and London

Printed in the United States of America

Contributing Authors

W. STEWART AGRAS, M.D.
*Professor and Chairman, Department of Psychiatry,
University of Mississippi School of Medicine,
Jackson*

TEODORO AYLLON, Ph.D.
*Professor of Psychology, Georgia State University,
Atlanta*

DAVID H. BARLOW, Ph.D.
*Assistant Professor of Psychiatry, University of
Mississippi School of Medicine, Jackson*

JOHN PAUL BRADY, M.D.
*Professor of Psychiatry, The University of Pennsylvania
School of Medicine; Hospital of University
of Pennsylvania, Philadelphia*

HAROLD LEITENBERG, Ph.D.
*Associate Professor of Psychology and Psychiatry,
Department of Psychology, University of
Vermont, Burlington*

ISAAC M. MARKS, M.D.
*Senior Lecturer, Institute of Psychiatry (University of
London); Consultant Psychiatrist, Maudsley
Hospital, London, England*

MICHAEL D. ROBERTS, M.A.
*Research Associate, Laboratory for Applied Behavior
Analysis, Department of Psychology, Georgia State
University, Atlanta*

v

Preface

This book is written for the clinician interested in the behavioral therapies, to provide an overview of findings from the behavioral sciences that have application to clinical problems and also to provide selected descriptions of behavior therapy techniques. A short account of these therapies is given in the editor's introductions to each chapter, together with the pages referred to therein. These introductions omit much of the experimental and theoretic material, concentrating on the therapeutic techniques, their indications, and a brief review of their efficacy. Finally, the annotated therapeutic index serves to recommend therapeutic approaches for particular clinical problems.

The contributing authors of this volume acknowledge the help of colleagues and funding agencies in the preparation of this book and of journal editors who have allowed reproduction of figures originally published elsewhere. The preparation of Chapter 2 was aided by a grant from the National Institutes of Mental Health, MH13651, which also supported some of the research reported in Chapters 1 and 2. Drs. Ayllon and Roberts wish to thank Mrs. Nancy Roberts for her indefatigable efforts in the completion of the manuscript for Chapter 3. Dr. Barlow thanks Mrs. Anita Batman for translating the Russian journal articles cited in Chapter 4. The editor of the *British Medical Journal* kindly allowed reproduction of Figure 2 from Volume 2, p. 722, 1969; while the editor of the *British Journal of Psychiatry* gave permission to reproduce Figure 3 from Volume 119, p. 353, 1971, an article by I. M. Marks, J. C. Boulougouris, and P. Marset. Dr. Marks thanks Drs. M. Crowe, S. Rachman, and R. Stern for valuable comments on the manuscript of Chapter 6. The annotated therapeutic index was prepared with the very great assistance of Joy Reynolds, M.A. Finally, I am grateful to Miss Sue Noblin who organized and typed the final manuscript for the book.

W. S. A.

Contents

CONTRIBUTING AUTHORS   *v*

PREFACE   *vii*

1. THE BEHAVIORAL THERAPIES: UNDERLYING
   PRINCIPLES AND PROCEDURES   *1*
   W. Stewart Agras

2. POSITIVE REINFORCEMENT AND EXTINCTION
   PROCEDURES   *27*
   Harold Leitenberg

3. THE TOKEN ECONOMY: NOW   *59*
   Teodoro Ayllon and Michael D. Roberts

4. AVERSIVE PROCEDURES   *87*
   David H. Barlow

5. SYSTEMATIC DESENSITIZATION   *127*
   John Paul Brady

6. FLOODING (IMPLOSION) AND ALLIED TREATMENTS   *151*
   Isaac M. Marks

   ANNOTATED THERAPEUTIC INDEX   *215*

   SUBJECT INDEX   *223*

Behavior Modification

Principles and Clinical Applications

1

The Behavioral Therapies: Underlying Principles and Procedures

W. STEWART AGRAS

EDITOR'S INTRODUCTION

The clinician interested in using a new therapeutic procedure requires an adequate description of the technique, an elucidation of underlying principles so that he may use the therapy flexibly, and an evaluation of its effectiveness. The following behavioral therapies are described in this volume: shaping, extinction, the token economy, aversive procedures including covert sensitization, systematic desensitization, and flooding, which includes implosion, prolonged exposure, paradoxical intention, and response prevention. Other techniques such as modeling are referred to in several chapters.

The major principles underlying the behavioral therapies are described on pages 13–23 and are amplified in each chapter, where their specific relationship to a therapeutic procedure is discussed. An important aspect of the behavioral therapies is that they provide a medium for the application of knowledge from the experimental behavioral sciences to the clinic. This has generated much applied research and promises a more adequate scientific basis for psychotherapeutics than has existed in the past.

The contributors to this volume have reviewed much of this research to shed light on the mode of action and efficacy of the be-

havioral therapies. Two main lines of research exist. The first is the single case experiment in which subjects are used as their own control. In such studies the relatively immediate effect of a particular therapeutic variable can be assessed. Such experiments can be used to sort out effective from ineffective procedures and to discover how a therapy works. Effective procedures can then be embodied in a therapeutic program which must then be tested, either against no treatment or a standard therapy. Overall, more is known about the immediate effect of the behavior therapies than their long-term effect, although enough is known to generate some optimism about these new therapies.

W.S.A.

In this chapter we will review the development of the behavioral therapies, examine what they consist of, and define the principles and procedures of the experimental behavioral sciences underlying their development.

The rise of behavior therapy has stimulated conflict and research. Early developers often attacked the traditional psychotherapies, producing a strong defensive reaction and a rejection and criticism of behavior therapy. Such antagonism is unfortunate, since it diverts attention from the contribution that behavioral sciences such as experimental psychology and social psychology can make to practice and research in psychotherapy. These sciences contribute experimental methods and new therapeutic possibilities that may strengthen the efficacy of traditional psychotherapies and lead to the development of new forms of therapy more effective than present techniques. This should be welcomed by therapists of all persuasions, none of whom can be satisfied with the results of present-day techniques.

Naturally the viewpoint of the experimental behavioral scientist differs from that of the clinician. Overt measurable behavior is emphasized while thinking and feeling are de-emphasized, a point of view often opposite to that of the clinician. Yet this new emphasis may shed light upon aspects of behavior that have been neglected. Similarly, different concepts are used by the behavioral scientist who emphasizes the environmental antecedents or consequences of behavior rather than explanatory internal concepts such as defense mechanisms or ego structure. Again, the fresh viewpoint may stimulate new thinking and creative insight.

EARLY DEVELOPMENT

Most historians of the behavioral therapies point to scattered empiric use of the concepts and techniques of behavior modification in the past. In the nineteenth century, the era of moral therapy, rehabilitation toward normal behavior was stressed. Thus Dr. John S. Butler is described [7] as relying on positive attention to build up desired behaviors; if a patient tore at her clothing, he provided her with a new dress and took every opportunity to compliment her on her appearance. A nice example of the use of social reinforcement! Later Simmel [37] used procedures such as banishing patients to their rooms if they showed undesirable behaviors, a procedure now more technically known as "time out" from reinforcement. Such techniques made no impact on the field of psychotherapy, due partly to the demise of moral therapy but mainly to the lack of an experimental or theoretic framework.

Psychotherapeutic techniques in fact developed as an extension of the case history method of data collection and analysis. This approach is shared with other medical specialties and has shaped the thinking and practice of psychiatry and clinical psychology. To an internist the patient complains of a symptom which is viewed as secondary to organic dysfunction. To a psychiatrist the patient or his relatives complain of a change in behavior (although this may be phrased as change in feeling or thinking). Sharing the viewpoint of medicine, psychiatry came to view abnormal behavior as being secondary to internal changes.

This viewpoint was incorporated in the most important theoretic system to predate the behavioral approach, namely, psychoanalysis. However, many notions about behavior are shared by the two schools of thought, including the view that the history of an individual is important in understanding present behavior, that maladaptive behavior is largely acquired through learning in a social environment, and that the basic scientific aim is to understand the factors that influence abnormal behavior so as to modify it more effectively. Freud developed psychoanalysis without reference to psychology because psychology, in its infancy at the turn of the century, was unable to investigate complex human behavior. The first attempts to integrate the developing knowledge about learning with psychoanalytic theory consisted of translating one set of concepts into the other [15]. Later translations were more sophisticated [11] but did not change the research tactics or therapeutic procedures of psychiatry or clinical psychology.

More important were the clinical applications of behavioral techniques based on Pavlov's work. Watson [43] experimentally produced a phobia in an infant by pairing a noxious stimulus (noise) with a neutral stimulus (a white rat). After a few pairings crying and avoidance of the rat occurred, as well as avoidance of other animals such as a rabbit and materials such as fur and, to a lesser extent, cotton and wool. Soon afterward Jones [20] described a number of direct techniques that eliminated children's fears; these included gradual approach to the feared object and social imitation in which a child was exposed to children not afraid of the same object as himself and who modeled normal approach behavior.

More therapeutic applications were those of Kantorovich [21] in alcoholism and Max [29] in the case of a homosexual. Both paired electric shock with the deviant behavior. However, these isolated usages made little or no difference to treatment methods. Indeed, the only treatment based on learning theory that had gained some acceptance by the midforties was aversion therapy for the treatment of alcoholism [25] in which the taste and smell of alcohol was paired with nausea induced by the injection of apomorphine.

LATER DEVELOPMENT

Recent developments in the behavioral therapies derive from two sources: dissatisfaction with the results of the verbal psychotherapies and the growth of alternative approaches to treatment, particularly Wolpe's systematic desensitization [44], and extensions of Skinner's experimental work [38] from the laboratory to the clinic.

Dissatisfaction with the results of verbal psychotherapy grew slowly, since there was little research on the efficacy of such therapy. Eysenck's review articles [12, 13] highlighting this problem produced an unfortunate furor, and his later writings on behavior therapy were interpreted as being antagonistic to psychoanalytic psychotherapy, placing proponents of such therapies in a defensive position. Nevertheless, Eysenck's position that psychotherapy had not been shown to be more effective than no treatment was solidly based. His critics identified many of the methodologic difficulties in evaluating the effects of psychotherapy but could not rebut his main conclusion. Later Bergin [6], in a reanalysis of the data of controlled outcome studies of psychotherapy, found that patients treated with psychotherapy show both negative and positive change when compared to untreated control subjects who show slight improvement and cluster about the mean. This evidence suggests that behavioral change does occur during psychotherapy but is masked in group studies where the positive and negative effects cancel out.

The realization that verbal psychotherapy has uncertain effects left an opening for new forms of therapy. One such form was described by Wolpe in his book *Psychotherapy by Reciprocal Inhibition* [44]. Wolpe, an enthusiastic developer of new ideas, based this therapy on observations derived from animal experiments in which he successfully used feeding to reduce learned avoidance behavior in cats who were gradually led to approach a feared situation. He hypothesized that "if a response incompatible with anxiety can be made to occur in the presence of anxiety evoking stimuli, it will weaken the bond between the stimuli and the anxiety response." Instead of using feeding to inhibit anxiety in humans, Wolpe found that relaxation was seemingly as good Thus, patients with neurotic avoidance behavior imagine a series of gradually more fear arousing scenes while deeply relaxed. Supposedly anxiety will be inhibited by relaxation as the patient progressively is able to approach the object of his fear, first in imagination and then in reality.

The second class of new therapies derives from B. F. Skinner's [38] experimental analysis of behavior. Skinner and his associates were able to gain precise control of certain aspects of animal behavior in the laboratory by varying the consequences of the animals' behavior. One of the first applications to the clinic was that of Fuller [17], who shaped a simple arm-raising response in a "vegetive idiot" by making a sugar-milk solution contingent on successively nearer approximations of this behavior. Later Lindsley [26] used the techniques of operant conditioning to investigate the behavior of schizophrenics, following which a rapid expansion to various kinds of behaviors in children and adults occurred (see Chapters 2, 3, and 4).

Since then a number of other techniques such as implosive therapy, flooding, and paradoxical intention have been included within the behavior therapies, because they either are based on procedures derived from experimental psychology or aimed at direct behavior change. At this point it can be seen that a number of forces have influenced the development of behavior therapy and that some way of defining the field and differentiating the approach from the verbal psychotherapies is necessary.

DEFINITION

There are two ways to define the behavioral therapies. One is to list the therapeutic procedures which purport to be derived from experiments in learning. Such a list includes:

1. Systematic desensitization
2. Shaping by positive reinforcement including token economies

3. Aversive therapies
   a. Punishment techniques
   b. Escape and avoidance conditioning
   c. Classical conditioning
   d. Covert sensitization
4. Implosion-flooding
5. Modeling
6. Paradoxical intent

This technique-oriented approach has the disadvantage of making behavior therapy a "school" of psychotherapy in parallel with but divorced from other schools of therapy.

An alternative is to use the techniques of the behavioral sciences to tease out the principles underlying therapeutic behavior change. In the beginning it would seem wise to determine the efficacy of variables known to affect normal behavior. Later, discoveries unique to the modification of deviant behavior will doubtless be made. As effective variables are identified, they may be combined into therapeutic procedures testable in controlled outcome studies. Unfortunately, the behavioral sciences are not advanced enough to allow a comprehensive compilation of the variables that cause behavior change. For the time being, then, it is necessary to blend these two approaches, moving from therapeutic technique to experiments analyzing the effective ingredients of such techniques, and from variables which affect behavior to new therapies.

RELATIONSHIP TO PSYCHOANALYTIC PSYCHOTHERAPY

As noted earlier, psychoanalysis, following the theories of medicine, hypothesized that internal events explain disturbed behavior. Constructs such as ego, id, and superego, and hypothetical energy such as libido are used in a series of somewhat loosely arranged hypotheses to explain behavior. The experimental behavioral sciences, on the other hand, consider behavior to be maintained by environmental events. Skinner [39] objects to the use of inner constructs to explain behavior on the ground that such constructs can be misleading. Thus, while a functional analysis of behavior is interested in the direct effect of punishment on behavior, a mental psychology views punishment as inducing anxiety which in turn causes behavioral change. The danger in such a formula is that there is a tendency to view anxiety as causing the behavior change, i.e., a symptom, and forget to specify what caused the anxiety in the first place. The more complex the internal hypotheses, the more likely is this to happen. Skinner therefore argues for the simpler approach in which the environmental factors prompting and maintaining abnormal behavior are defined.

Psychoanalytic psychotherapies usually assume that the following factors are essential to change symptoms: emotional and intellectual understanding or insight, resolution of the conflict underlying the symptom, and the use of transference behavior to achieve the first two aims. These assumptions have been essentially untested; however, they derive from psychoanalytic observations and hypotheses. The aims of psychoanalytic therapy according to Knight [22] are:

1. Disappearance of presenting symptoms.
2. Real improvement of mental functioning, e.g.,
   a. The acquisition of insight, intellectual and emotional, into the childhood sources of conflict, the part played by precipitating and other reality factors, and the methods of defense against anxiety that have produced the type of personality and the specific character of the morbid process.
   b. Development of tolerance, without anxiety, of the instinctual drives.
3. Improved reality adjustment, e.g.,
   a. More consistent and loyal interpersonal relationships with well-chosen objects.
   b. Free functioning of abilities in productive work.

The main drawback to this list is that with the exception of change in symptoms, most of the aims are unmeasurable. Particularly difficult are aims such as development of tolerance of instinctual drives, which are based on hypotheses concerning inner mental events.

The behavioral therapies, on the other hand, assume that deviant behavior is maintained by its consequences. Thus to change behavior it is necessary to change these consequences so that deviant behavior will disappear, and to arrange an environment in which appropriate new behavior can be learned. The aims of behavior therapy, therefore, are to:

1. Eliminate deviant behavior (symptoms) directly, either in the life situation in which it occurs or within a specially designed artificial situation.
2. Build up desired behaviors in small progressive steps in a specially designed program.

EXAMPLE OF PROCEDURE

A simple example of the differences in procedure between the psychoanalytic psychotherapies and a behavioral therapy is illustrated by a case of agoraphobia in a married woman aged 23 years. She had not been able to leave her home alone for over a year and had associated fears of crowds, choking, and dying. Her past history revealed that she had had a brief episode of a fear of choking and dying in childhood. At that time her mother was in hospital having a thyroid operation, and the patient who was "very close to her" recalled being afraid that her mother might die. Her agoraphobia started shortly after marriage and progressively worsened.

Psychoanalytically oriented treatment would aim at elucidating the conflicts underlying her symptom, using verbal interchange and the transference relationship to enable the patient to gain insight into her problem. An initial hypothesis might be that this patient was overdependent upon her mother and that separation through marriage replicated the frightening situation in childhood when mother deserted her and was in danger of dying. Further hypotheses might involve exploration of ambivalent feelings and fantasies toward her parents and her husband. Change in symptoms would be expected to occur as insight developed and was reflected in changes in interpersonal relationships and in the therapeutic transference.

From a behavioral viewpoint the behavior to be changed is that of not being able to leave home alone, which was the patient's presenting problem and which she wished to change. Several approaches are possible. One might be to identify factors in her environment which maintain her deviant behavior, such as the attention given the patient by her mother and husband for not leaving home. One or other of them was always with her. Changing this might lead to a reduction in her phobic behavior.

The approach decided on, however, was to teach the patient to leave a safe situation (in this case, hospital) by herself. As a first step an objective measure of agoraphobia was devised. Since the central symptomatic behavior was the patient's difficulty in leaving a dependent situation, distance walked from the hospital alone was used as a measure. A course was laid out from the hospital to downtown, and landmarks were agreed upon by patient and staff at about 25-yard intervals for over a mile. The patient was asked to stay on the course and to note the point at which she turned back. Two 30-minute treatment sessions were held each day. At the end of each attempted walk the patient reported how far she had gone. Since much of the course was observable, checks were made that confirmed the accuracy of the patient's report.

The second step was to determine her initial level of behavior by having her attempt to walk alone over the course for a few sessions, following which treatment was begun. This simply consisted of praising the patient enthusiastically on each trial that she met the criterion for reinforcement. This was determined as follows: if the patient was praised for walking 100 yards alone on one trial and then walked 120 yards on the next, the criterion for reinforcement became 110 yards, i.e., the mean value between the previous criterion and the next trial in excess of it. The patient now had to meet or exceed 110 yards to receive praise.

As can be seen in Figure 1, the patient was able to walk further alone each session during reinforced practice in the first phase. Although this is not essential clinically, it is useful to test whether the treatment being used is responsible for the behavioral change. Thus, for the next few days the therapist no longer praised her for improvements in performance. After a brief spurt her performance declined, and only picked up again following further reinforcement in the final phase. At this point the patient was able to walk downtown alone, and she was then encouraged to walk elsewhere which she found she could do. In addition, her associated fears of crowds, choking, and dying had also vanished. Follow-up 2 years later showed her to be symptom free and also showed that her family life had improved considerably, probably as a result of losing her incapacitating phobic behavior.

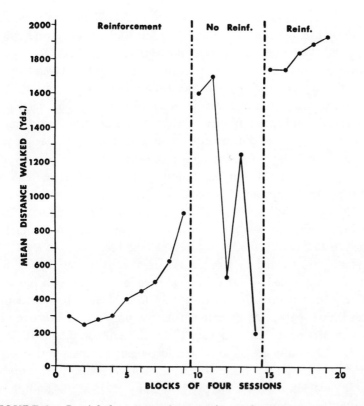

FIGURE 1. *Partial data from the experimental treatment of an agoraphobic patient, showing the effect of introducing, removing, and reintroducing praise given contingent on walking alone. That reinforcement was responsible for improved performance is demonstrated by worsening in the middle phase when it was withdrawn.*

COMPARISON OF BEHAVIORAL AND INSIGHT-ORIENTED THERAPIES

The major difference, then, between insight-oriented therapy and the behavioral therapies is that the former first changes attitudes and feelings as expressed in a verbal interchange, expecting life behavior to change later, while the latter first changes behavior, expecting that attitudes and feelings will follow. Little experimental

work has been done on which is the most effective approach to behavior change, or which combination of attitude, insight, and emotional and behavioral change is most effective.

However, some evidence suggests that the insight and behavioral
psychotherapies do not differ in practice as much as appears on the
surface. In both types of therapy a relationship exists between patient and therapist, the quality of which has been shown in certain
contexts to affect the outcome of therapy. In both, therapeutic instructions and suggestion that improvement will occur are given.
Frank [14] has shown that persuasion is an effective ingredient in
verbal psychotherapy, while recent work [2, 23, 35] suggests that the
same holds true for behavior therapies. Positive reinforcement has
also been found to occur within a verbal psychotherapy, namely,
Rogerian therapy. Truax [41] analyzed tape recordings of a single
long-term case treated by Rogers. He unexpectedly found that the
therapist responded differentially to five of the nine behaviors
studied and that the rate of emission of four of these behaviors increased during therapy, demonstrating the presence of selective social reinforcement. This appears to be the only study which has
looked at the influence of social reinforcement within a verbal psychotherapy, although a number of authors have examined this question in analogues of verbal psychotherapy [42], again finding a
definite effect of contingent social stimuli.

Finally, a quotation from Freud's collected papers [16] in which
he is discussing the psychoanalytic treatment of agoraphobia suggests that insight is not enough and that the therapist must pay attention to direct behavioral change. "One can hardly ever master a
phobia if one waits till the patient lets the analysis influence him to
give it up. . . . One succeeds only when one can induce them . . .
to go about alone and to struggle with their anxiety while they
make the attempt." Similarly, Terhune [40], in his description of
an apparently successful form of psychotherapy, considers that direct
approach to the feared object or situation in reality is of great importance and benefit. Undoubtedly, both Freud and Terhune paid
attention to and praised their patients' progress.

If there are procedures common to the verbal and behavioral psychotherapies, then the scientific problem becomes the identification

of those that improve the patient's condition. Behavioral science research has already led to the discovery of a number of variables that alter deviant behavior. Such variables or procedures are based first on principles of learning that have been elucidated by experimental psychology, and second on social and cognitive variables. Some of these will be described in the next section. Although the coverage will not be complete, it will form an adequate introduction to the subsequent chapters where the application of the principles in the form of the behavioral therapies will be described.

PRINCIPLES AND PROCEDURES DERIVED FROM EXPERIMENTAL PSYCHOLOGY

Two main learning paradigms have been formulated by experimental psychology—respondent and operant conditioning.

Respondent Conditioning

Respondent conditioning, or learning based on classical conditioning, is important because it deals with autonomic responses that often form part of neurotic behavior. The basic notions of the conditional reflex are familiar enough; certain inborn responses are regularly elicited by certain stimuli. For example, food in the mouth (unconditional stimulus) induces salivation (unconditional response). If another stimulus is paired with the presentation of food, e.g., a buzzer (conditional stimulus), it will, after a number of pairings, come to elicit salivation (conditional response). Similarly, a rapid heart rate initially in response to a painful stimulus may subsequently be induced by a tone.

STIMULUS GENERALIZATION. It seems possible that various kinds of environmental stimuli initially paired with frightening events could come to elicit a rapid heart rate or other visceral responses characteristic of an anxiety reaction. Moreover, in humans capable of symbol formation words can become conditional stimuli and may elicit the same responses. Thus, punishment by overly strict parents might evoke a cardiac response in a child, while associated stimuli such as the sights or sounds of quarreling, authority figures, or words with aggressive connotations may later elicit the same response. This phenomenon is known as stimulus generalization; the further the stimulus is removed from the original conditioned reflex, the less the autonomic response.

EXTINCTION. Extinction of a conditional response occurs if the conditional stimulus is presented a number of times without being followed by the unconditional stimulus. After an interval of time, presentation of the conditional stimulus will once more elicit the conditional response in a weaker form, a phenomenon known as spontaneous recovery. Thus, repeated exposure to a fear-arousing stimulus either in reality or in imagination would lead to a decline in heart rate.

While extinction is one example of the therapeutic use of classical conditioning techniques, others, such as conditioning an aversive response, have been used more frequently. Thus, apomorphine, which elicits nausea, has been paired with the smell and taste of alcohol; approach to alcohol then elicits nausea and avoidance behavior. Similar notions led Mowrer [32] to propose the "bell and pad" method of treating enuresis, which has been shown to be a successful approach to this difficult problem if used correctly.

Although the principles of classical conditioning are useful in dealing with the autonomic aspects of neurotic behavior and in certain specific behavior therapies, it is clear that much human behavior is not reflex in character. Human behavior is goal directed, rather than being simply elicited by environmental stimuli. For this type of behavior, generally regarded as voluntary, the work of B. F. Skinner is relevant.

Operant Conditioning

The term *operant* derives from the fact that certain behaviors "operate" on the environment to produce consequences. These consequences, often called reward and punishment, in turn affect behavior and are usually grouped into three types; namely, positive reinforcers, negative reinforcers, and neutral events.

POSITIVE REINFORCERS. An event is considered to be a positive reinforcer if the behavior that precedes it is found to have an increased probability of occurring. Many events positively reinforce human behavior, although it is important to remember that what is positively reinforcing for one person may not be for another. Food, water, sexual activity, and warmth are all positive reinforcers. Social attention, praise, grades, and money are also reinforcers, and many others have been described in clinical studies, such as candies, cigarettes, treats of various kinds, and even access to a psychotherapist. Indeed anything that an individual engages in with any regularity can be used as a positive reinforcer.

NEGATIVE REINFORCERS. These reinforcers are usually defined in a slightly different way; namely, that when removed, it is observed that the behavior that preceded them tends to increase in probability of occurrence. Generally, painful stimuli such as excessive heat, blows, electric shock, noise, and social criticism are negative reinforcers.

Given the observed relationships between behavior and environmental events of various types, it obviously becomes possible to change behavior in a number of ways. This process of making environmental events contingent on behavior is known as operant conditioning, which includes procedures such as shaping, extinction, and aversive control.

SHAPING. Shaping has clear relevance for therapeutic behavior change since it involves building up desired behavior by applying selective positive reinforcement. It is necessary that the subject exhibit some initial behavior which is then built up by reinforcing closer and closer approximations to the desired final response. This is achieved by waiting for or by prompting the first response and immediately following it with positive reinforcement. The response probability is thereby increased and is also likely to overshoot

—that is, to come nearer the final desired behavior due to variations in the amplitude of response. By reinforcing sufficiently often to maintain a suitable response rate, and by increasing the criterion for reinforcement, the desired behavior is slowly built up. (This technique is described in detail in Chapter 2 in the section on the procedure of positive reinforcement.) During shaping, reinforcement is given for most responses meeting the slowly changing criterion. Once established, the frequency of reinforcement is changed to one that is sufficient to maintain behavior of the desired strength.

EXTINCTION. While desirable behavior can be encouraged by shaping, it is often necessary to eliminate undesirable behavior. One way to do this is to determine what reinforcer is maintaining it and then to remove that reinforcer. This procedure is called extinction. Upon removal of reinforcement the behavior will weaken and will finally disappear. At times the behavior in question will strengthen before falling off. This is shown in Figure 1 during the middle phase in which praise for walking further was withheld. The patient at first actually doubled her distance walked before showing a decline in this behavior.

AVERSIVE PROCEDURES. Another way to reduce the frequency of unwanted behavior is to use aversive procedures. Negative reinforcement can be used in three main arrangements: escape procedures, avoidance training, and punishment. In an escape procedure the individual can turn off negative reinforcement by performing an action. In an avoidance paradigm the individual prevents the onset of negative reinforcement by making a response. Both arrangements lead to strengthening of the escape or avoidance behavior. Avoidance behavior can be extremely persistent since by its very nature the organism can never discover that the aversive stimulus has been discontinued—i.e., the behavior is 100 percent successful in avoiding negative reinforcement and is therefore maintained in the total absence of such reinforcement. Many persistent neurotic behaviors may be the product of avoidance training. Thus, ritualistic behavior such as handwashing that may be aimed at avoiding an unwanted consequence by its very continuance prevents the discovery that the avoided contingency will no longer occur. Avoidance training has been extensively used in the treatment of sexual perversions (see Chapter 4).

Punishment refers to the procedure of making negative reinforcement contingent upon a particular behavior. This has the effect of reducing the frequency of behavior, often very rapidly. It is therefore a very useful procedure when it is important to gain quick control of a subject's behavior, e.g., unruly or aggressive behavior in children. However, it has some drawbacks. First, behavior is only temporarily suppressed; remove the punishment and the behavior recurs. This can be overcome by reinforcing behavior that is not compatible with the punished behavior; thus, aggressive behavior might be punished to prevent the response, and cooperative polite behavior reinforced at the same time. Second, the subject can learn an avoidance response that is just as undesirable as that which was punished. Punishing stealing might lead to the person's hiding his crime more efficiently to prevent discovery and avoid punishment. Third, punishment can produce unwanted side effects such as general social withdrawal, fear responses, and aggressive behavior.

STIMULUS CONTROL. Shaping, extinction, and aversive control all deal with the manipulation of the consequences of behavior. Behavior can, however, also be controlled by antecedent stimuli, a paradigm known as stimulus control. An example of this is the traffic light. When red, traffic is stopped; when green, moving. The driver makes a response depending upon which signal is lighted. It is possible that behavior such as homosexuality is an example of stimulus control since sexual behavior only occurs in the presence of a male stimulus for male homosexuals and a female stimulus for lesbians.

Techniques to change stimulus control exist. One of these is known as stimulus fading; in this technique a new stimulus is slowly increased in strength during performance of the behavior while the first is decreased. Behavior then comes under control of the second stimulus. It was recently shown [5] that the penile response of a male homosexual to slides depicting nude males could be transferred at full strength to slides of nude women by overlapping the two slides and slowly increasing the heterosexual stimulus while decreasing the homosexual stimulus. The picture of a woman to which the subject had shown no response now elicited penile erection. This suggested that fading may be of therapeutic value.

Finally, recent work suggests that reinforcement procedures affect autonomic responding, a sphere of interest usually reserved for classical conditioning. It has been shown that operant conditioning procedures systematically affect responses such as heart rate [8], blood pressure [36], and galvanic skin response [10]. At first the question was raised as to whether an intermediate voluntary response such as respiration or muscular changes was being affected; however, carefully controlled work with animals [31] indicates that autonomic responding is being directly changed. In humans it has been shown, for example, that salivation was increased in one group of volunteers when money was made contingent on salivating, while no change was observed in a group rewarded for minimal salivation. Similarly, Shapiro [36] was able to produce differences in blood pressure between two groups of subjects, one reinforced for raising, the other for lowering blood pressure. This development is most interesting and may open the way for direct modification of autonomic behavior in neurotic and psychosomatic conditions.

Respondent and operant conditioning are not the only ways to modify behavior. Humans respond to verbal contingencies such as instructions that are best viewed in the context of cognitive or social learning.

VARIABLES DERIVED FROM SOCIAL AND COGNITIVE PSYCHOLOGY

Private events such as thinking are difficult to investigate, for they can only be observed by one person, the subject himself. However, reports of inner events can be useful under certain circumstances, and other events usually considered as being within the person, such as expectancy, perception of progress, and self-control, can be objectified to some extent.

Expectancy

Expectancy, which is induced in part by the instructions given about a particular situation and partly by prior experience with similar situations, is important in behavior change. The effectiveness of placebo administration depends upon these factors; thus, it was shown that a group of outpatients who had reached maximum improvement with brief psychotherapy showed further improvement following the administration of a course of inert medication given with instructions suggesting that improvement was to be expected [18]. In another study of neurotic outpatients Hoehn-Saric et al. [19] found that patients given a brief prepsychotherapy interview in which the goals of therapy were outlined improved more following subsequent psychotherapy than a group of patients not given the interview.

Therapeutic instructions, however, produce different responses in different subjects. Figure 2 shows the data for three agoraphobic patients who were given instructions suggesting to them that they should steadily improve simply by practicing in their phobic situation. There were three patterns of behavior; no effect (S1), a transient effect (S2), and steady improvement (S3). The most common patterns seem to be the first and second; they have now been observed in a number of patients with severe neurotic disorders. Overall, the findings regarding instructions and expectancy indicate that strongly induced expectancy confers a benefit upon a group receiving such instructions, although individual responses will vary considerably. Findings regarding expectancy appear to hold for verbal psychotherapy [14], systematic desensitization [1, 23, 30, 35], hypnosis [34], and perhaps for all therapies.

It also appears that the more precisely instructions define the expected behavior change, the better. Thus, precise problem identification and exact instructions regarding therapeutic aims and proce-

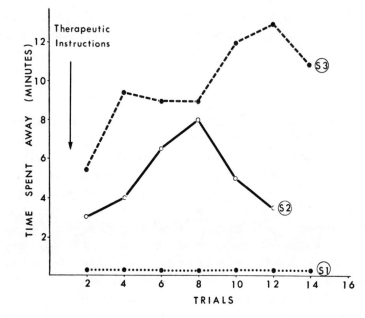

FIGURE 2. *The effect of therapeutic instructions on the ability of three agoraphobic subjects to walk alone as measured by time spent away on each trial. As can be seen three different patterns occur; no effect (S1), a transient effect (S2), and steady improvement (S3).*

dures, both of which enhance expectancy of a beneficial outcome, are an important beginning for any therapy.

Perception of Progress

A second variable of some importance appears to be adequate and exact feedback of information regarding therapeutic progress. Such feedback has been shown to enhance progress in applied learning situations such as training in motor skills, programmed instruction, and most recently in the experimental modification of autonomic functions [8, 36]. Simply allowing subjects to see how they are progressing modifies their behavior. A simple means of accomplishing this is to have a patient record the frequency of a behavior he wishes to change such as cigarette smoking. Such recording reliably leads to a decline in such behavior, although it is unusual for the behavior to be eliminated completely. Feedback of performance has recently been shown to modify complex neurotic behavior (see Chapter 2, p. 41).

If a patient expects to improve and then perceives improvement, he will be pleased or, to put it another way, will reinforce himself for improved performance.

Self-control

Recently several studies have been reported in which subjects learned to administer reinforcement to themselves without any direct external control [28]. The usual technique involves instructing the subject as to the correct response, reinforcing the correct responses, and then arranging the situation so that the individual reinforces his own responses. It has been found that individuals positively reinforce themselves at a slightly higher rate than the emission of correct responses, while negative self-reinforcement (self-punishment) tends to be at a lower rate than the response to be reinforced. Presumably self-reinforcement can occur at a symbolic level (in the form of self-praise) and also by the person arranging things so that he has access to a particular reinforcement only after completing a certain task. In this way self-control of behavior is achieved. Techniques such as this may be very important in obtaining permanent therapeutic behavior change.

Modeling

The final procedure to be discussed is modeling, which leads to learning by imitation. One of the techniques most used to induce behavioral change is to show people how to do things. Learning can occur in a variety of ways with this technique. Subjects can observe both the modeled behavior and its consequences, describe it verbally, or practice the behavior that then comes under the control of its consequences.

Bandura and his colleagues have investigated a number of aspects of the modeling process, particularly as it applies to the elimination of fearful behavior. In one study [3] children who showed severe fear of dogs on a behavioral approach test were divided into a number of differently treated groups. In two of these they observed a fearless child approach a dog during some eight sessions, in either a party or neutral context. Both groups improved considerably more than two other groups who simply saw a dog or saw the party without a dog. Sixty-seven percent of children in the modeling group were able to remain alone in a room with a dog while very few of the children in the control groups were able to.

The ability to imitate is notably deficient in some types of behavioral disorders such as childhood autism. However, it has been shown [4] that imitative responses can be shaped by reinforcement of approximations to imitation, and the newly developed class of behavior, i.e., a tendency to imitate, used to generate new responses. Exposure to a model may more effectively build up complex repertoires of behavior than shaping each piece of the repertoire item by item. Thus, college students [27] were not able to acquire a complex sequence of behavior when it was taught by differential reinforcement of correct and incorrect responses, while they rapidly acquired the behavior when exposed to models.

This form of learning probably occurs in the verbal psychotherapies. Although therapists restrict the range of their behavior during psychotherapy, they do offer model solutions to problems in verbal form, especially in the more directive supportive therapies and in the later phases of psychoanalytic psychotherapy where identification with the therapist may become important. The concepts of identification and imitation are related, identification usually referring to behaviors performed in the absence of the model and restricted to the class of interpersonal behaviors.

Other forms of psychotherapy use imitative learning in a more planned way. Role-playing techniques are an excellent example of this; the therapist and patient enact problem situations, at times the therapist switching roles with the patient to demonstrate more adaptive ways of behaving. Similarly, Mowrer [33], in integrity therapy, consistently models more straightforward and more adaptive ways of behaving described as self-disclosure and personal accountability.

SUMMARY AND OVERVIEW

As noted, the behavioral therapies developed out of the coincidence of a growing dissatisfaction with the efficacy of the prevailing verbal psychotherapies and the increasing relevance of the experimental behavioral sciences for the clinic. Some of the techniques that have been mentioned, such as the application of selective positive reinforcement and extinction, are direct applications of procedures that have been investigated in the laboratories of experimental psychology, often across a wide range of organisms. Others that appear to have been derived from animal experiment, such as systematic desensitization, have been radically altered in the transition from animal to human so that the relationship to the original experiment appears strained. Yet others such as implosive therapy, in which patients are exposed to intensely imagined fear-arousing situations, have an even looser connection with the findings of the experimental behavioral sciences. The task in such therapies as desensitization and implosion is to first assess their effectiveness and, if effective, then to find out how they work.

The experimental behavioral sciences can contribute ideas for potential therapeutic developments together with methods for the experimental analysis of existing therapies. Already, there have been interesting developments, and we can expect more. At the least we can expect a better understanding of how therapies work. Hopefully, new and more effective therapies will be devised. But most important, the field of psychotherapy will become one in which findings in basic sciences will be tested in an applied setting, namely, the clinic, fostering an interaction that will be mutually beneficial.

In the following pages the various therapeutic procedures which make up the behavioral therapies will be described from the view-points of procedure, relationship to the findings of the experimental behavioral sciences, and evidence of efficacy.

REFERENCES

1. Agras, W. S., Leitenberg, H., Barlow, D. H., Curtis, A., Edwards, J., and Wright, D. The role of relaxation in systematic desensitization therapy. *Archives of General Psychiatry* 25:511, 1971.
2. Baer, D. M., Peterson, R. F., and Sherman, J. A. The development of imitation by reinforcing behavioral similarity to a model. *Journal of Experimental Analysis of Behavior* 10:405, 1967.
3. Bandura, A., Grusec, J. E., and Menlove, F. L. Vicarious extinction of avoidance behavior. *Journal of Personality and Social Psychology* 5:16, 1967.
4. Bandura, A., and Kupers, C. J. The transmission of patterns of self-reinforcement through modeling. *Journal of Abnormal and Social Psychology* 69:1, 1964.
5. Barlow, D. H., and Agras, W. S. An experimental analysis of fading to increase heterosexual responsiveness in homosexuality. Southeastern Psychological Association, Miami, 1971.
6. Bergin, A. E. The effects of psychotherapy: Negative results revisited. *Journal of Counseling Psychology* 10:244, 1963.
7. Bockhoven, J. S. *Moral Treatment in American Psychiatry.* New York: Springer Publishing Co., 1963.
8. Brener, J., Kleinman, R. A., and Goesling, W. J. The effects of different exposures to augmented sensory feedback on the control of heart rate. *Psychophysiology* 5:510, 1969.
9. Brown, C. C., and Katz, R. A. Operant salivary conditioning in man. *Psychophysiology* 4:156, 1967.
10. Crider, A., Shapiro, D., and Tursky, B. Reinforcement of spontaneous electrodermal activity. *Journal of Comparative and Physiological Psychology* 62:20, 1966.
11. Dollard, J., and Miller, N. E. *Personality and Psychotherapy.* New York: McGraw-Hill, 1950.
12. Eysenck, H. J. The effects of psychotherapy: An evaluation. *Journal of Consulting Psychology* 16:319, 1952.
13. Eysenck, H. J. *The Effects of Psychotherapy.* New York: International Science Press, 1966.

14. Frank, J. D. *Persuasion and Healing.* Baltimore: Johns Hopkins Press, 1961.
15. French, P. M. Relations between psychoanalysis and the experimental work of Pavlov. *American Journal of Psychiatry* 12: 1165, 1933.
16. Freud, S. Turnings in the ways of psychoanalytic therapy. In *Collected Papers,* Vol. 2. New York: Basic Books, 1959.
17. Fuller, P. R. Operant conditioning of a vegetative human organism. *American Journal of Psychology* 62:587, 1949.
18. Gliedman, L. H., Nash, E. H., Imber, S. D., Stone, A. R., and Frank, J. D. Reduction of symptoms by pharmacologically inert substances and by short-term psychotherapy. *Archives of Neurology and Psychiatry* 79:345, 1958.
19. Hoehn-Saric, R., Frank, J. D., Imber, S. D., Nash, E. H., Stone, A. R., and Battle, C. Systematic preparation of patients for psychotherapy. I. Effects on therapy behavior and outcome. *Journal of Psychiatric Research* 2:267, 1964.
20. Jones, M. C. Elimination of children's fears. *Journal of Experimental Psychology* 7:382, 1924.
21. Kantorovich, N. V. An attempt at associative reflex therapy in alcoholism. *Psychological Abstracts,* No. 4282, 1930.
22. Knight, R. P. Evaluation of the results of psychoanalytic therapy. *American Journal of Psychiatry* 98:434, 1941.
23. Leitenberg, H., Agras, W. S., Barlow, D. H., and Oliveau, D. C. Contribution of selective positive reinforcement and therapeutic instructions to systematic desensitization therapy. *Journal of Abnormal Psychology* 74:113, 1969.
24. Leitenberg, H., Agras, W. S., Butz, R., and Wincze, J. Heart rate and behavioral change during treatment of phobia. *Journal of Abnormal Psychology* 78:59, 1971.
25. Lemere, F., and Voegtlin, W. L. An evaluation of the aversion treatment of alcoholism. *Quarterly Journal of Studies on Alcohol* 11:199, 1950.
26. Lindsley, O. R. Operant conditioning methods applied to research in chronic schizophrenia. *Psychiatric Research Reports* 5:118, 1956.
27. Luchins, A. S., and Luchins, E. H. Learning a complex ritualized social role. *The Psychological Record* 16:177, 1966.
28. Marston, A. R., and Cohen, N. J. The relationship of negative self reinforcement to frustration and intropunitiveness. *Journal of General Psychology* 74:237, 1966.
29. Max, L. W. Breaking up a homosexual fixation by the condi-

tioned reaction technique: A case study. *Psychological Bulletin* 32:723, 1935.

30. McGlynn, F. D., Mealiea, W. L., and Nowas, M. M. Systematic desensitization of snake avoidance under two conditions of suggestion. *Psychological Reports* 25:220, 1969.

31. Miller, N. E. Learning of visceral and glandular responses. *Science* 163:434, 1969.

32. Mowrer, O. H. Apparatus for the study and treatment of enuresis. *American Journal of Psychology* 51:163, 1938.

33. Mowrer, O. H. Integrity therapy: A self-help approach. *Psychotherapy Theory Practice and Research* 3:114, 1966.

34. O'Connell, D. N., Shor, R. E., and Orne, M. T. Hypnotic age regression: An empirical and methodological analysis. *Journal of Abnormal Psychology* (Monograph) 76:1, 1970.

35. Oliveau, D. C., Agras, W. S., Leitenberg, H., Moore, R. C., and Wright, D. E. Systematic desensitization, therapeutically oriented instructions and selective positive reinforcement. *Behavioral Research and Therapy* 7:27, 1969.

36. Shapiro D., Tursky, B., Gershon, E., and Stern, M. Effects of feedback and reinforcement on the control of human systolic blood pressure. *Science* 163:586, 1969.

37. Simmel, E. Psychoanalytic treatment in a sanatorium. *International Journal of Psychoanalysis* 10:70, 1929.

38. Skinner, B. F. *The Behavior of Organisms.* New York: Appleton-Century-Crofts, 1938.

39. Skinner, B. F. Behaviorism at Fifty. In T. W. Wann (Ed.), *Behaviorism and Phenomenology.* Chicago: University of Chicago Press, 1964.

40. Terhune, W. B. The phobic syndrome. *Archives of Neurology and Psychiatry* 62:162, 1949.

41. Truax, C. B. Reinforcement and nonreinforcement in Rogerian psychotherapy. *Journal of Abnormal Psychology* 71:1, 1966.

42. Ullman, L. P., Krasner, L., and Collins, B. J. Modification of behavior through verbal conditioning: Effects in group therapy. *Journal of Abnormal and Social Psychology* 62:128, 1961.

43. Watson, J. B., and Rayner, P. Conditioned emotional reactions. *Journal of Experimental Psychology* 3:1, 1920.

44. Wolpe, J. *Psychotherapy by Reciprocal Inhibition.* Stanford: Stanford University Press, 1958.

2

Positive Reinforcement and Extinction Procedures

HAROLD LEITENBERG

EDITOR'S INTRODUCTION

The psychotherapeutic application of the procedures of positive reinforcement and extinction is one of the clearest demonstrations of the direct relevance of the experimental behavioral sciences to the clinic. There have been many demonstrations in the laboratory—with a range of organisms—that the probability of a behavior occurring is increased when the behavior is followed by a rewarding event, and lessened by the removal of such events. It now appears that much animal behavior, normal human behavior, and deviant human behavior follows the same laws, although the demonstrations have been most numerous in the case of animal behavior and least in the case of deviant human behavior.

Reinforcement as used in the clinic implies that the behavior to be changed must be accurately defined, and preferably measured. Thus, in the case described in the section on positive reinforcement, withdrawal and its desired opposite, socialization, were not discussed; rather, the latter was defined as the amount of time that the patient spent in talking to the nursing staff at certain times of day. This was measured by timing the amount of such conversation. Once the baseline rate of conversation was established, then an environmental event hypothesized to be reinforcing could be made contingent upon his conversing; in this case tokens that gave the patient an oppor-

27

tunity to do things he enjoyed were given for every two minutes that he talked to a nurse. Conversely, he could not engage in such activities without earning them by talking. By keeping an ongoing measure, the effect of the contingent application of tokens could be followed (see Figure 3), permitting continuous assessment of the efficacy of therapy.

Extinction simply means the removal of a reinforcing event. In the clinic this implies that an adequate behavioral analysis can be made so that the events reinforcing the behavior to be changed can be defined. Although this can be done from the history on occasion, it is much better to observe the deviant behavior directly and to see what the consequences of the behavior are. Usually these turn out to be attention of one kind or another. It is noted that what might appear to the observer to be undesirable attention may, in fact, be reinforcing. Test of the hypothesis is made by measuring the behavior to be changed and observing the effect of removing the hypothesized reinforcer; for example, instructing a mother not to attend to the unwanted behavior. A practical point to be noted is that the unwelcome behavior may first increase in frequency following removal of the reinforcer before decreasing.

In recognition that variables other than reinforcement play a part in a therapeutic program, Leitenberg points to evidence of the separate and additive effects of therapeutic instructions, feedback of information on progress, and the opportunity to practice adaptive behaviors (pp. 41–44). This implies that therapeutic programs should contain at least all the above ingredients, but it appears that opportunity to practice adaptive skills is of paramount importance.

All this is very different from the more traditional role with which many therapists feel comfortable. It is a different way of thinking about and observing behavior and involves a more active therapeutic role. Failure (and success) is immediately apparent from the ongoing measures. Is it a practical therapy? Seemingly so, if the therapist is willing to work with the staff of institutions and with family members, for they become the therapists, making the measures and carrying out the therapeutic conditions while the professional therapist

supervises progress and makes changes to carry out the overall thera-
peutic plan (which of course has been evolved in discussion with
the patient and his relatives).

The applications of these procedures are many: from psychosis to
neurosis; children to adults; in institutions and the home. If it is cor-
rect that much deviant behavior is learned in the natural environ-
ment, namely, the home, and is maintained by that or other envi-
ronments, then the logical place to work is in those environments
or with that part of the environment that can be brought to the
therapist. Working with family members, enabling them to change
their behavior toward the patient in order to change his behavior,
may prove to be one of the most effective ways to apply reinforce-
ment and extinction procedures. Leitenberg sketches out one such
application on page 50. To date, however, very little work with adult
interpersonal problems has been done; but clearly reinforcement
techniques could be used, perhaps with videotape feedback of per-
formance in a setting similar to that of family or role-playing thera-
pies.

The evidence that reinforcement and extinction procedures are
successful is derived from single case-controlled studies. There is no
doubt that very severe deviant behavior such as delusional talk and
phobic or compulsive behavior have been dramatically altered as a
result of applying such procedures. The single case study shows that
immediate and powerful effects occur. However, several problems
exist. The first is that using a behavioral definition, most patients
appear to have a cluster of loosely related behavioral disorders. Al-
tering one may not alter others. Altering behavior in one environ-
ment may not ensure transfer to another. Finally, the long-term
effects of these procedures are not known. No controlled outcome
study of the application of selective reinforcement procedures in
clinical disorders (token economies excepted) has been done. Pre-
liminary evidence from the follow-up of treated cases suggests that
long-term benefits do occur, but this has yet to be tested.

W.S.A.

As noted in the previous chapter, a main assumption of behavioral therapy is that many neurotic and perhaps even psychotic behavior patterns are due to inappropriate or insufficient learning. Therapy, therefore, should consist of arranging environmental conditions to facilitate the elimination of maladaptive behavior and the acquisition of adaptive behavior.

The present chapter is concerned with *positive reinforcement* techniques designed to establish and maintain desirable behavior and with *extinction* procedures designed to reduce or eliminate unwanted behavior. These two aims are, of course, complementary, and as a result reinforcement and extinction procedures are often combined in a therapeutic program. For purposes of clarity, however, they will be discussed separately. Selected case studies will be used to illustrate procedural details, and wherever possible, mention will be made of experimental attempts to explore the effects of varying a given technique in a particular way.

A major premise of operant conditioning is that behavior can be generated and maintained by its consequences. According to this premise the way in which a person acts in a situation and the frequency of his acts are largely controlled by the events that follow such action. One common consequence of behavior is referred to colloquially as a rewarding or satisfying event. Numerous laboratory demonstrations using organisms ranging from flatworm to man have shown that the *frequency of an act is increased* if that act is followed by a rewarding event [20, 24]. This is what is meant by a positive reinforcement effect. Similarly, there have been a vast number of empiric demonstrations showing that the frequency of an act decreases when the former rewarding (reinforcing) consequence is omitted [24]. This is what is meant by the term *extinction*.

Since one of the problems facing psychotherapy is to devise more effective and more rapid methods for either increasing the frequency of occurrence of a given piece of behavior such as social interaction, or decreasing the frequency of a behavior such as undue expression of interpersonal hostility, it would seem that systematic use of reinforcement and extinction procedures might have something to contribute. The following sections outline the progress made so far.

THE PROCEDURE OF POSITIVE REINFORCEMENT

There are four steps in the therapeutic application of positive reinforcement. First, in agreement with the patient the behavior to be developed is precisely defined so that the occasion for reinforcement is clear and so that changes in frequency of occurrence can be easily monitored. There is nothing more central to the behavioral approach than this. The target behavior and the specific changes desired must be precisely defined. There should also be some way to observe *continuously* whether or not *measurable* changes are taking place in the direction of the ultimate behavioral objective. This should be an ongoing measure, not one that awaits the conclusion of a therapy.

The second task is to define those objects or activities that serve as positive reinforcers. In the case of hospitalized psychiatric patients, food, cigarettes, access to privacy, the opportunity to watch television, to go into town, to walk on hospital grounds, to earn money, to have more time with a social worker, and so on have been used. In the case of outpatients, praise from the therapist and patient-arranged contingencies have been employed. For example, the patient may arrange to go bowling only if a certain behavior occurred at X frequency that week. The variety of social and material reinforcers for children is almost unlimited, from time-honored gold stars, to grades, to smiles, to money.

The third step is to arrange conditions favoring the emission of the behavior to be strengthened. This may be done by giving instructions; by demonstration, or by observation of other patients performing the behavior in question; or, as is more likely in the case of behavior that has long been absent or that arouses anxiety in the patient, through a gradual *shaping* procedure. Shaping by means of the method of successive approximation involves reinforcing in sequence those behaviors leading to the execution of the desired act.

Fourth, once the behavior has been generated, it must be strengthened through appropriate reinforcement *schedules* in order to reduce the likelihood of its disappearance when the control maintained during therapy over the consequences of behavior is removed, as it may be in the "real" world. This involves providing reinforcement intermittently rather than after each occurrence of the desired behavior. Of course, it is also hoped that once established, desirable behaviors (e.g., punctuality or lucid conversation) will continue to elicit reward, since society tends to reinforce "normal" rather than "abnormal" behavior. This goes back to the first critical step—the choice of target behaviors to reinforce. They should be ones that are likely to be maintained by society. If, however, the patient is being returned to the environment that caused him to enter treatment in the first place, an environment that failed to reinforce desirable behavior, then it may be beneficial to involve family members in the therapeutic procedure, so they can learn to be more effective positive reinforcing agents (see Russo [33]).

POSITIVE REINFORCEMENT: A CLINICAL EXAMPLE

To illustrate the four critical steps in the application of positive reinforcement, the case of a 21-year-old male inpatient will be described [3]. He had been hospitalized almost continuously for 4 years and had shown a steadily worsening trend in his behavior. He spent all his time in his room or in solitary occupations, rarely approached others or initiated conversation, and answered questions logically but extremely tersely. Following the slightest criticism or physical hurt he would walk off the ward and engage in ritualistic swearing. Treatment including psychotherapy, ataractic drugs, and electroconvulsive therapy had not helped his condition. Diagnosed as having a severe obsessive compulsive disorder, his behavior appeared to be an effort to avoid any possibility of physical injury or social rebuff.

The first problem chosen to work on was his avoidance of social interaction. The target behavior was therefore defined as self-initiated conversation with nursing staff outside his room. During three 90-

minute sessions each day, one or more nurses were made available for the patient to approach. They were instructed not to initiate conversation and simply to respond appropriately to his attempts at talking with them. Once the target behavior was defined, an ongoing measure of it was made by having the nurses time by stopwatch the duration of each of his conversations with them, so that a daily total for the three sessions could be plotted. During a baseline period (see Figure 3) he was instructed at the beginning of each session to talk as much as possible with the nursing staff. As can be seen, this did not meet with much success.

The second step was to find a reinforcer. Observation of the patient revealed that he enjoyed leaving the ward and sitting in the lobby of the hospital "watching the world go by," listening to the radio, and watching television. It was decided to use the opportunity to do these things as reinforcement. He was told that every 2 minutes that he talked with a nurse during the three daily sessions would earn him a token exchangeable for 5 minutes of any of the above-mentioned activities, which he would otherwise not be allowed to engage in. The similarity of this procedure to a job was pointed out to him, an analogy which he appeared to accept, and which may have been important in avoiding a hostile reaction to the deprivation of these pleasurable activities. The token was given to him by the nurse after each 2 minutes of talking, providing immediate reinforcement for the target behavior.

The effect of this procedure was dramatic, as can be seen in the first reinforcement phase. In Figure 3 the usefulness of an ongoing behavioral measure is nicely demonstrated, since it it clear that during the baseline no progress was being made, and that only after the institution of reinforcement did he begin to converse longer with the nurses. To prove conclusively that contingent application of reinforcement was responsible for the therapeutic effect, a control procedure was instituted for the next few days. During this period the patient was given 25 tokens (which had been the highest amount earned) every morning; that is, no response was required from him in order to obtain reinforcement. As can be seen in Figure 3, after a brief spurt his conversational ability showed a steadily declining trend during this phase, demonstrating that it had been under the control of the reinforcement procedure. Then, in the final phase the original procedure was reinstated, giving rise to a further increase in conversational ability.

Following this, the final step in a reinforcement program was carried out. Instead of holding sessions the nursing staff observed the patient at randomly chosen times throughout the day. If he was seen talking either to staff or to other patients at one of these times, he was given tokens. Slowly, the intervals between reinforcement were lengthened, and finally, token reinforcement for conversing was

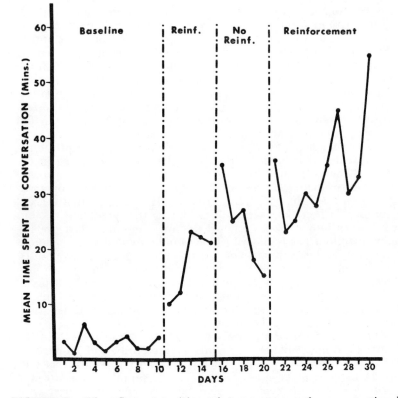

FIGURE 3. *The effect of positive reinforcement on the conversational ability of a severely withdrawn compulsive patient. The introduction of contingent tokens led to a gain in conversational ability, removal (noncontingent tokens) to a decline in conversation, and reintroduction to a steady gain.*

withdrawn. At this point no decline in talking was noted, suggesting that this activity had become reinforcing in itself.

Representative literature on the use of the selective positive reinforcement procedure is reviewed in the following pages. Excluded from this presentation is a discussion of token economies that are ward-wide applications of positive reinforcement procedures; these will be described in the next chapter. Special emphasis will be given to treatment of adult behavioral disorders since reinforcement techniques have been used so often with children that "equal time" would make this chapter unmanageable.

POSITIVE REINFORCEMENT:
APPLICATION TO THE PSYCHOSES

There have been a number of examples of the successful use of positive reinforcement to build up desired behaviors in psychotic patients, most usually with the diagnosis of schizophrenia. Thus, several investigators have attempted to reinstate verbal behavior in mute psychotic patients. Isaacs, Thomas, and Goldiamond [28] worked with two catatonic schizophrenics, who had been mute for 14 and 19 years, respectively. In each case the method of *shaping* via successive approximation was employed using chewing gum as a reinforcer. In the first case, during the first 2 weeks a stick of gum was held before the patient's face, and when his eyes moved, the therapist gave him the gum. Then only lip movements and later vocalization, a croak being considered sufficient at first, resulted in reinforcement. At the end of the sixth week, the patient suddenly said, "Gum, please." He then responded to questions, and partial transfer to people other than the therapist was noted. Unfortunately, attendants and nurses continued to react to his nonverbal requests, thereby preventing any extensive change in his verbal behavior. No follow-up is reported.

The second patient did not accept the gum offered to him until the third session. Shortly after this he was informed that gum would be given him only when he attended group therapy. He agreed to this. In the third group therapy session (all the other members talked) receipt of gum was made contingent upon his participation in a group activity. Patients were seated in a semicircle, and each had to name an animal when his turn came. If they did, they were given a piece of gum. The patient did not respond on the fourth or fifth sessions. During the sixth session, the patients were asked to name a city or town in Illinois. The nonverbal patient said "Chicago." He was given gum, and two members of the group spontaneously praised him. From then on he answered in the group. Although gum was discontinued after the tenth session, selective verbal praise maintained responding in the group setting. There was no transfer to the ward, however, and he did not initiate any conversation in the group setting. Although no attempt was made to shape such transfer, it seems likely that this could have been done since the first and most difficult hurdle had already been overcome.

Sherman [35, 36] used similar procedures to shape verbal behavior in four long-term mute psychotics. For one patient, mute for 26 years, pennies and praise were used as reinforcement. After only 16 sessions he returned to the ward and spoke to one of the attendants. The attendants were then told not to respond to notes written by the patient asking for something, but only to respond to verbal requests. The patient's verbalization increased until he was talking between 9 and 24 times daily with the attendants. There was no other concurrent treatment to which this improvement could be attributed.

In a recent study [23] social greeting responses of three withdrawn and chronic schizophrenic patients were shaped using cigarettes as reinforcers. After the subjects were reliably greeting several experimenters, the use of cigarettes was gradually decreased to see if this verbal behavior could be maintained by natural social contingencies. A 3-month follow-up indicated that it was being maintained at a high level.

Attempts have also been made to modify the content of psychotic patients' speech by selective positive reinforcement procedures. Thus, Wincze, Leitenberg, and Agras [46] examined the effectiveness of reinforcement in modifying verbal expressions of delusional belief in 10 chronic paranoid schizophrenic patients. The mean age of the 6 male and 4 female patients was 45 years, and they had been hospitalized for a mean period of over 12 years. No changes were made in the patients' medication before or during the experiment, although occasional changes were made at the end of the study if the patients' behavior had improved sufficiently to warrant this.

Each patient's verbal behavior was recorded during (1) training sessions with a therapist during which time the therapist asked questions directed at the delusional system and depending on the phase of the experiment provided different consequences for patients' answers; (2) conversations with the nursing staff on the ward; and (3) interviews with a psychiatric resident unfamiliar with the design of the study. The percentage of total talk that was delusional could be calculated in each instance and was used as the main measure in the study. Reliability checks with multiple judges were made using the tape-recorded sessions. The agreement in these checks always exceeded 85 percent.

The results can be summarized as follows. Simple instructions, i.e., telling a patient when he is and when he is not speaking delusionally, had a transient beneficial effect in several patients. However, when patients received tokens for speaking nondelusionally—tokens that could be exchanged for time in their room, time watching television, for cigarettes, and so on—the effect was much more clear-cut. In seven of the nine patients where this could be done (one subject's delusional behavior had declined substantially before the reinforcement phase could be introduced) frequency of delusional behavior in the training sessions declined at least 20 percent below the level of the preceding nonreinforcement phases. If reinforcement was provided only during training sessions with a therapist, there was little transfer to the ward, and even when reinforcement procedures were instituted in both these places, changes in delusional behavior still did not usually transfer to the conversations patients had with a psychiatrist. The most dramatic and most generalized changes were likely to appear if delusional talk on the ward fell to within 0 to 10 percent of total talk. It should be noted that reinforcement phases lasted no longer than 14 days, so there is no way of knowing from this study if declines in delusional talk could be sustained for longer periods. The data, however, offer some hope in this regard; long-term schizophrenics very quickly changed their pattern of talking when such changes produced positive gains from their environment. And subjects with the largest decline in delusional talk were likely to generalize the change to other settings.

One of the more interesting questions raised by this study is the relationship between verbal behavior and belief. Preliminary research in our laboratory suggests that when the percentage of delusional talk is reduced to below 10 percent, then beliefs are indeed changed as verbal behavior changes. Lesser changes do not seem to be accompanied by changes in belief.

In addition to the modification of the frequency and content of the speech of schizophrenic patients, several other classes of behavior have been altered by the use of selective positive reinforcement. For example, Ayllon [6] reported the case of a chronic schizophrenic woman who wore excessive amounts of clothing—including some half-dozen dresses, several pairs of stockings, sweaters, and so on. In order to gain entrance into the dining room to eat, she had to meet while dressed a progressively decreasing weight requirement. Within 10 weeks she was wearing a normal amount of clothes.

Some behaviors do not require a prolonged shaping procedure for redevelopment. These are behaviors that do not provoke much anxiety, the major reason for their absence being that they have not been sufficiently reinforced. For example, in a study reported by Ayllon and Azrin [7] patients received candy or extra dessert if they picked up utensils at meals. Instructions to pick up utensils without any added reinforcement resulted in 25 percent of the patients engaging in this behavior. Reinforcement without instructions resulted in only 10 percent of the patients picking up the utensils. However, when both instructed and reinforced, all the patients picked up the utensils.

POSITIVE REINFORCEMENT: APPLICATION TO THE NEUROSES

A number of attempts to treat classic neurotic disorders with selective positive reinforcement have been reported. In one of the earliest examples Schmidt [34] described the case of a 42-year-old man with a long history of phobic symptoms such as avoidance of crowds, trains, and heat. Treatment consisted of two parts: verbal conditioning and "practical" behavior-training. First the patient made up a hierarchy of illness statements graded toward normal. Thus, if the original statement was, "I am usually very apprehensive when traveling on a bus," a series of statements were constructed leading up to the final one of "I am usually quite at ease when traveling on a bus." These were typed upon 75 cards, and each day the patient had to read the one out of the four statements on each card which best described his condition. Social reinforcement (a smile, nod, and the word "good") was delivered when he chose a statement representing clinical improvement. In the second part of the experiment "practical behavior training" was applied to 12 graded travel situations. At each step he traveled first with the therapist, then with the therapist at a distance, and then several times by self. It was found that a combination of both verbal and behavior training produced the most significant and the most persistent changes. Interestingly, the same finding has been made in the use of aversive therapy (see pp. 106–109).

In another early example of the use of selective positive reinforcement in neurotic conditions Bachrach, Erwin, and Mohr [11] demonstrated that eating behavior could be restored in a chronic case of anorexia nervosa. At the beginning of the study the patient was in danger of death and weighed 47 pounds, down over several years from a customary 120 pounds. She presented the classic picture of anorexia nervosa with amenorrhea, cachexia, and indifference to her physical condition. Previous medical treatment had failed entirely, although no psychiatric treatment had been attempted. The patient was placed in a room that was empty apart from a bed, a nightstand, and a chair. All visitors were restricted. The three experimenters each ate a meal with her. At first movements associated with eating and then eating itself were reinforced by the experimenter paying attention to her. Other reinforcements used were access to a radio, television, or phonograph. When weight gain reached a plateau for several weeks (possibly due to vomiting), reinforcement was made contingent upon weight gain instead of eating. The patient then gained a total of 40 pounds and maintained this weight during a 2-year follow-up, allowing her to function adequately outside of the hospital. In a replication of this study Leitenberg, Agras, and Thomson [28] also used a positive reinforcement approach in the treatment of two female adolescent cases of anorexia nervosa. The first girl weighed 76 pounds, down 25 pounds from her usual weight.

The second patient weighed 69 pounds, down 22 pounds from her usual weight. In both cases an initial baseline period in hospital without reinforcement procedures indicated no weight gain. Following introduction of the reinforcement regime, however, caloric intake and weight increased in a regular manner. We have since used this technique successfully in four other cases with no relapses so far recorded on follow-ups ranging from several months to 2 years.

A relatively extensive research program at the University of Vermont has been examining the application of positive reinforcement and related behavioral techniques to the treatment of chronic neurosis. The research carried out with inpatients at the Medical Center Hospital Clinical Research Center aimed to discover variables that effectively modify chronic neurotic behavior. Because of the small size of the sample of patients, the research strategy was not a conventional group outcome design. Instead, an alternative approach was used in which the subject served as his own control and different experimental conditions were compared *within* rather than between subjects.

In the first chapter the treatment of an agoraphobic patient within this program was described (see pp. 9–11). This patient was one of the three chronic agoraphobes [1]. Prior to treatment two of the subjects had been unable to leave their homes alone for 1 and 16 years, respectively; the third had been able to manage only a 5-minute drive to work alone but had not walked anywhere on his own for 15 years. A 1-mile "course" from the Clinical Research Center to downtown was developed with designated landmarks at 25-yard intervals. The subjects were asked to stay on the course, to note the point at which they turned back, and were told: "We would like to see how far you can walk by yourself without experiencing undue tension. We find that repeated practice in a structured situation often leads to progress." Two sessions were held each day in the first case and five in the other two cases. Occasional checks of the patients' behavior were made to confirm the accuracy of their verbal report of distance walked. The duration of each walk was also timed by the therapist using a stopwatch.

The variable of interest in this study was the therapist's selective use of praise for progress in distance walked. The criterion was established as the mean between the previous criterion and the next highest trial. Thus, if the patient had been praised (reinforced) for 200 yards and then walked 400 yards on the next trial, the new criterion for praise became 300 yards. In each case this systematic praise, given contingent upon walking further, was introduced, removed, and reintroduced in sequential phases of several days' duration. Following the introduction of social reinforcement (praise), distance walked increased. When reinforcement was withdrawn, progress halted, and when it was reinstated, there was rapid and sustained improvement. It should be noted that the effect of social reinforcement was separated from the effects of instructions and general therapeutic support since both the latter variables were kept constant; only the presence or absence of contingent reinforcement was varied. We have since similarly demonstrated the importance of social reinforcement in treatment of claustrophobia and astasia-abasia [2] and phobia of various mechanical and electrical equipment [3].

In another study [28] with two phobic patients it was found that precise knowledge of small gains in performance had a facilitating effect similar to that of social reinforcement. This is best illustrated in one of the cases, a severe claustrophobic, a 51-year-old woman who reported that she could not stay in a house by herself, in a room with a closed door, a cinema, a church, or drive in a car alone for more than 3 or 4 miles. Her son indicated that for years he had to stand outside ladies' rooms holding the door ajar because she was afraid to have it closed.

A small, dimly lit room provided a situation in which the patient's claustrophobia could be measured and thus worked with. There were three sequential phases in the experiment: performance feedback, no feedback, and feedback again. Each phase lasted 6 days with between two and four sessions each day and a total of 22 sessions per phase; there were five trials per session. During feedback conditions the patient kept track of her time spent in the room, using a stopwatch we had provided under the guise of needing to check the accuracy of our automatic timer. This was done to control against an expectation that the stopwatch was needed for her to make progress. In the intervening no-feedback phase the stopwatch was not provided, the subject being told that it was broken and had been sent out for repairs. Although all other conditions were kept constant, improvement in each of the feedback phases was greater than in the intervening no-feedback phase.

In another study [26] we investigated the therapeutic effect of simply providing the opportunity for graded practice in the feared situations with five severely phobic inpatients. The experimental approach can be illustrated by the case of a crowd phobic. During certain phases of his hospital stay he was taken to a crowded store and given the opportunity to practice going in with instructions to come out as soon as he felt unduly anxious. He was told that such repeated practice would help him overcome his phobia. In other phases of equal length he was given psychotherapy sessions to explore his attitudes and interpersonal difficulties with his wife that might have contributed to his problem. He was told that the psychotherapy sessions would also help him overcome his phobia and that "we had found it best to alternate these two types of treatment procedures." Progress, as measured by the amount of time he spent in the store, was only made when he was able to practice. During the psychotherapy phase when he did not practice, he made no further improvement. The other patients in this series were two knife phobics, an agoraphobe, and a claustrophobe. As in the first case, each experiment was designed to determine whether phobic behavior could be reduced by practicing approach to the feared situation or object and whether or not a specific measure of phobic behavior would show as much change without practice as with practice. In all cases no improvement was found in the phases without practice, in spite of an equal amount of time in hospital, an equal amount of therapist attention, and an equally valid rationale for the patient to expect change.

In general, our work with neurotic disorders suggests that more emphasis needs to be placed on developing structured opportunities for patients to practice adaptive skills and social behavior in situations where this behavior is lacking. If possible, precise feedback of performance and selective application of therapist praise, or other types of reinforcement, for small gains in progress should also be provided. In addition, it is essential to provide instructions which suggest to the patient that such repeated practice in situations which he formerly avoided will be therapeutic. My colleagues and I have found in two studies with another form of behavior therapy, systematic desensitization, that omission of such expectations of therapeutic gain substantially reduces the extent of benefit a patient receives from the therapeutic procedure [25, 30].

When expectations of success are combined with repeated practice in the feared situation together with praise and feedback, all the ingredients for an effective treatment of phobia are present. For example, Callahan and I [15] combined these ingredients into a treatment procedure called *reinforced practice* and have started a series of controlled outcome studies with a variety of nonclinical fears. In the first study individuals who responded to a local newspaper advertisement for people afraid of heights and who could not climb more than 44 of a fire escape's 88 steps participated in the experiment. The mean number of steps climbed on the pretest was 23. Subjects were matched on the basis of pretest scores and then assigned at random to treatment and control conditions. When treatment subjects completed ten sessions or reached the top of the fire escape (whichever came first), both subjects were posttested. (The control subjects had previously been told there might be a delay before they were seen.)

Reduction of height phobia was explained to each subject as a situation analogous to acquiring a new skill. The rationale was supplied that they could learn to act in the feared situation by gradual practice in a supervised setting. In this way they would make contact with the feared situation that they normally avoided. Examples were given of the success of this approach with such a fear as claustrophobia. Subjects were also told that learning would transfer to other height-fear situations although the transfer might not be immediate.

Subjects began treatment on the day that they were given therapeutic instructions. Treatment consisted of six trials per session with feedback and contingent praise. On a given trial a subject was told to climb the fire escape as high as possible without feeling any undue anxiety, and to remain at his highest point as long as reasonably comfortable. He was then told to return to a level that did not evoke anxiety for a brief rest before the next trial. After each trial the experimenter (who remained on the ground) yelled up to the individual the total number of steps climbed.

Following each trial, a subject was also praised if he exceeded his criterion for that particular trial. This was first established as the subject's mean pretest score and was advanced by one-half the improvement on any praised trial. Thus, if S started by climbing 10 steps and improved to 20 steps on the next trial, the new criterion for praise was raised to 15 steps.

When change from pretest to posttest was compared for treatment and control groups, it was found that the mean change for the treatment group was 43.6 steps while the mean change for the control group was 2.2 steps. This difference was statistically significant ($t = 5.34$, $p < .001$). A 1-year follow-up evaluation is scheduled for this study, and, in addition, other fears in adults (fear of animals such as snakes, claustrophobia, fear of electric shock) and in children (darkness, thunder and lightning) are being studied. The results are still incomplete, but the tentative suggestion is that although fears may originate from different sources and be maintained by different variables, they can all be reduced by the same *reinforced practice* procedure.

As mentioned in the introduction to this chapter, there has been a great deal of effort expended in applying reinforcement procedures to the treatment of behavior disorders in children. This ranges from work with the autistic [21, 29, 48], to the retarded [12], to the delinquent [13], to the hyperactive [31], to the academic underachiever [16], but because of space limitations this literature will not be reviewed here. The interested reader is referred to a review article by Gelfand and Hartmann [17] and to Ullman and Krasner's edited book of case studies [40].

THE PROCEDURE OF EXTINCTION

Extinction refers both to a procedure and a behavioral effect. The procedure consists of the removal of the reinforcing stimulus maintaining a particular behavior. The effect is a decline in frequency of the behavior. As a simple laboratory example, if a hungry animal has been trained to press a bar for food and then food is no longer provided for this behavior, bar-pressing will decline to near zero. Similarly, if an organism learns to press a bar to avoid shock and then shock is completely removed, bar-pressing will again decline. There are a number of variables that determine how resistant the act will be to extinction (see Kimble [24], pp. 281–320). Two of these, in particular, are important: the effect of partial reinforcement and the nature of the reinforcing event.

In the absence of reinforcement, behavior previously established on a partial reinforcement schedule will be maintained for a longer time than behavior established on a continuous reinforcement schedule (e.g., Weinstock [45]). Partial reinforcement in the bar-press situation means that the animal does not receive a food pellet each time he presses the bar. Instead, food might be delivered after completion of a fixed or variable number of presses (ratio schedule), or after a fixed or variable time from the last reinforced response (interval schedule). The most important lesson to be learned from this is that on any given occasion some behavior may occur, not receive any obvious reward, and yet still be under the control of reward. Pigeons, for example, can be taught to peck at a circular plastic disc over 500 consecutive times with brief access to grain occurring only *after* each series of 500 pecks are completed (Zimmerman and Ferster [50]).

If any neurotic or psychotic behavior is being maintained by positive reinforcement, extinction procedures (removal of the positive reinforcement) can only be started when one knows what the reinforcement is and can control its delivery. Frequently, the reinforcement may not be very obvious, or it may be difficult for the therapist to control. Also, if positive reinforcement has been provided on an intermittent basis, which is most likely, then extinction effects will be delayed.

The second important variable is the nature of the reinforcing event. If the "deviant" behavior has been maintained because it serves to avoid or terminate aversive or frightening stimuli, then the extinction procedure is likely to be slower than in the case of positively reinforced behavior. Thus, dogs trained to jump a hurdle to avoid brief electric shocks will continue to jump in response to the signal for shock even after the experimenter has withdrawn all shock from the situation (Solomon and Wynne [38]). It might be said that the dogs do not reality test. Once having learned to avoid shock, they do not wait to find out if they will still be shocked if they fail to jump. It is safer to jump. Similarly for the neurotic. Even if the original traumatic event or cumulative punishing interpersonal experiences are gone, he may continue to avoid situations, people, and objects associated symbolically or actually with these psychologically painful stimuli. This, of course, prevents new learning from taking place and exacerbates the problem further. The most useful extinction procedure in such cases is to prevent the organism from making the avoidance response so that he can discover that there is no longer anything painful to avoid. However, since this is what systematic desensitization (see Chapter 5), implosion and flooding (see Chapter 6), and reinforced practice ultimately try to do, the topic of extinction of negatively reinforced behavior will not be discussed in this chapter. We will only be concerned in this chapter with extinction of positively reinforced maladaptive behaviors.

Social approval and signs of attention and concern may be as important determiners of certain neurotic and psychotic behavior patterns as they are of normal behavior patterns. Most textbooks of psychiatry and abnormal psychology make passing recognition of this in their discussion of the "secondary gain" from symptoms. These may be material in nature, for example, payments of disability insurance, or they may be purely social, such as an increase in attention from relatives and staff. As will be seen in the case studies to be described, these so-called secondary gains may be far more relevant in the maintenance of abnormal behavior than has previously been thought possible. Indeed, they may often be of primary importance.

EXTINCTION: APPLICATION TO THE PSYCHOSES

A number of the symptomatic behaviors shown by psychotic patients have been treated by the use of extinction. In a typical example reported by Ayllon and Michael [10], a schizophrenic woman interfered with the nurses' work by entering their office some 16 times daily over a 2-year period. All attempts to persuade her to stay out of the office failed. Each time she had to be escorted back to the ward, and upon occasion she was even "pushed back bodily" out of the office. Ayllon and Michael instructed the nurses to ignore her completely whenever she entered the office. Following this, the average number of entries per day dropped to two over an 8-week period. Certainly, this cannot be considered a core symptom of schizophrenia. Nevertheless, this case indicates that part of the behavior of schizophrenic patients is maintained by pleasant or even unpleasant attention.

The next case presented by Ayllon and Michael [10] is more impressive in that it deals with a more central symptom of paranoid schizophrenia. The patient incessantly talked in a delusional way about her illegitimate child and the men who were pursuing her. This delusion had been present for 3 years and in several instances had been so annoying to other patients that they beat her to try to keep her quiet. The nurses were asked to check the patient every 30 minutes, to pay no attention to her if she engaged in delusional talk, but to respond if she talked rationally. They were also told to stop her fighting with other patients in a matter-of-fact way. Psychotic talk showed a significant decline, except for one occasion following the patient's visit to one of the social workers. The patient later said to one of the nurses: "Well, you're not listening to me. I'll have to go and see Mrs. ——— [the social worker] again, 'cause she told me that if she would listen to my past she could help me."

Other workers have also reduced the delusional speech [32] and also the hypochondriacal complaints of chronic schizophrenic patients [8], while Ayllon and Haughton [9] reinstated self-feeding behavior in a group of 32 back ward chronic schizophrenics using extinction. The nurses were asked to stop feeding them, thereby no longer providing reinforcement for this type of dependent behavior. The patients had to enter the dining room within a half-hour period; if they failed to enter in this time, they could not eat. Although there was an initial drop in the number of meals taken, each patient soon learned to enter the dining room on time and to feed himself.

In none of these cases was there a striking change in the patients' overall behavior. Since such a change was not the intent, however, this cannot be considered fair criticism. One requirement of any conditioning therapy, and this includes extinction, is a clear and precise definition of the symptom to be treated. The patient as a whole is not treated; only a specific behavior pattern. Nor is it suggested that the extinction procedure is the most effective for all the symptoms exhibited by any one patient. These studies only suggest that the extinction technique may be a reliable and effective way to eliminate or reduce the frequency of occurrence of some symptoms.

EXTINCTION: APPLICATION TO THE NEUROSES

The extinction procedure has also been used, although less frequently, in neurosis. Walton [44] described a case of neurodermatitis in a 20-year-old woman who had suffered from that condition for 2 years. Various treatments, including ointment, pills, lotion, and x-ray therapy, had proved unsatisfactory. Walton noted that scratching of the affected areas was reinforced by the attention of her family and fiancé, who also put ointment upon the sores. The family and the fiancé were instructed to discontinue this attention. Over a period of 2 months the frequency of scratching decreased until it stopped altogether, and after 3 months her skin had returned to normal. A follow-up of 4 years revealed no relapse nor any symptom substitution.

Allen and Harris [4] report a similar case in a 5-year-old child.

For a year she had been scratching herself until she bled. The scratching had resulted in large sores and scabs upon her forehead, nose, cheek, and chin. Neither previous pediatric nor psychiatric consultation had eliminated the scratching. It was noted that the child's mother spoke only to criticize, direct, or correct the child; otherwise, she paid no attention to her. The mother was instructed to discontinue all efforts to correct her daughter's misbehavior and to ignore all episodes of scratching. In addition, for every 20 or 30 minutes that the child went without scratching she was instructed to reinforce the child by giving her a small star. Candy or food was also given together with the second or third star. The stars were pasted in a booklet, counted twice a day, and exchanged for special trinkets. The child was also allowed to buy clothes for her doll on each afternoon of a scratch-free day. As the scratching decreased, the frequency of reinforcement was reduced. At the end of 6 weeks the child's face and body were clear of all scabs and sores, and after 4 months the scratching behavior had not recurred nor had any other symptom taken its place. Notice that the extinction procedure in this case was combined with positive reinforcement for nonscratching behavior.

Leitenberg, Agras, and Thomson [27], in describing a case of anorexia nervosa, reported how physical complaints occurring initially at a rate of over 20 each day were completely eliminated via an extinction procedure. During the baseline period nurses were instructed to act "normally," whereas in the extinction period they were told to ignore (by staring blankly and not responding, or by walking away from the patient) complaints of headaches, pains, fainting, and insomnia.

Another example of an extinction procedure was reported by Wolf, Birnbrauer, Williams, and Lawlor [47]. The patient was a 9-year-old girl suffering from cerebral palsy and associated mental retardation, aphasia, and hyperirritability. She vomited almost daily in class, a behavior that had built up over a period of 3 months. The authors speculated that the practice of returning the girl to her dormitory whenever she vomited was a positive reinforcement. Extinction procedures were therefore started in which the girl was not returned to the dormitory. In addition, the teacher praised her and gave her M & M candies for desired classroom behavior. Vomiting extinguished in 6 weeks and did not recur throughout the rest of the school year. During the next school year, however, the child vomited once and was returned to her dormitory. This was allowed to continue, and as expected, she began to vomit in class as often as before. When extinction procedures were reintroduced, vomiting again disappeared. Wolf and his associates have also reported a number of studies in which it was found that teacher attention and concern were maintaining inappropriate behavior in nursery-age children. In one of the studies [5] it was found that a teacher approached the child who was a social isolate to "find out what was bothering her," to console, to persuade, and so forth, when the child was alone. However, when the child did actually play with other children, she received no attention from the teacher. When the contingencies were reversed, the frequency of each behavior was reversed, i.e., playing alone decreased and playing with other children increased. This was repeatedly altered simply by switching which behavior the teacher attended to.

Finally, one aspect of a case study of marital discord reported by Goldiamond [18] is worth mentioning. A husband could not be in the presence of his wife without either berating her or sulking in a conspicuous manner. It was suggested that whenever he had the urge to engage in such behavior he should go into the garage and sit on a "sulking stool." There are, of course, numerous elements in this program in addition to an extinction procedure. There is humor, distraction, and communication that the sulking behavior was not only inappropriate and silly but under his control. The extinction element was there, however. If the husband sulked in the garage, the former interpersonal consequence presumably maintaining this behavior (distress by wife) was no longer present.

These few examples make one point extremely clear. In order to apply an extinction procedure one must properly identify the reinforcing events maintaining the deviant behavior. While this may be possible from the history elicited either from the patient or relatives, it is more likely that direct observation of the patient during occurrence of the symptomatic behavior will lead to such identification. Such observation may be carried out on a hospital ward or by watching the interaction between the patient and members of his family, either at home or in the clinic. Usually the reinforcing events will be social in nature, such as verbal or nonverbal attention given to symptomatic behavior. It is important to note that what may seem to be unwelcome attention may be positively reinforcing. A clear demonstration of this point is presented in a recent study on disruptive classroom behavior by Thomas, Becker, and Armstrong [39]. They report that a teacher's command to "sit down" caused the immediate desired effect, i.e., the child would sit down. Unfortunately, he also started to stand up more frequently. Only praising sitting increased sitting behavior.

Once the probable reinforcing event is delineated, it can hopefully be eliminated. Usually this involves giving detailed and specific instructions to members of staff, or to the teacher, or to other pertinent members of the family. Training these "reinforcing agents" may require demonstrations or even preliminary role-playing sessions to practice ignoring the unwanted behavior and attending to the desired behavior. There is no question, however, that it can be done. Exciting recent examples of how parents and other significant members of the child's environment were trained to apply both reinforcement and extinction procedures to deal with serious problems in children can be found in studies by Wahler et al. [43], Wahler and Erickson [42], and Hawkins et al. [19].

How much maladaptive behavior is maintained by positive reinforcement is not known. Although the studies so far reported have dealt with only a small number of neurotic and psychotic behaviors, they appear to indicate that further attempts to apply the extinction procedure are deserving of support; the progress so far is promising. Of course, further studies need to be mindful of the need for experimental controls and long-term follow-up.

REINFORCEMENT AND EXTINCTION: SUMMARY AND OVERVIEW

The complementary psychotherapeutic techniques of reinforcement of adaptive behaviors and extinction of maladaptive behaviors reviewed in this chapter are still in an early stage of development. Applications have been made to only a small fraction of psychotic, psychoneurotic, personality, and psychosomatic disorders. Not only must applicability to a greater variety of behavior disorders be determined, but within the confines of those disorders already studied the sample size needs to be considerably expanded in order to be able to judge the generality of findings. Furthermore, there is a striking need for well-controlled *outcome* studies with adequate follow-up periods. Future workers in this area will have less recourse to the "excuse" that they are "pioneering" a new approach.

It should be noted that the circumscribed aims of behavior therapy provide one essential ingredient for making serious scientific evaluations possible. The objectives of therapy are not diffuse and ambiguous. They are not personality restructuring, self-actualization, ego-strength, or insight (see pp. 8–13). Unlike many other psychotherapeutic endeavors, the behavior therapist has the ability to quantify the form and frequency of the desired behavioral change. This limited objective is sometimes denigrated as "mere" symptom relief, likely to provoke "symptom substitution." However, as several recent papers have cogently argued [14, 49], there is no empiric evidence for the notion of symptom substitution in the context of behavior therapy. The more likely form of failure is relapse of the old symptoms rather than the development of new ones.

The "mere symptom removal" argument is perhaps best addressed by reference to a physical analogy. If a man breaks his leg skiing, the first priority is to mend the broken leg. Subsequently, there may or may not be call to teach the man to ski better, to develop his physical condition to his fullest potential, and to correct poor conditions on the slope. No matter what else is done, the first order of business is to fix the leg. Similarly, the first order of business for treatment of an obsessive-compulsive handwasher is to help her to be able to stop washing without experiencing overwhelming anxiety; the first order of business for a patient who complains of feeling of inadequacy is to train him to define his terms behaviorally and subsequently to help train him to act in ways that can be considered adequate. The behavior therapist is not unaware that patient's complaints are often stated in the realm of feelings (e.g., dissatisfaction, loneliness) and attitudes (e.g., alienation), but the hypothesis is that if these feelings and attitudes can be expressed in behavioral terms, then something direct can be done about the problem. One need not change feelings and attitudes in order to change behavior. Rather, if one can change behavior, then thoughts and values and feelings about oneself and others change as well. In addition, it is obvious that since patients may make multiple complaints, then multiple therapeutic techniques may be called for. We are reaching a level of sophistication where specific interventions are designed to produce specific rather than global therapeutic effects.

Positive reinforcement and extinction procedures appear to be powerful shapers of behavior. It seems to make little difference whether the behavior in question is labeled "normal" or "abnormal." The consequences of behavior are the means by which most behavior is molded to meet the physical and social requirements of the environment in which the organism lives. A systematic application of reinforcement and nonreinforcement contingencies may therefore serve to modify many of the significant behaviors of the behaviorally ill patient. The ever-increasing work in this area, the results so far obtained, and the exciting interaction with some of the basic research in experimental psychology all indicate that this expectation may be realized.

Although guarded optimism does not appear misplaced at this time, many more controlled and objective studies will have to be done before it is completely clear that applications of reinforcement principles are not just another passing fad in the difficult area of psychotherapy.

REFERENCES

1. Agras, W. S., Leitenberg, H., and Barlow, D. H. Social reinforcement in the modification of agoraphobia. *Archives of General Psychiatry* 19:423, 1968.
2. Agras, W. S., Leitenberg, H., Barlow, D. H., and Thomson, L. E.

Instructions and reinforcement in the modification of neurotic behavior. *American Journal of Psychiatry* 125:1435, 1969.

3. Agras, W. S., Leitenberg, H., Wincze, J. P., Butz, R. A., and Callahan, E. J.   Comparison of the effects of instructions and reinforcement in the treatment of a neurotic avoidance response: A single case experiment. *Journal of Behavior Therapy and Experimental Psychiatry* 1:53, 1970.

4. Allen, E. K., and Harris, F. R.   Elimination of a child's excessive scratching by training the mother in reinforcement procedures. *Behaviour Research and Therapy* 4:79, 1966.

5. Allen, E. K., Hart, B. M., Buell, J. S., Harris, F. R., and Wolf, M. M.   Effects of social reinforcement on isolate behavior of a nursery school child. *Child Development* 35:511, 1964.

6. Ayllon, T.   Intensive treatment of psychotic behavior by stimulus satiation and food reinforcement. *Behaviour Research and Therapy* 1:53, 1963.

7. Ayllon, T., and Azrin, N. H.   Reinforcement and instructions with mental patients. *Journal of the Experimental Analysis of Behavior* 7:327, 1964.

8. Ayllon, T., and Haughton, E.   Modification of symptomatic verbal behavior of mental patients. *Behaviour Research and Therapy* 2:87, 1964.

9. Ayllon, T., and Haughton, E.   Control of the behavior of schizophrenic patients by food. *Journal of the Experimental Analysis of Behavior* 5:343, 1962.

10. Ayllon, T., and Michael, J.   The psychiatric nurse as a behavioral engineer. *Journal of the Experimental Analysis of Behavior* 2:323, 1959.

11. Bachrach, A. J., Erwin, W. J., and Mohr, P. J.   The Control of Eating Behavior in an Anorexic by Operant Conditioning Techniques. In Ullman, L. P., and Krasner, L. (Eds.), *Case Studies in Behavior Modification*. New York: Holt, Rinehart & Winston, 1965.

12. Birnbrauer, J. S. Wolf, M. M., Kidder, J., and Tague, C.   Classroom behavior of retarded pupils with token reinforcement. *Journal of Experimental Child Psychology* 2:219, 1965.

13. Burchard, J. D., and Tyler, V. O.   The modification of delinquent behavior through operant conditioning. *Behaviour Research and Therapy* 2:245, 1965.

14. Cahoon, D. D.   Symptom substitution and the behavior therapies. *Psychological Bulletin* 69:149, 1968.

15. Callahan, E. J., and Leitenberg, H.   Reinforced practice as a

treatment for acrophobia: A controlled outcome study. Paper presented at American Psychological Association, Miami, 1970.

16. Clark, M., Lachowicz, J., and Wolf, M. M.   A pilot basic education program for school dropouts incorporating a token reinforcement system. *Behaviour Research and Therapy* 6:183, 1968.

17. Gelfand, D. M., and Hartmann, D. P.   Behavior therapy with children: A review and evaluation of research methodology. *Psychological Bulletin* 69:204, 1968.

18. Goldiamond, I.   Self-Control Procedures in Personal Behavior Problems. In Ulrich, R., Stachnik, T., and Mabry, J. (Eds.), *Control of Human Behavior*. Glenview, Ill.: Scott, Foresman, 1966.

19. Hawkins, R. P., Peterson, R. F., Schweid, E., and Bijou, S. W. Behavior therapy in the home: Amelioration of problem parent-child relations with the parent in a therapeutic role. *Journal of Experimental Child Psychology* 4:99, 1966.

20. Honig, W. K. (Ed.)   *Operant Behavior: Areas of Research and Application*. New York: Appleton-Century-Crofts, 1966.

21. Hudson, E., and DeMyer, M. K.   Food as a reinforcer in educational therapy of autistic children. *Behaviour Research and Therapy* 6:37, 1968.

22. Isaacs, W., Thomas, J., and Goldiamond, I.   Application of operant conditioning to reinstate verbal behavior in psychotics. *Journal of Speech and Hearing Disorders* 25:8, 1960.

23. Kale, R. J., Kaye, J. H., Whelan, P. A., and Hopkins, B. L. The effects of reinforcement on the modification, maintenance, and generalization of social responses of mental patients. *Journal of Applied Behavior Analysis* 1:315, 1968.

24. Kimble, G. A.   *Hilgard and Marquis' Conditioning and Learning*. New York: Appleton-Century-Crofts, 1961.

25. Leitenberg, H., Agras, W. S., Barlow, D. H., and Oliveau, D. C. Contribution of selective positive reinforcement and therapeutic instructions to systematic desensitization therapy. *Journal of Abnormal Psychology* 74:113, 1969.

26. Leitenberg, H., Agras, W. S., Edwards, J. A., Thomson, L. E., and Wincze, J. P.   Practice as a psychotherapeutic variable. *Journal of Psychiatric Research* 7:215, 1970.

27. Leitenberg, H., Agras, W. S., and Thomson, L. E.   A sequential analysis of the effect of selective positive reinforcement in modifying anorexia nervosa. *Behaviour Research and Therapy* 6:211, 1968.

28. Leitenberg, H., Agras, W. S., Thomson, L. E., and Wright, D. E. Feedback in behavior modification: An experimental analysis in

two phobic cases. *Journal of Applied Behavior Analysis* 1:131, 1968.

29. Lovaas, O. I., Berberich, J. P., Perloff, B. F., and Schaeffer, B. Acquisition of imitative speech by schizophrenic children. *Science* 161:705, 1966.

30. Oliveau, D. C., Agras, W. S., Leitenberg, H., Moore, R. C., and Wright, D. E. Systematic desensitization, therapeutically oriented instructions and selective positive reinforcement. *Behaviour Research and Therapy* 7:27, 1969.

31. Patterson, G. R., Jones, R., Whittier, J., and Wright, M. A. A behavior modification technique for the hyperactive child. *Behaviour Research and Therapy* 2:217, 1965.

32. Rickard, H. C., Dignam, P. J., and Horner, R. F. Verbal manipulation in a psychotherapeutic relationship. *Journal of Clinical Psychology* 16:364, 1960.

33. Russo, S. Adaptations in behavioural therapy with children. *Behaviour Research and Therapy* 2:43, 1964.

34. Schmidt, E. A comparative evaluation of verbal conditioning and behavior training in an individual case. *Behaviour Research and Therapy* 2:19, 1964.

35. Sherman, J. A. Reinstatement of verbal behavior in a psychotic by reinforcement methods. *Journal of Speech and Hearing Disorders* 28:398, 1963.

36. Sherman, J. A. Use of reinforcement and imitation to reinstate verbal behavior in mute psychotics. *Journal of Abnormal Psychology* 70:155, 1965.

37. Skinner, B. F. *Science and Human Behavior*. New York: Macmillan, 1953.

38. Solomon, R. L., and Wynne, L. C. Traumatic avoidance learning: The principle of anxiety conservation and partial irreversibility. *Psychological Review* 61:353, 1954.

39. Thomas, D., Becker, W., and Armstrong, M. Production and elimination of disruptive classroom behavior by systematically varying teacher's behavior. *Journal of Applied Behavior Analysis* 1:35, 1968.

40. Ullman, L. P., and Krasner, L. (Eds.) *Case Studies in Behavior Modification*. New York: Holt, Rinehart & Winston, 1965.

41. Ullman, L. P., Krasner, L., and Collins, B. J. Modification of behavior through verbal conditioning effects in group psychotherapy. *Journal of Abnormal Social Psychology* 62:128, 1961.

42. Wahler, R. G., and Erickson, M. Child behavior therapy: A

community program in Appalachia. *Behaviour Research and Therapy* 7:71, 1969.

43. Wahler, R. G., Winkel, G. H., Peterson, R. F., and Morrison, D. C. Mothers as behavior therapists for their own children. *Behaviour Research and Therapy* 3:113, 1965.

44. Walton, D. The Application of Learning Theory to the Treatment of a Case of Neurodermatitis. In Eysenck, H. J. (Ed.), *Behavior Therapy and the Neuroses*. London: Pergamon, 1960.

45. Weinstock, S. Acquisition and extinction of a partially reinforced running response at a 24-hour intertrial interval. *Journal of Experimental Psychology* 56:151, 1958.

46. Wincze, J. P., Leitenberg, H., and Agras, W. S. A sequential analysis of the effects of token reinforcement and instructions on the delusional verbal behavior of chronic paranoid schizophrenics. Paper presented at American Psychological Association, Miami, 1970.

47. Wolf, M. M., Birnbrauer, J. S., Williams, T., and Lawlor, J. A Note on Apparent Extinction of Vomiting Behavior of a Retarded Child. In Ullman, L. P., and Krasner, L. (Eds.), *Case Studies in Behavior Modification*. New York: Holt, Rinehart & Winston, 1965.

48. Wolf, M. M., Risley, T., Johnston, M., Harris, F. R., and Allen, E. K. Application of operant conditioning procedures to the behavior problems of an autistic child: A follow-up and extension. *Behaviour Research and Therapy* 5:103, 1967.

49. Yates, A. J. Symptoms and symptom substitution. *Psychological Review* 65:371, 1958.

50. Zimmerman, J., and Ferster, C. B. Some notes on time out from reinforcement. *Journal of the Experimental Analysis of Behavior* 7:13, 1964.

3

The Token Economy: Now

TEODORO AYLLON AND
MICHAEL D. ROBERTS

EDITOR'S INTRODUCTION

The token economy is a special case of the application of rein-forcement and extinction procedures. Exactly the same principles apply; namely, definition of the behavior desired, measurement, con-tingent application of a hypothesized rewarding event, and monitor-ing the effect via performance measures. Instead of using reinforcers directly, tokens that can later be exchanged for a variety of consumer goods and pleasurable activities are used. Instead of being applied to an individual, the procedure is applied to a group in a whole en-vironment: a ward, a home for delinquents, a classroom. Adaptive behaviors are built up by reinforcement with tokens and, if neces-sary, undesirable behaviors are eliminated by using the technique of response cost, namely the contingent loss of tokens. The pioneer-ing token economy at Anna State Hospital is clearly described on pages 72–79.

Instituting such an economy implies total environmental control. If privileges are used as reinforcers, then they must only be obtain-able via a token exchange. This means that the hospital or school administration must agree with the aims of the project and take the necessary administrative measures to allow for such control. More-over, staff at all levels must be educated in the use of the token system and be convinced enough of its advantages to work willingly within it. Thus, the first steps in starting a token economy are to seek administrative support and to educate the staff. The newcomer to the field is advised to seek consultation with someone who has directed such a program or to visit an operating token economy to familiarize himself with the myriad of small operational details that can make or break such an endeavor. The mere giving of tokens is not a token economy. Properly done, the token economy is a complex motivating environment.

Ayllon and Roberts present a bold argument that traditional psychotherapists have come to limit their activities, preferring to treat the verbal, the intelligent, and the less handicapped. This is a sound argument; 98 percent of private patients seen by members of the American Psychoanalytic Association are white, and 78 percent have at least a college education [1]. State hospitals have many unfilled positions, both for psychiatrists and psychologists. Ayllon and Roberts consider the token economy to be an antidote to this trend. The role of the professional therapist is altered more drastically than with other applications of reinforcement procedures. The main therapy is provided continuously by aides, nurses, guards, teachers, houseparents, or even fellow patients. The professional therapist designs the economy, teaches the staff, supervises the results by way of ongoing, objective behavioral measures, and makes changes based on these observations. He can also conduct experiments to achieve maximum cost efficiency and evaluate the overall efficiency of the program.

Ayllon and Roberts (p. 75) argue that shaping adaptive behavior, particularly the ability to work at relevant tasks, tends to eliminate deviant behavior since the requirements of work are incompatible with maladaptive behavior. However, most economies also pay attention to the elimination of generally undesirable behaviors, usually, as noted previously, in a punishment or extinction paradigm. Of course, unique problems can be worked out within the token economy on an individual basis, but to date most applications have been to relatively homogeneous groups, the back ward patient, the delinquent, the mentally retarded, or the educationally handicapped.

Once maximum performance is achieved within a token economy, the problem of transfer to the natural environment occurs. Ideally,

*a series of environments each more closely approximating the termi-
nal environment should be available, all run along the same lines,
perhaps with money gradually replacing tokens. For the back ward
patient, a series of more open wards, a halfway house, and an independent group living situation might be considered. Again, the
family is a natural group for the application of the token economy,
particularly for the disturbed child or adolescent. In such instances
a behavioral contract is often drawn up between parents and child
(ren) forming a vehicle for the exact specification of desired and
undesired behaviors and the reinforcers and punishments. This technique appears to help families to reorganize themselves and to com-
municate better, allowing positive behaviors (and therefore feelings)
more chance to occur.*

*As in the case of reinforcement and extinction procedures, there
is much experimental data demonstrating the immediate powerful
effects of the contingent application of tokens. At least a fourfold increase in work behavior can be expected from the application of
these procedures in a back ward environment. However, nearly all
the studies have been single-case controlled experiments, and again
we find a paucity of controlled outcome studies. Moreover, the outcome studies that have been published to date are not conclusive in
that they have been beset with methodologic problems. As noted in
one critique [2], patients treated within a token economy program
should be compared with patients treated in an exactly similar way
except that tokens be given noncontingently in the control group.
Preferably the staff in the control treatment should feel that they
can produce equally good results as the token economy to control
for expectancy and ward morale, factors which enhance therapeutic
outcome. An alternative experimental design is to compare an optimal treatment program with a similar program plus a token economy. Measures of patient performance over a follow-up of at least
1 year should be made. In this way the practical question as to the
extra benefit conferred by the token economy can be answered and
some judgments as to cost efficacy made. Unfortunately, no study
approximates either of these designs; doubtless this will be remedied,*

but until then the long-term usefulness of the procedure must re-
main in doubt. Nevertheless, the token economy is an effective way
of organizing a therapeutic environment to maximize patient per-
formance. This is an important contribution in itself and should be
considered an extension of the concepts and methods of milieu
therapy.

W.S.A.

REFERENCES

1. Hamburg, D. A.   Report of ad hoc committee on central fact-
   gathering data of the American Psychoanalytic Association. *Jour-*
   nal of the American Psychoanalytical Association 15:841, 1967.
2. Hersen, M., and Eisler, R. M.   Comments on Heap, Boblitt,
   Moore, and Hord's "Behavior-Milieu Therapy" with chronic
   neuropsychiatric patients. *Psychological Reports,* in press.

The token economy is rapidly becoming one of the "in" topics in
the behavioral sciences. The demand for effective tools of behavior
management has led to a reevaluation of traditional therapeutic
and educational procedures in such settings as hospitals, clinics,
prisons, schools, and even the U.S. Army.

What is the token economy? Like the application of positive reinforcement described in the preceding chapter, it involves four steps.
First, the definition of treatment objectives in performance terms, as
contrasted to vague, global concepts; second, ongoing observational
recording of these behaviors; third, the use of a wide range of incentives to which the individual patient gains access upon meeting specific behavioral objectives; and finally, the use and exchange of a
tangible currency, such as tokens, for incentives. In short, the token
economy represents a new methodologic, conceptual, and theoretic
approach to the treatment of mental illness, as compared to what
may be termed *traditional* or *mainstream* psychotherapy.

RATIONALE

But why a new approach? And why should hospitals, clinics, prisons, schools, and the U.S. Army try it? What are the traditional therapeutic and educational systems failing to do? According to a report of the Joint Commission on Mental Health in 1961, psychotherapists, psychiatrists, and clinics devote most of their time to minor and the more easily treatable forms of mental illness, tending to ignore those suffering from serious mental disorders. Further, they tend to treat the college-educated, upper-middle-class, white segment of the population. A report issued by the National Institute of Labor Education in 1963 demonstrates that the state hospital population is drawn mainly from the lower socioeconomic groups; yet, the psychotherapeutic methods used by the scarce professional are based on services to middle- and upper-class individuals, surely an unsound basis for the treatment of the great majority of patients.

Why did therapists come to limit themselves in this way? The authors suggest that it was a function of the training of these professionals. Psychology was an offspring of medicine, psychiatry a medical field of specialization. It was natural, therefore, that the therapist assume a disease-oriented or medical-model concept of behavioral disturbance. The psychotherapist, therefore, arranged his treatment methods for the "sick" who came to him. The patient was considered to be sick either when he emitted behavior that was judged to be abnormal or failed to do something considered normal. Being mentally ill, he sought or was brought to the therapist to be cured. The medical view of mental illness suggested that treatment should not be concerned with eliminating the abnormal behavior but with the hypothesized underlying cause. Psychotherapy, therefore, consisted of discovering and treating this cause, thus allowing the emergence of a healthy personality.

An alternative approach to the treatment of institutionalized persons was, however, developing during the midfifties. This approach is best described as clinical-experimental psychology rather than psychopathology. It focused on the direct measurement of specific, observable behaviors of severely mentally ill individuals. These behaviors were regarded as problematic rather than symptomatic, and their treatment was based on the concepts of operant psychology.

Operant psychology attends to those behaviors that affect the surrounding environment. Such behaviors are maintained, and often shaped, by the feedback a person receives from the environment as a consequence of his behavior. There is no firm discrimination made between normal and abnormal operant behaviors, as both are maintained and formed by identical processes. Operant methodology and techniques for the experimental analysis of behavior were developed in the laboratory after extensive work with animals [15, 24].

The methodology of operant conditioning was successfully applied to the study of chronic psychotic behavior by Lindsley [18] and Lindsley and Skinner [19]. Lindsley's pioneering work showed that a behavioral dimension, which could be identified and defined reliably, provided the basic datum for study and analysis. Systematic alterations of the environment could then be studied in terms of their effect on the behavior. Indeed, initial results from Lindsley's work showed that the behavior of chronic schizophrenic patients in the laboratory setting was susceptible to environmental influence.

BEHAVIORAL MEASUREMENT

Extension of this general finding to clinical problems required that the concept of mental illness be redefined in terms of observable behavior rather than psychic manifestations. Although a trained professional may be capable of observing psychic correlates such as obsession or delusion with some degree of reliability, untrained nurses and attendants cannot be expected to do so. However, the use of behavioral observations made it possible to use nonprofessionals effectively since (1) behavior could be tightly and objectively defined, (2) its occurrence could be reliably recorded, and (3) its consequences could be systematically and consistently determined, all by *nonprofessionals*. When this methodology was developed, it was easily learned and applied; and, because it was administered by the nonprofessional staff and not by a single therapist, a built-in reliability check over several observers avoided the problem of bias.

At first behavioral researchers did not record behavior directly. Although radical in theoretic conception, they shared a common methodologic background with traditional psychotherapy. Their training had demonstrated to them that the richness and complexity of human behavior made direct measurement difficult. Therefore, they sought a shortcut by using indirect, interpretive, or inferential means. The most objective psychological measurement was the I.Q. test, so it was here the researchers first sought the shortcut. They found I.Q. tests to be reliable, but of little value, however, in measuring specific behaviors. Personality tests seemed to offer more, but the correlation between such tests and actual behavior proved too low to be useful. The testing procedures seemed too insensitive for the objectives of the behavioral psychologists. When administered in the usual pre- and posttest fashion, they sometimes indicated no change, even though the researchers had a "feeling" that the patient's behavior had changed. And even when a change was indicated, they could not say with assurance that it was due to the methods they had used and not to another variable such as time, insight, or spontaneous recovery. The psychiatric interview was tried next. Interview techniques, however, sacrificed a great deal of reliability, and it was found that how the patient *described* his behavior often varied greatly from observations of how he in fact *did* behave. Already partially in use, rating techniques were the next measures to be tried. Ratings, however, were not reliable, as they were affected by the rater's personality, mood, interpretation, and even the time of rating.

Thus, behavioral psychologists, finding no suitable indirect methods, returned to the only sensitive and reliable methods of which they were sure—the arbitrary laboratory responses that had been used to develop operant theory. But was it fair to the patient who had real-life problems to treat him in terms of lever presses and chain pulls? No! Treatment and measurement methods had to be made relevant to the patient's problems. Researchers had to face the fact that if they were to use observable behavior in the methodology, there were no shortcuts; they all had drawbacks in that they necessitated the sacrifice of reliability in the name of relevance, or the sacrifice of relevance in the name of reliability with the further possibility of suffering from insensitivity to moment-to-moment change. Thus, if specific behavior was the objective of their methodology, it would have to be directly observed. By defining the behavior to be observed in terms that made it easier to record reliably, and by restricting observations to a certain time and place, measurement could be made easier than they had presumed.

While researchers were interested in identifying and recording psychotic behavior, they gradually became aware that psychotic behavior is not unidimensional but multidimensional. What was needed was a chance to record a dimension that had both clinical relevance and a high degree of stability from measurement to measurement. In the mental hospital this criterion was met by patients whose behavior seemed to provide continuous stress or discomfort to the ward staff or appeared to interfere with therapeutic efforts. Thus, early efforts were directed toward elimination of behaviors that were a chronic problem to the staff.

The operant conditioners were certainly psychologic heretics. Their concepts of behavior and therapy were radically different from those prevailing in the field of psychology. Like any group of heretics or radicals, they faced an immense problem in getting themselves heard. Although they had new ideas that they wished to put into practice, the traditional majority controlled the institutions in which they might work. Unlike many heretics and radicals, they realized that a compromise had to be made. They agreed to take the most difficult psychological problems and with their new methods eliminate these problem behaviors. Still skeptical but having nothing to lose, the traditionalists allowed a few researchers and clinicians to tackle these problems. Given the opportunity, the operant heretics set about proving themselves.

PRELIMINARY RESEARCH

As noted in Chapter 2, research workers and clinicians began to apply the procedures of operant conditioning to a variety of problem behaviors. Directly relevant to the development of the token economy was a series of experiments by Ayllon and others [3–10] in a hospital setting through which the effectiveness of such principles and procedures as used by nonprofessionals in the treatment of severely disturbed institutionalized patients was demonstrated.

Social Reinforcement

Verbal behavior is often considered the most bizarre feature of the mentally ill. Ayllon and Haughton [8] trained nurses and aides to identify and record the bizarre verbal behavior of a psychotic patient. It was found that selective withholding or application of the nurses' attention, interest, and concern to the patient's verbal behavior was a controller of the content of the patient's speech. When the nurses' attention, interest, and concern were selectively applied to "healthy" talk and withheld from bizarre talk, bizarre talk quickly decreased and healthy talk increased from 50 percent to 80 percent of the patient's total verbal output, stabilizing at more than 30 percent above its original level.

It was found that many other disruptive psychotic behaviors, when considered and treated as would be any learned "normal" behavior, could be controlled by social feedback, including situations in which the lack of a particular behavior is problematic. Ayllon [2] described such a situation in which nursing attention seemed to be necessary for the physical survival of the patient. This patient had been spoon-fed, tube-fed, and on extreme occasions intravenously fed. Her refusal to eat, it had been assumed, was an integral part of her psychosis. This "treatment" had been going on for 14 years. The nurses' assistance was entirely withdrawn, and within 4 days the patient, by then ravenous, ran to the dining room and proceeded to eat on her own.

These and other experiments indicated that many behaviors displayed on institutional wards were maintained by feedback given to the patient by those with whom he was in social contact. In the institution the patient is in almost constant social contact with the nurses and attendants. Therefore, researchers began to train the nurses and attendants to treat patients within their charge by consciously manipulating the social feedback they gave to the patients. This approach presented two significant advantages; first, actual treatment of patients was no longer limited exclusively to professionals, and second, treatment was no longer limited to an hour or so a week but could be administered up to 24 hours a day by nurses and attendants.

Stimulus Satiation

An alternative to the extinction procedure to eliminate undesirable behavior was also discovered, namely, stimulus satiation [3]. This technique was used to treat a psychotic female patient who had displayed obsessive-compulsive behavior for 9 years.

The most prominent feature of the patient's illness was hoarding towels. Each day she collected towels from the other 40 patients on the ward and kept them in her small room; and every day the staff asked the patient very politely for the towels that belonged to other patients, but she refused to give them up. This obviously represented a logistic problem to the ward staff; how to give baths to 40 patients when one patient kept 30 towels for herself. The only solution previously attempted was to go to her room each time and take all the towels away from her. Often such symptoms are interpreted as reflecting a deep need for love. Hoarding towels was thus regarded as a symptom of this need. While this analysis may be useful as a way of conceptualizing a problem, it certainly was not very helpful to the attendants or nurses who were faced with a real, practical problem of a ward-wide towel shortage. In this case the problem was further complicated because the patient refused to talk and therefore was regarded as unsuitable for psychotherapy.

Treatment began by directly measuring the problem behavior, namely, towel hoarding. A constant count of the towels possessed by the patient was initiated so as to minimize guesswork and provide a check on the effectiveness of the treatment procedures. The first procedure tried was to discontinue the old method of telling the patient not to collect towels or taking them away from her. The attendants, in fact, were instructed to give the patient an average of seven towels a day. At first she was very happy to receive the towels, and for the first time in 12 years coherently indicated her pleasure and welcomed the attendants with words like, "Oh, you found my towels, that's wonderful, thank you, nurse, thank you." This situation seemed delightful to the patient, but the staff became increasingly impatient to find a solution to their problem. So, after a few days the daily average of towels given to the patient was increased to 60. The patient's attitude toward towels began to change: "It takes me all day to put my things away now, you know . . . I don't think I need so many towels, maybe I have enough now." Since the problem behavior was defined in terms of number of towels, this change in verbal behavior was not enough. The towels kept on coming since the researchers wanted the patient to decide to get rid of them, not just to complain about them.

The patient had previously folded the towels and neatly placed them on her bed, her bureau, and her chair, but when the number of towels reached about 700, she complained that she could not stay up the whole night folding and caring for them. The staff still refrained from coercion and understandingly reassured the patient to "do the best you can; we'll just try to give you what you need." But the patient became less efficient in arranging the towels and was even irritated by their presence, as was evidenced by her throwing a couple of towels at a nurse after 4 weeks of treatment. She then found that no one picked up the towels and no one brought them in again, so she tried another two or three towels and put them outside her room. Again they did not come back. Within a few days she had disposed of towels, literally by the hundreds, until she was left with only one.

Methodologic Problems

Although extinction and stimulus satiation were effective in eliminating some undesirable behaviors, methodologic problems, particularly in measurement, occurred. Problematic behaviors were especially suited for operant treatment as they are by definition observable, and therefore recordable. The definition of the behavior that is necessary prior to reliable recording can, however, present a formidable task. Self-abuse, for example, presents a typical problem of dimension, definition, and recording. Is it anytime the patient strikes, pinches, or bites himself, or only when such behavior leaves a physical result? When does normal scratching become self-injurious? Assuming that the response can be defined, how should it be recorded? It is impractical to follow the patient around 24 hours a day. A time-sampling technique may be applied, but how does one handle the situation when no self-abuse is observed, but the physical evidence, such as torn-out hair, is seen?

Assuming that these methodologic problems can be solved, what should one do with the patient who displays many inappropriate behaviors? They could be eliminated in series or perhaps even in tandem, but for maximal effectiveness each must be treated as a separate behavior with its individual methodologic problems to overcome. Fortunately, an alternative tactic was possible.

Selective Positive Reinforcement

Undesirable behavior was often found to be diminished by reinforcing a competing behavior. This was done by using the procedure of selective positive reinforcement (see Chapter 2, pp. 31–35), following desirable behavior with a stimulus that causes its rate to increase. Originally, the reinforcers used were consumable items such as peanuts, cigarettes, M & M's, cookies, ice cream, candy, and chewing gum [9, 11]. These applications of operant conditioning to treat institutional behavior used one or, at most, a few of these reinforcers in any one procedure. Doing so was convenient, and with care, satiation could be postponed for a time. But in general, consumable reinforcers were found unsatisfactory because of the satiation problem and because their use required preselection of individuals who were affected by such events. Although cigarettes were useful with some patients, others did not smoke. There was an obvious need for reinforcers of wide applicability.

Multiple Reinforcers

Direct observation of daily ward behaviors indicated great differences in the frequency of any particular behavior among different individuals. Based on this observation, Premack [21] expressed a general principle that of any two behaviors, the one having a higher probability of occurrence can be used to reinforce the lower probability one. Researchers began to strengthen low-probability, desirable behaviors by reinforcing them with the opportunity to engage in high-probability behaviors. Many reinforcers could be offered, and the patient was allowed to select the one he wanted at that particular time. Ferster and De Myer [14] made many different types of reinforcing objects and events available to autistic children at one time. As a consequence of desirable behavior, the children were allowed to select among drinking a cold beverage, playing a pinball machine, playing a phonograph record, running an electric train, and so on.

Conditioned Reinforcers

A problem, even with multiple reinforcers, occurred. In general, reinforcement is optimal when the presentation of the reinforcer immediately follows the emission of the desired response [25]. But, it is often impractical to offer a reinforcer without causing numerous interruptions of the patient's ongoing behavior. This problem led researchers to develop conditioned reinforcers to bridge the delay between the occurrence of the response and availability of the reinforcing stimulus. The use of conditioned reinforcers was well founded in experimental studies [16]. Consider the plight of the old country doctor. He practiced among the rural population, setting broken limbs, delivering children, and curing disease. For his efforts he was often "paid" by being asked to supper (which meant he could not continue his rounds), offered a dozen eggs (although he already had a dozen at home) or some canned peaches (even though he did not especially care for peaches). What the doctor needed was medical supplies, a new car, electricity to light his house, and probably a quart of his favorite Bourbon. Even the most dedicated physician would prefer to receive payment for his services in cash, which he could later exchange for supplies, a new car, and so on.

Ayllon and Azrin [4–6] used tokens (specially manufactured, distinctive, metal, coinlike objects) as conditioned reinforcers in an institutional project. The attendants were trained to reinforce the patients with tokens when the appropriate behavior was displayed. A methodologic advantage provided by the use of tokens was that they minimized the subjective aspects of the patient-attendant interaction at the time of reinforcement delivery. In addition, the token allowed the development of a standardized procedure for the delivery of the reinforcer and its exchange and opened the way for the treatment of groups rather than individual patients with nonprofessionals as the main therapeutic agents.

THE TOKEN ECONOMY AT ANNA STATE HOSPITAL

Subjects

The first large-scale use of conditioned reinforcers was in the applied behavior research project conducted at Anna State Hospital [6]. The objective of this research was to design a complex motivating *environment* to achieve specific objectives of treatment and rehabilitation; the project was called "The Token Economy." The subjects of the study were psychotic mental patients. According to White [28], schizophrenia is the most common form of psychosis, exhibited in a multitude of varying symptoms. "The disorder can be understood only when constitution, physiology, the nervous system, mental changes, emotional changes, adjustment and defense, and the character of the social environment are all spread upon the canvas. Only workers who can grasp subtleties in all of these fields can solve the problem of schizophrenia" (pp. 509–510). The varieties of psychosis are several, but some of the general symptoms include loss of interest, ineffectiveness in meeting social demands, a lack of assertiveness, delusions, loss of contact with reality, catatonic-stupor with or without catatonic excitement, extreme passivity, disorganization of the personality, incoherency, a definite failure to interact effectively with other people, withdrawal, and loss of contact with the environment. It is also generally held that psychotics are unable to function in environments requiring moderate-to-fine discriminations of time, space, and consistency. These, then, were the subjects of a series of experiments [4] to determine the effectiveness of behavioral procedures in maintaining desired behaviors.

Target Behaviors: Choice

Psychopharmaceuticals were also used to eliminate certain kinds of behaviors. Unfortunately, although these drugs eliminated certain undesirable behaviors, they also affected desirable behaviors.

Token economy systems, of course, are no panacea either; they have been and will be misused. For example, tokens could be used to reinforce patients for sitting quietly in their rooms all day as a method of ward management—not a particular fruitful use of the procedure. It must be kept in mind that tokens are only a means to an end, namely, behavior. The critical part of an applied program, then, is the selection of the terminal or target behavior.

The Anna State Hospital project focused on behaviors that were functional, not only in the ward environment but further and more importantly in other environments. The aim was to shape behaviors relevant to life both within and outside the hospital. In order to discover the dimensions of these useful behaviors the researchers evaluated the performance of the attendants in those terms. They observed that employees (i.e., *normal* people) worked on jobs such as serving meals, washing dishes, cleaning, mopping, and general housekeeping duties. In addition, they picked up the dirty linen, counted the pieces, wrote the number on the appropriate slip, and then took the bundle of clothes to a collection place for pick-up service by the laundry people. The attendants also made beds, gave baths, conducted patients outside the ward, ran errands, and performed sundry other duties during most of their 8 hours of shift work. Undoubtedly necessary for the functioning of the ward, these were useful behaviors. Ayllon and Azrin decided to regard much of the work of the attendants as target behaviors for the patients. In order to assess the functionality and usefulness of such target behaviors it was further decided that the behaviors must lead to an enduring change in the environment in which they occur. As an example, washing dishes may be considered useful and necessary, functional in the ward or outside of the hospital; and the result of this behavior is clean dishes. (That is, a change in the physical environment, as from dirty to clean dishes.)

Other behaviors, which may seem functional in the ward or outside it, including personal care behaviors such as keeping clean, cutting fingernails, and combing hair were not directly reinforced. As in the outside world, these behaviors were treated as prerequisites for the target behaviors. The nurse is not allowed to work unless she is dressed in her uniform; the chef must have clean hands before preparing food; the fashion model cannot pose with an unkempt appearance.

Target Behaviors: Relevance

The question of relevance must also be answered in considering the target behavior. Will the response be maintained outside or after the training situation? No matter how objectively defined the behavior is, and how clearly specified as a target, that behavior cannot be expected to be maintained outside or after the training situation unless it will be reinforced there. The relevance of training, or teaching, is a much argued topic in education today, and with good reason; who cannot remember expending great effort in learning Latin, Greek, or Sigmund Freud's birthplace (Moravia) only to forget or abandon these hard-earned skills because they had no usefulness? This is not to say that frequency of future usage is the only criterion of relevance. Mouth-to-mouth respiration is a skill infrequently used by most laymen, but if the situation for its use arises, the skill may save a life. Similarly, the use of the proper exits during a fire is a rarely reinforced response as is movement to an air raid shelter. The importance of these responses, however, may justify the time and effort spent in training. A response may also be useful after training in situations other than the original training situation or as a prerequisite for further training. Thus, a patient may be trained in general mechanical skills that in turn allow acceptance into telephone lineman's training school. He may also have been trained in proper interview behavior which, although used only once in his lifetime, may get him a job. In general, before selecting a target behavior one must not merely assume, but demonstrate its usefulness to the patient.

Stimulus Control

Even with an effective reinforcement procedure and useful and necessary target behaviors that are functional within and outside of the hospital, still another problem must be considered—stimulus control [26]. In the hospital environment it is impossible to observe each patient every moment of the day and night in order to record when and whether the patient is mopping, mowing the grass, or setting the table. The solution to the problem is to arrange the environment such that the target behavior can only take place at the designated time and place. Ayllon and Azrin [6], for example, made the mop available only at a specified time of the day and for a specific duration. The same kind of requirement was imposed on other behaviors, and in this manner the attendants could easily identify a behavior since it was usually restricted to a certain time and place.

Stimulus control is also relevant to behaviors outside the hospital environment. To return to the dish-washing example, this behavior is only reinforced when it occurs at the appropriate time and place. Washing one's dishes in the bathtub may not be considered an appropriate place, nor would washing the dishes immediately after a guest had placed his food on them be considered the appropriate time. Nearly any behavior may be considered abnormal when it occurs at an inappropriate time or place (laughing at a funeral, non-aggressiveness at a prizefight, sleeping through a lecture).

Work as Target Behavior: Reasons for Selection

In summary, work was selected as the target behavior for: (1) Sociologic reasons: the working person is a functional unit in society; conversely, to function in society one must be able to work. (2) Psychologic reasons: the person emitting relevant working behavior instead of bizarre behavior is not likely to be labeled or diagnosed pathologic, as reliable working behavior is itself a demonstration contrary to current conceptions of psychosis. (3) Methodologic reasons: work behaviors can easily be defined, observed, and recorded. They can also be limited in time and place, therefore making them less difficult to modify.

Experimental Design

The studies by Ayllon and Azrin followed an experimental design consisting of careful measurements of the desired work behaviors for a period of time during which they were followed by token reinforcement. The next stage of the design required that the reinforcement procedure be discontinued. In the third stage it was reinstated. Measurements of work behavior throughout these periods made it possible to evaluate the role of the reinforcement procedure in maintaining the desired behaviors.

Job Selection

One of the first experiments was designed to answer the question: What determines the choice or selection of jobs? Intangible factors associated with job satisfaction were often offered as explanations for a patient's specific job selection. After familiarizing themselves with several jobs, patients tended to prefer some over others. Ayllon and Azrin wondered what would happen if token reinforcement were made available only to the least preferred jobs. Would patients continue to work at their preferred jobs because of the intrinsic factors involved in the jobs themselves? Or would they quit working as a natural reaction against someone manipulating their environment? Neither happened; patients now selected the least preferred jobs, those for which tokens were available. Previously preferred jobs which now paid no tokens were not selected. When token reinforcement was reinstated for the preferred jobs, the patient resumed full-time work on them. The tasks selected for study in that experiment were full-time jobs resembling those performed by normal individuals in the hospital. This made it possible to evaluate the strength of uncontrolled subjective likes and dislikes in selecting a job versus the reinforcement procedure.

Reinforcing Potential of Work

These results indicated that patients shifted their work selection depending on which job resulted in token reinforcement. The next question asked was: Is work reinforcing enough in itself to be continued without payoff? One job was preferred over another because of the payment, but just how reinforcing was the job in and of itself?

Because the attendants paid the patients for working, the patient-attendant interaction was an additional factor that was considered in a design testing the reinforcing properties of work. If payment of tokens at the end of the job had been simply discontinued, this relationship would automatically have been terminated, and it would have been impossible to determine whether the tokens or the interaction was responsible for the changes in work patterns. The solution was an experimental design in which the patient-attendant interaction continued.

In this design the attendants, instead of waiting for the completion of the desired performance to reinforce the patient, anticipated the patient and gave her the usual number of tokens at the beginning of the day—*before* her job was to be performed. The results showed that the performance of full-time jobs by patients decreased to zero when token reinforcement was given independent of performance. On the first day that the reinforcement procedure was reinstated, so that the patient was given tokens following the completion of the job, there was an immediate return to the previous high level of performance.

Reinforcement: Other Variables

At this point the experimenters wondered if these results were an artifact of the type of patients involved in full-time work. The question was: What would happen if the same procedure was used with more disturbed patients—that is, with those who worked as little as 15 minutes and perhaps only as long as 3 hours each day? The next design included all 44 patients on the ward. Although the jobs varied in complexity from sweeping the floors to running an automatic dishwasher and operating a movie projector, the results were similar to those obtained with the full-time jobs. When token reinforcement was delivered independent of the performance, the number of hours at work decreased to a near-zero level. When token reinforcement was reinstated for completion of the desired performance, the number of hours at work returned to its original level.

The researchers then attempted to simulate the typical ward environment quantitatively—one in which token reinforcement was absent and where privileges and other desirable items were available freely and generally independent of the patient's performance. The results obtained indicated that freely available privileges do not help to maintain high-level performance. Quite the contrary; during this period patients in general "lost interest" in their work, that is, they worked fewer hours. In fact, their work behavior decreased to less than one-fourth of its original level. These results offer a good estimate of the probable level of performance in a typical ward: the patient's level of productivity in a sense is underestimated; he is likely to be working at one-fourth of his potential level of performance.

Since up to this point one feature of the experimental manipulation was the all-or-none use of reinforcement procedures, the researchers wondered what the effect of relative amounts of reinforcement of the desired behaviors would be. To study this situation they designed an experiment in which the patient was given experience with two different jobs. The completion of each was followed by two different amounts of reinforcement, one larger than the other. Given that both resulted in tokens, which job would the patient select? The patients, as it turned out, selected the job that resulted in the larger amount of reinforcement. And, when the magnitude of payoff was reversed so that the job which initially paid least came to pay the most, the patients then switched to that job. These results indicated that the presence or absence of reinforcement was not the only determinant of the high level of performance, but that the relative amount available for the job was also important.

Reinforcement: Summary

In summary, the reinforcement program was effective in maintaining performance because tokens were given for the desired performances. When tokens were no longer given, then those performances decreased. When the token delivery was changed from one job to another, the performance of the job for which tokens were not available decreased immediately to a near-zero level. The mere act of giving tokens did not maintain the high level of performance, as seen in the experiment in which tokens were given before completion of the job. The payment had to be *contingent* upon job completion. These results demonstrated that the reinforcement procedure used was so effective that the influence of other factors was relatively minimal when reinforcement was absent. Further, the results indicate that this motivational system was extremely potent for a wide range of psychiatric problems.

First of all, the population of patients included mental retardates, schizophrenics, paranoids, organic psychotics, manic depressives, and so on. Such a wide range of diagnostic classifications might have been expected to reveal some differential effect depending upon the diagnosis. Yet, the results showed that patients from all these classifications had a higher level of performance under the reinforcement procedure. While the number of years of hospitalization ranged from 1 to 37 years, this factor did not affect the patients' performance either. Neither age, which ranged from 24 to 74 years, nor level of education seemed to be a significant factor. The reinforcement program was effective with young and old and for patients whose education ranged from primary school to college.

OTHER TOKEN ECONOMIES

Token economy systems are not limited to those variables selected by Ayllon and Azrin. A review, by no means exhaustive, of current applications reveals that token economy systems have been applied in many environments, along many variables, and with many subjects. Most of these studies have demonstrated the effect of reinforcement by the use of control procedures.

Use with Children and Adolescents

One of the earliest applications was that of Ferster and De Myer [14] who worked in a mental hospital with three autistic children to sustain and widen their behavioral repertoire. Target behaviors were reinforced by access to vending machines dispensing candy and food, to record players, television, telephone, toys, and a trained monkey, using coins as conditioned reinforcers. Further studies with children include that of Wolf, Giles, and Hall [30] who applied token economy concepts to develop and maintain the academic behavior of 16 low-achieving fifth and sixth grade children in a community setting (urban poverty area). The conditioned reinforcer used in this study was points given in the form of trading stamps, which could later be exchanged for field trips, consumables, money, toiletries, or clothing, or could be saved for larger items such as inexpensive watches, and second-hand bicycles. The school environment proved to be eminently suitable for the use of the token economy, and low achievers were able to make significant academic progress.

Token systems have also been used with older and more disturbed children. Burchard [12] operated an intensive training program with 12 adolescent, antisocial, institutionalized, retarded boys. The target behaviors were reading, writing, time telling, using public transportation, buying and washing clothes, and using a telephone. Tokens, used as conditioned reinforcers, could be exchanged for meals, snacks, smoking articles, grooming and hygienic articles, clothing, books, recreational activities, and bus tickets for trips to town or home. Punishment in the form of seclusion and loss of tokens was made contingent upon behaviors such as fighting, lying, stealing, cheating, assault, and property damage. In a similar study [17] 27 teen-age, moderately retarded girls were worked with in an institutional setting. Target behaviors were those deemed necessary for life outside the institution; these included ironing, sewing, personal self-care, letter writing, assisting aides, housekeeping, engaging in proper social interaction, and clothing selection. Token reinforcers, points kept on a card, were backed up by activities: movies, canteen, swimming, dances, sports, phone calls, pictures, late television, parties, dates, walks, picnics, shopping trips, dinner at a restaurant, and skating. Intensive training was given in personal appearance and personal hygiene, and response cost, that is, loss of tokens (see p. 96), was added to reduce undesirable behaviors.

More delinquent behaviors have also been modified successfully.

Phillips [20] reported a small study of three "predelinquent" boys in a "home situation" institution. Target behaviors in general were in social, self-care, and academic areas, useful in and outside of the institution, such as watching the television news, reading the newspaper, cleaning one's room, keeping one's person clean and neat, reading books, completing homework, and obtaining desirable report card grades. These behaviors were reinforced with points tallied on cards. Points were exchangeable for an allowance, use of a bicycle, television, games and tools, snacks, and privileges such as going downtown, staying up past bedtime, and choice of seat in the car. Phillips also developed a manager system in which one boy who was assigned responsibility for a daily job such as bathroom cleaning selected and reinforced others for performing the job, and was in turn reinforced himself, depending upon their performance. Like many of the other studies, response cost was also added as a form of punishment for undesirable behaviors such as failing grades, arguing, stealing, being late, and speaking aggressively, a loss of points being made contingent on these responses.

Rose and his associates [22] also worked with juvenile offenders, age 8 to 16, in a community setting in a large-scale program called the Hartwig project. Many behavioral procedures were used to decrease the frequency of socially defined maladaptive behaviors. Tokens in forms of poker chips, painted blocks, play money, clicks on a counter, tally marks on a tabulation sheet, and stars were used to reinforce appropriate behaviors and could be exchanged for store items, tickets to sporting events, trips, and snack bar purchases. The authors reported tokens to be particularly potent with these subjects, as most of them were economically deprived. Finally, Cohen, Filipczak, and Bis [13] worked with 16 student-inmates at the National Training School for Boys. In general, the target behavior was an attitude toward academics approximating that established for students in the public schools. Token reinforcement, in the form of points, was given for specific test and homework completion behaviors. Points were exchangeable for soft drinks, milk, potato chips, Polaroid snapshots, entrance and time in a lounge-recreation area of library, smoke breaks, rental of private office space, books or magazines, purchase of additional classroom time, private tutoring, and mail-order catalog materials.

USE WITH ADULTS

In addition to the Anna State Hospital project, several applications of the token economy to psychiatric populations have been made. In one of these, Atthowe and Krasner [1] worked with 60 predominantly chronic schizophrenic patients in a Veterans Administration hospital closed ward to produce attendance at group activities and therapy classes, engagement in social interaction, certain self-care activities such as making one's bed, and following rules against antisocial behavior. The target behaviors were reinforced by watching television, canteen articles, and obtaining a "carte blanche" which functioned in place of the conditioned reinforcer: tokens. In another study within a state hospital, Schaefer and Martin [23] worked with 40 adult patients with varying diagnoses, all of whom were regarded as "apathetic." Personal hygiene, social interaction, and adequate work performance were reinforced with brass tokens that could be exchanged for meals, commissary items, television, doctor's visitations, recreation programs, and ward "health insurance." Similarly, Winkler [29] established a program with 66 patients of varying diagnosis in a chronic psychiatric ward. Responses such as attendance at morning exercises, finishing morning exercises, getting up, dressing, and bed making were reinforced with plastic tokens exchangeable for desired goods and activities. In addition, disruptive behavior such as noise making and violence were punished by loss of tokens. Finally, perhaps the largest token economy system ever attempted is currently being applied by the United States Army at Fort Ord, California [27]. Developed by Major General Phillip Davidson, Jr., the program initially involved two battalions of trainees (about 2,500 men), with target behaviors of inspection performance, physical fitness, marksmanship, and other military skills. The conditioned reinforcing stimulus is points punched on individual plastic "merit cards" which can be exchanged for weekend movies, a Sunday off post, a weekend pass, and other privileges.

OVERVIEW

To repeat, "What then *is* the token economy?" For clarity we will first describe what it is *not*. It is *not* the distribution of tokens. The mere use of tokens or other such conditioned reinforcers by no means defines the term. It is *not* a closed economic system. The behavior of the individual must affect the consequences of that behavior so as to prevent loss of motivation. It is *not* an inflexible system. It cannot be "set up" *a priori*. It must be subject to constant adjustment in order to maximize motivation, learning, and growth. It is *not* designed to facilitate passive participation. It is *not* independent of the individual's needs.

What is it then? The token economy *is* the determination of target behaviors that are directly measurable, have functional characteristics, and have relevance for the individual not only in the treatment environment but also in outside, normal, or posttraining environments. It *is* the specification of a certain time and place in which the target behavior will be followed by certain conditioned reinforcers (tokens, points). It *is* the availability of a wide range of "back-up" reinforcers (consumables, cosmetics, activities, priorities). It *is* a system of exchange in which the ratio of conditioned reinforcers to "back-up" reinforcers is based on the behavior of the individual. It *is* the continuous analysis of the relationship between behavioral requirements and their consequences and adjustments based on this analysis. It *is* a continuous self-corrective procedure that enables the therapist to abandon any misconceptions about the presumed effectiveness of the ongoing therapeutic procedures. It *is* a system that protects the individual from capriciousness on the part of those whose job is to care for, train, or teach him. It *is* a system that recognizes the individuality of those involved, designed to strengthen behaviors useful to the *individual*, not merely those that will benefit the staff or the therapist.

Having answered the questions of what the token economy is and is not, the next question to pose is, "What *could* the token economy be?" It *could* facilitate any form of rehabilitation. Because it facilitates the maintenance of behavior at maximal levels of motivation, it *could* be used to help achieve vocational, educational, and therapeutic objectives in prisons, schools, and hospitals. In effect, this system *could* be a means through which the individuals concerned become responsible for the functioning of their therapeutic, educational, vocational, or training environment. Again, this system *could* be used to assure transfer of the individual's newly acquired behaviors to the outside world. Last but not least, the development and maintenance of complex social behaviors will continue to be a major practical problem to existing institutions. It is here that the methodology of the token economy can help. Indeed, the behavioral methodology can help not only in conceptualizing the social objectives of institutions, but also in evaluating the effectiveness of current methods to achieve them.

REFERENCES

1. Atthowe, J. M., and Krasner, L.   A preliminary report on application of contingent reinforcement procedures (token economy) on a "chronic" psychiatric ward. *Journal of Abnormal Psychology* 73:37, 1968.
2. Ayllon, T.   Some behavioral problems associated with eating in chronic schizophrenic patients. Paper read at American Psychological Association, Chicago, September, 1960.
3. Ayllon, T.   Intensive treatment of psychotic behavior by stimulus satiation and food reinforcement. *Journal of Behavior Research and Therapy* 1:53, 1963.
4. Ayllon, T., and Azrin, N. H.   The measurement and reinforcement of behavior of psychotics. *Journal of Experimental Analysis of Behavior* 8:357, 1965.
5. Ayllon, T., and Azrin, N. H.   Reinforcer sampling: A technique for increasing the behavior of mental patients. *Journal of Applied Behavior Analysis* 1:13, 1968.
6. Ayllon, T., and Azrin, N. H.   *The Token Economy: A Motiva-*

tional System for Therapy and Rehabilitation. New York: Appleton-Century-Crofts, 1968.

7. Ayllon, T., and Haughton, E. Control of the behavior of schizophrenic patients by food. *Journal of the Experimental Analysis of Behavior* 5:343, 1962.

8. Ayllon, T., and Haughton, E. Modification of symptomatic verbal behavior of mental patients. *Journal of Behavior Research and Therapy* 2:87, 1964.

9. Ayllon, T., Haughton, E., and Hughs, H. Interpretation of symptoms: Fact or fiction? *Journal of Behavior Research and Therapy* 3:1, 1965.

10. Ayllon, T., and Michael, J. The psychiatric nurse as a behavioral engineer. *Journal of the Experimental Analysis of Behavior* 2:323, 1959.

11. Bijou, S. W., and Sturges, P. T. Positive reinforcers for experimental studies with children—consumables and manipulatables. *Child Development* 30:151, 1959.

12. Burchard, J. D. Systematic socialization: A programmed environment for the habilitation of antisocial retardates. *Psychological Record* 17:461, 1967.

13. Cohen, H. L., Filipczak, J., and Bis, J. A Study of Contingencies Applicable to Special Education: Case I. In R. Ulrich, T. Stachnik, and J. Mabry (Eds.), *Control of Human Behavior: II. From Cure to Prevention.* Glenview, Ill.: Scott, Foresman, 1970.

14. Ferster, C. B., and De Myer, M. K. A method for the experimental analysis of the behavior of autistic children. *American Journal of Orthopsychiatry* 32:89, 1962.

15. Ferster, C. B., and Skinner, B. F. *Schedules of Reinforcement.* New York: Appleton-Century-Crofts, 1957.

16. Kelleher, R. T. Chaining and Conditioned Reinforcement. In W. K. Honig (Ed.), *Operant Behavior: Areas of Research and Application.* New York: Appleton-Century-Crofts, 1966.

17. Lent, J. R., Leblanc, J., and Spradin, J. E. Designing a Rehabilitative Culture for Moderately Retarded Adolescent Girls. In R. Ulrich, T. Stachnik, and J. Mabry (Eds.), *Control of Human Behavior: II. From Cure to Prevention.* Glenview, Ill.: Scott, Foresman and Company, 1970.

18. Lindsley, O. R. Operant conditioning methods applied to research in chronic schizophrenia. *Psychiatric Research Reports* 5:118, 1956.

19. Lindsley, O. R., and Skinner, B. F. A method for the experi-

mental analysis of the behavior of psychotic patients. *American Psychologist* 9:419, 1954.

20. Phillips, E. L. Achievement place: Token reinforcement procedures in a home-style rehabilitation setting for "pre-delinquent" boys. *Journal of Applied Behavior Analysis* 1:213, 1968.

21. Premack, D. Toward empirical behavior laws: I. Positive reinforcement. *Psychological Review* 66:219, 1959.

22. Rose, S. D., Sundel, M., Delange, J., Corwin, L., and Polumbo, A. The Hartwig Project: A Behavioral Approach to the Treatment of Juvenile Offenders. In R. Ulrich, T. Stachnik, and J. Mabry (Eds.), *Control of Human Behavior: II. From Cure to Prevention.* Glenview, Ill.: Scott, Foresman, 1970.

23. Schaefer, H., and Martin, P. Behavioral therapy for "apathy" of hospitalized schizophrenics. *Psychological Reports* 19:1147, 1966.

24. Skinner, B. F. *The Behavior of Organisms.* New York: Century-Crofts, 1938.

25. Skinner, B. F. *Science and Human Behavior.* New York: Macmillan, 1953.

26. Terrace, H. S. Stimulus Control. In W. K. Honig (Ed.), *Operant Behavior: Areas of Research and Application.* New York: Appleton-Century-Crofts, 1966.

27. *Time* 95:15 (June 29, 1970).

28. White, R. W. *The Abnormal Personality.* New York: Ronald, 1964.

29. Winkler, R. C. Management of chronic psychiatric patients by a token reinforcement system. *Journal of Applied Behavior Analysis* 3:47, 1970.

30. Wolf, M. M., Giles, D. K., and Hall, R. V. Experiments with token reinforcement in a remedial classroom. *Behaviour Research and Therapy* 6:51, 1968.

4

Aversive Procedures

DAVID H. BARLOW

EDITOR'S INTRODUCTION

As noted in Chapters 2 and 3, some maladaptive behaviors can be reduced in frequency or eliminated altogether, either by reinforcing competing adaptive behaviors or by using extinction procedures. However, it is not always possible to identify or remove the reinforcer or to identify a competitive behavior. At other times, as in the case of self-destructive behaviors, it is necessary to bring behavior under control rapidly, which is not usually possible with reinforcement or extinction procedures. In such cases aversive procedures are applicable.

Three main paradigms for their use exist. The first is classical conditioning in which a stimulus eliciting the maladaptive behavior is paired with a noxious stimulus. In the case of an alcoholic the sight or smell of alcohol might be paired with painful electric shock. Theoretically, anxiety or fear comes to be associated with the once-pleasurable stimulus. The second is punishment. Here a behavior, for example, drinking alcohol, is followed by the noxious stimulus. This procedure also contains elements of classical conditioning, since the smell or taste of alcohol is automatically paired with the noxious stimulus in a punishment paradigm. The third procedure is avoidance training in which the subject avoids punishment by, for example, pushing away a glass of alcohol within a certain time limit.

There are many aversive stimuli: electric shock, chemical substances such as apomorphine which produce nausea and vomiting, or even noxious odors. More recently, verbal aversion consisting of descriptions of disturbing scenes have been used in the procedure known as covert sensitization. Here scenes of the behavior to be eliminated are paired with the aversive scenes. Finally, as noted earlier, response cost or fines within a token economy can be used, as can time-out from positive reinforcement. In the latter procedure, particularly useful with children, the subject is contingently placed in isolation for a few minutes. In this way he cannot obtain reinforcement during that time and also suffers the noxious effects of being alone. Interestingly, social aversive stimuli have rarely been used, although criticism and mockery would appear to be powerful aversive events.

The application of a particular aversive stimulus within one of the three paradigms described earlier constitutes the aversive therapies. Again, the same principles of behavior modification apply, namely, precise definition of the behavior to be changed and continuing measurement to allow for ongoing analysis of the efficacy of the procedure. This is especially necessary when strong aversive stimuli are being used in a punishment paradigm. Such a procedure should be effective very quickly and should be discontinued if not effective so that undue pain is not inflicted. The aversive therapies raise a number of ethical issues that must be faced squarely by every therapist using them. Naturally, no aversive stimulus that causes tissue damage should be used. As with all therapies, the informed consent of the patient or parents in the case of a minor should be obtained. This should entail a discussion of the aversive stimulus and procedure, the side effects of the procedure, the chance of success, and the methods used to evaluate the efficacy of therapy. Application within captive populations raises special problems. Here, the informed consent of the director of the institution is necessary; but in addition, the formation of an advisory committee, which should include nonprofessionals to monitor the use of such therapies, should be considered.

The aversive therapies have a number of applications of which the more important are for the severely oppositional or self-destructive child, the alcoholic, and the sexual deviate. Barlow insists that *aversive procedures form only part of a therapeutic program and that attention should be directed toward building up behaviors to replace the suppressed behavior—heterosexual behavior in the case of homosexuals, more successful coping with social and work problems for the alcoholic, and cooperative constructive behaviors for the oppositional child. In the case of alcoholism chemical aversion (pp. 93–94, 99–100) appears to be potentially the most useful therapy, giving in clinical series a 1-year abstinence rate of 60 percent, and with the use of periodic booster sessions, 95 percent abstinence. These are impressive results since few alcoholics improve without treatment. Unfortunately, there is no controlled outcome study comparing this therapy with other methods (or with no treatment) to allow definite conclusions regarding its efficacy. In an outpatient setting covert sensitization might be considered when treating alcoholics, although one controlled outcome study suggests that only modest results (40 percent abstinence at 6-month follow-up) will be obtained.*

With sexual deviation (pp. 104–110) electrical aversion in a punishment or avoidance paradigm has been used most frequently, punishing both deviant fantasies and, where possible, actual sexual behavior as in the case of cross-dressing. Again, there are few controlled studies. However, Feldman compared classical conditioning, avoidance training, and psychotherapy in the treatment of homosexuality, finding no difference between the two aversive therapies (approximately 60 percent recovery), although both were superior to psychotherapy (approximately 20 percent recovery). This suggests that electrical aversion should become the treatment of choice in homosexuality, although longer-lasting results will probably be obtained by using booster sessions and by building up heterosexual behavior. The latter might consist of assertive training, role playing in social approach behavior to heterosexual partners, and desensitization of fear of heterosexual intercourse.

The oppositional or self-destructive child has been dealt with by using time-out and electrical aversion (pp. 113–116). Many studies have included control procedures in a single case analysis demonstrating the immediate effectiveness of the aversive procedure, but again, no long-term controlled outcome studies exist. However, this is less critical in the case of such children since immediate manage-ment is often the most difficult problem, one with which aversive procedures have been shown to be effective.

Once behavior is brought under control in a treatment setting, the problem of transfer to other environments is again raised. Barlow suggests that there is a difference between voluntary and nonvolun-tary patients in this regard. Transfer is rarely found in the captive subject but is often seen in the case of the voluntary patient. He suggests that the motivated patient may use the effects of the pro-cedure to control his own behavior. Thus, in the presence of the stimulus eliciting the deviant behavior the patient might imagine the unpleasant effects of the aversive procedure, thus controlling his tendency toward deviant behavior. This is an interesting hypothesis worthy of further study. It is of direct clinical relevance since pa-tients can be instructed to maximize the efficacy of aversive therapy by using the procedure for self-control.

W.S.A.

Aversive techniques have been used to treat behavior disorders such as alcoholism, sexual deviation, shoplifting, ruminative vomit-ing, hallucinations, and violent or aggressive behaviors. In this chapter the nature of aversive control will be discussed, and the ap-plication of aversive techniques to several classes of disorders de-scribed. Research on the effectiveness of the techniques will be re-ported, as well as suggestions for improving the procedures in the light of recent knowledge.

In the last several decades, and particularly since the application of the basic behavioral sciences to the clinic has become more popu-lar, basic and applied research has discovered some of the critical conditions necessary for the use of aversive stimuli in modifying be-havior. However, the use of aversion is not a unitary process. There are different paradigms in which aversive stimuli can be applied and a wide assortment of aversive stimuli from which to choose.

THE MAJOR PARADIGMS

The assumption underlying the use of aversive techniques, like other behavior modification procedures, is that the maladaptive behavior is learned. Therapy thus consists of unlearning inappropriate responses, thoughts, and feelings and learning more appropriate behavior. A number of different ways in which aversive stimuli can be used to facilitate learning have been discovered in the laboratory and applied to maladaptive behavior. These paradigms and examples of their use are described below.

Classical Fear Conditioning

This procedure, developed by Pavlov, involves pairing two stimuli, the conditioned stimulus (CS) and the unconditioned stimulus (UCS). For example, in treating homosexuality the homosexual stimulus (CS), usually a picture or slide, is presented to the patient followed immediately by an aversive stimulus (UCS), perhaps a brief electric shock. Theoretically, after repeated pairings of the two stimuli the patient will develop a similar feeling to the homosexual image that he experiences to the shock, often described as "anxiety." If the conditioned response is strong enough, the patient will avoid these feelings of anxiety now associated with homosexuality by avoiding situations in which homosexual behavior occurs. Another possible explanation is that the attractive stimulus is devalued so that the patient perceives the stimulus as less attractive.

Punishment

In punishment the aversive stimulus follows occurrence of a clearly defined *behavior*. This differs from classical fear conditioning where no behavioral response is required. For example, in treating alcoholism using a punishment paradigm, the patient pours whiskey, picks up the glass, and begins to drink before receiving a shock. In classical fear conditioning the sight and smell of alcohol would be paired with the shock without the occurrence of a behavioral response. These two procedures are often confused and are in fact difficult to separate since during punishment classical conditioning is also taking place. Each time a response is punished, the sensory cues associated with the behavior are being paired with the aversive stimuli in a classical conditioning paradigm. If drinking a glass of whiskey is punished by shock, then seeing and smelling whiskey are also being paired with the aversive stimuli.

Avoidance and Escape Learning

A third procedure allows the patient to avoid the aversive stimulus. For example, an alcoholic beverage might be placed in front of an alcoholic with a shock programmed to follow 10 seconds later. If the patient pushes the drink away, however, he does not receive the shock. This is called avoidance conditioning. The notion is that with repeated trials the patient will develop a habit of actively avoiding alcohol.

A variant of this procedure is escape conditioning where the subject can terminate the aversive stimulus by engaging in another, but usually more adaptive behavior. In practice this paradigm has been little used in clinical settings.

Aversion Relief

Another way to use an aversive stimulus in a clinical setting is aversion relief. The cessation of an aversive stimulus such as shock produces a period of "relief" subjectively reported as pleasant. If a formerly neutral or undesirable object is associated with this relief, the object hypothetically picks up pleasurable qualities and becomes more attractive. For example, the offset of shock has been associated with heterosexual slides to increase heterosexual responsiveness.

Since this paradigm involves simple pairing of a pleasant state (relief from shock) with a formerly neutral stimulus, it is essentially a classical conditioning paradigm. Furthermore, the purpose is not to suppress directly an undesirable behavior but rather to strengthen a desired behavior. Thus, this paradigm uses an aversive stimulus in a different way than other paradigms.

Investigators are just beginning to examine the most efficient and effective way to apply aversive techniques to maladaptive human behavior; in the meantime, aversive stimuli are being used in various combinations of the previously described paradigms to treat maladaptive behavior.

THE AVERSIVE STIMULI

A variety of stimuli have been employed in aversive therapy, including nausea-inducing chemicals and painful electrical stimuli as well as verbal aversion in which upsetting scenes are described. Milder aversive stimuli such as removal of positive reinforcement have also been used.

Chemical Aversion

Usually this refers to the use of drugs such as apomorphine hydrochloride or emetine hydrochloride that induce nausea and vomiting.

In a typical procedure the patient drinks 20 ounces of lukewarm saline solution containing 1.5 grains of oral emetine. This fluid provides an easily regurgitable substance. The patient is then given an injection of 3.25 grains of emetine hydrochloride, 1.65 grains of pilocarpine hydrochloride to produce sweating and salivation, and 1.5 grains of ephedrine sulphate to guard against a fall in blood pressure. Emesis occurs in about 10 minutes, and the dosage has to be adjusted as sessions continue. The usual dosage for apomorphine is 5 mg. subcutaneously which produces emesis in approximately 20 minutes although Raymond [46] has successfully used smaller doses starting with 0.05 grain which is increased to 0.1 grain, with nausea and not emesis the desired response.

Chemical aversion has some disadvantages: (1) It is very unpleasant and may lead to refusal or premature termination of treatment.

(2) The onset of nausea and vomiting does not always occur at the desired time. Since it seems important that the sight or drinking of alcohol occur *just before* the nausea or vomiting, the unpredictability of the emetics may cause improper pairings and retard learning. (3) The patient develops tolerance to apomorphine. (4) Serious cardiovascular effects may occur, and extensive vomiting may lead to dehydration or occasionally gastrointestinal hemorrhage. (5) Since medical and nursing surveillance is necessary, the treatment is expensive and time-consuming.

Another chemical aversion is the drug succinylcholine chloride dehydrate. This drug, usually administered in an intravenous infusion, produces respiratory paralysis in humans through a curarizing effect at the motor endplates of the efferent neurons serving the skeletal muscles. This is extremely aversive on the first trial, and many patients think they are dying. Continuous medical supervision during administration is required.

Electrical Aversion

Nonconvulsive electric shock is currently the most widely used aversive stimulus. It is commonly administered through two electrodes approximately half an inch in diameter usually placed on the forearm, calf, or the fingertips, and held in place by snap fasteners or elastic or cloth strips. Electrode jelly is sometimes used. The intensity of shock is individually determined for each subject through his verbal report or by its effect on the inappropriate behavior. The desired intensity, as subjectively reported by the subject, can be from painful to a point just beyond that which is reported to be tolerable. A behavioral index of the appropriate intensity is the withdrawal or flinch reaction. Since most patients adapt to shock, the intensity must be increased from session to session to maintain a sufficient level of aversive stimulation. Shock is usually generated from batteries, and recently small portable devices have been used.

Shock shares with chemical aversion, however, the problem of unpleasantness to the patient, resulting in occasional refusal or termination of treatment.

Verbal Aversion

A recent innovation is the use of verbal aversion in a therapeutic procedure known as covert sensitization [11]. Vivid descriptions of extremely noxious scenes such as vomiting and nausea are described to the patient in conjunction with descriptions of the undesirable behavior. For example, in the treatment of a homosexual the following scene of the patient approaching his boyfriend was described:

As you get closer to the door you notice a queasy feeling in the pit of your stomach. You open the door and see Bill lying on the bed naked and you can sense that puke is filling up your stomach and forcing its way up to your throat. You walk over to Bill and you can see him clearly. As you reach out for him you can taste the puke, bitter and sticky and acidy on your tongue, you start gagging and retching and chunks of vomit are coming out of your mouth and nose, dropping onto your shirt and all over Bill's skin.

The description of the nauseous scene often lasts 1 to 2 minutes. The particular choice of adjectives is individualized to create optimal aversion. These scenes are most effective if some of the sensations or stimuli described actually occur during the undesirable behavior, or if the aversive consequences of the deviant behavior (occurring too long after the behavior to inhibit it) are added. Examples from homosexual behaviors would be the smell and taste of urine during fellatio or the guilt and fear of being caught.

This procedure has not been used as much as the previous techniques, but has the advantage of administration totally in imagination which results in flexibility in the choice of aversive images and facilitates self-administration of the technique outside of the therapist's office. Furthermore, the scenes can be tape recorded to save therapist time. It also seems less unpleasant than the previous two stimuli and may be less likely to cause termination of treatment.

Time-Out

Time-out from positive reinforcement is a term carried over from the experimental laboratory and refers to a procedure in which an individual earning reinforcement, e.g., food, at a high rate, is prevented from doing so. The procedure is often used with institutionalized patients or with children in the home or classroom. In a typical example a disruptive child or patient is removed, contingent upon disruptive behavior, from a situation when reinforcers such as other people or entertainment are present. Time-out has always been used in a punishment paradigm.

The time-out interval is usually 2 to 10 minutes, with release dependent on the absence of any undesired behavior, e.g., crying. Longer periods of time-out have the disadvantage of reducing the number of times the behavior is punished, thus lengthening the time necessary for the patient to learn to suppress the behavior, as well as reducing the number of potential reinforcements for behaving more appropriately. Time-out seems less aversive than other techniques but requires careful attention and consistency from the responsible attendant, such as a parent, teacher, or hospital aide. Most often, however, these are the people most affected by the behavior, ensuring a high degree of cooperation in a program designed to suppress the behavior.

Miscellaneous Aversive Stimuli

Loud noise has been used on occasion, usually in a punishment paradigm. White noise or tones have been used most often, e.g., Flanagan, Goldiamond, and Azrin [20], but other variations include a bicycle horn [48] which proved effective in suppressing disruptive behavior. The optimal decibel range for any of the above noises is from 100 to 120 db. Another, less frequently used aversive stimulus is a noxious odor in the form of sulfureted potash or some related substance, which has, for example, been used in treating obesity, e.g., Ashem [2]. Finally, in situations where control of positive reinforcement is possible, such as token economies in institutions, a system of fines can be imposed contingent on undesirable behaviors. The technical term for fines is response cost (see Chapter 3).

Which Aversive Stimulus?

The determination of the aversive stimulus to use is usually based on the therapist's familiarity with a particular aversive stimulus. The tendency has been to choose one aversive stimulus, such as chemical aversion in the early sixties, and apply it to every disorder. If this type of aversion proved to have shortcomings, as chemical aversion did, then researchers would suggest a wholesale switch to a "better" type, such as electrical aversion. Recently, however, guides for choosing a particular aversive stimulus to treat a particular disorder have emerged, based partly on clinical experience and partly on principles from general experimental psychology.

Briefly, it may be that some stimuli are more effective with certain behavior disorders, depending on the sensory modalities involved in the disorder. For instance, obesity and alcoholism, which involve mostly olfactory and gustatory stimuli, would be more effectively treated with aversive stimuli in these two modalities, such as drug- or imaginally produced nausea and vomiting, and perhaps in conjunction with noxious odors. On the other hand, self-destructive behavior or any disorder involving tactile stimulation may be best treated by electric shock. Following this line of speculation, auditory hallucinations might be treated by aversive noise, and cigarette smoking by smoke satiation. This notion has yet to be experimentally evaluated but follows from basic research in general psychology [59].

Side Effects of Aversive Procedures

Both positive and negative side effects result from the application of aversive techniques. Many negative side effects were first noticed in the experimental laboratories during work with lower organisms. However, not all of these have been observed in clinical settings. The most obvious side effect is the tendency to avoid the setting in which aversive stimuli are used. This leads to the loss of some voluntary patients who find aversive stimulation more frightening than the thought of continuing their undesirable behavior. A supportive relationship and reiteration of the benefits of treatment help to overcome this complication.

In lower organisms aversive stimulation often elicits aggression. With nonvoluntary patients an aversive stimulus that involves close physical proximity, such as leading a disruptive child to an isolation room (time-out), affords an opportunity for aggression and can occasionally produce aggressive behavior, as many a psychiatric aide has discovered. Bandura and Walters [5] also note that children imitate behavior they observe in adults. If one is attempting to control a disruptive child's behavior through physical punishment, the child may in turn control the behavior of his peers or parents with aggressive and punishing behavior. If this pattern develops, one should reinforce more appropriate social behavior.

A further side effect observed only in clinical settings -namely depression, may have implications for treatment. Depression sometimes occurs in patients who are attempting to control behavior that is maladaptive but intrinsically pleasurable, such as overeating, sexual deviation, or alcoholism. Such patients find it pleasing to visualize themselves without their problem. Only rarely do they realize the amount of pleasure that they gain from their behavior, and when this behavior begins to diminish during treatment, accompanying emotional reactions of ambivalence, frustration, a sense of loss, and occasionally a depressive reaction develop. These behaviors or emotions are not a result of the aversive stimulus per se, but are related to the accompanying loss of positive reinforcement. This points to a need to replace highly reinforcing deviant behavior with alternative behaviors from which the patient will derive equal pleasure. The instigation of alternative behaviors in conjunction with the use of aversive techniques will be a recurrent theme in this chapter.

Although the negative side effects of the application of aversive stimuli have rightly been emphasized, more positive, constructive side effects have also been observed. Some investigators have noted that as the target maladaptive behavior decreases, other maladaptive behaviors also decrease and more appropriate behaviors increase. This has been noted in both psychotic children [47] and voluntary adult patients [7].

CLINICAL APPLICATIONS

The clinical application of the aversive procedures will be discussed separately for each of the major behavioral disturbances for which such treatment has been used and seems to be indicated.

Alcoholism

All the major aversive stimuli, chemical, electrical, and verbal, have been used to treat alcoholism.

CHEMICAL. The most extensive application has been that of Voegtlin [55] who treated over 4000 cases of alcoholism at the Shadel Sanitorium in Seattle. Voegtlin and his colleagues used emetic drugs as the aversive stimulus in a punishment paradigm with the usual classical fear conditioning aspects present. Although apomorphine was employed with early cases, emetine was later used to avoid the sedative effect of apomorphine which was hypothesized to interfere with conditioning.

In the typical procedure [30] the patient was instructed that liquor is intrinsically obnoxious to the body and that the injection he was to receive was to *sensitize* his nervous system so that the true obnoxious characteristics of liquor would be more apparent. He was also told that after treatment he must never taste or experiment with liquor. Just before nausea and vomiting occurred, the patient was asked to take a glass containing 1 ounce of whiskey and to smell, taste, and swallow it. He was encouraged to swirl the liquor around in his mouth in order to appreciate fully the gustatory sensations. Two or three trials were held per session, and each session lasted about 45 minutes, usually being carried out on alternate days. The average number of sessions was between four and six so that the course of therapy lasted about 10 days. Counseling and practical advice on work and family stresses were also offered.

Lemere and Voegtlin [29] obtained follow-up data on 4096 of their patients, with some patients followed for 10 to 13 years after treatment. One year after treatment a remarkable rate of total abstinence, 60 percent, was found. Over the 13-year period 50 percent of those treated were totally abstinent, including patients who relapsed but who were then successfully retreated. The abstinence rate was significantly improved by booster sessions following treatment. Patients who received two or more booster sessions during the year following the initial treatment had a greatly improved chance of remaining abstinent for the full year [55]. Ninety-five percent of 84 patients remained abstinent, whereas the abstinence of a comparable group of 88 patients who did not receive booster sessions was 73 percent.

GROUP THERAPY.   This procedure has also been applied within a group therapy context where it was found that the gagging and retching of one member of the group facilitated nausea and vomiting by other members whether they had received emetic or simply placebo. Using this technique, Miller et al. [43] found that only 2 of 20 patients had relapsed to their former drinking habits at an 8-month follow-up, and then only after "strenuous effort at holding down the first drink," indicating that the conditioned response was still present. Three patients had brief lapses of between 1 and 3 days but stopped spontaneously. With a similar procedure Zvonikov [62] reported 66.5 percent total abstinence one year after treatment, and claimed his results to be the best obtained in Russia to that date.

These are high rates of success. It is possible that group procedures facilitate conditioning both by reinforcing the strength of the aversive stimulus and by providing mutual reinforcement for participation in therapy and incentive to remain sober after treatment, similar to that provided by A.A. groups. Furthermore, when therapy takes place in a group setting, it is possible that aversion is learned not only to the narrow stimulus situation consisting of a glass of whiskey, but also to the social setting in which others are drinking. Since much drinking occurs in social situations, this learning may transfer more easily to the environment.

SUCCINYLCHOLINE. A second chemical aversive stimulus used in alcoholism is succinylcholine, ususally applied in a punishment paradigm after a sip of alcohol has been taken. The patient is not warned of its muscle paralyzing effects, and only one trial is administered. Overall, the results of this procedure have been disappointing. Clancy et al. [12] reported no differences in abstinence rates between a group receiving treatment and a control group receiving the same procedure without Scoline. Farrar, Powell, and Martin [16] used a similar procedure and found that only two of the nine patients that they were able to follow were abstinent after one year. In one patient, however, the conditioned aversion, characterized by anxiety, dyspnea, and so on, was still present and had generalized to such substances as mouthwash and hair spray. This caused the patient to report the cure worse than the original condition.

ELECTRICAL AVERSION. This aversive stimulus was first used in the treatment of alcoholism by Kantorovich [23] in 1928, who treated 20 alcoholics in a punishment paradigm using between 5 and 20 sessions. Seventeen of the 20 patients acquired stable aversion reactions to alcohol. After a follow-up ranging from 3 weeks to 20 months, 14 (70 percent) of the treatment group remained abstinent. On the other hand, 7 out of a control group of 10 patients receiving hypnotic suggestion or medication reverted to their drinking pattern in a few days after release from hospital.

It was not until the midsixties that electrical aversion was again used, when Blake [8] devised an escape paradigm in which spitting out alcohol terminated shock. Twenty-five patients were treated in from 3 to 36 sessions over 4 to 8 days. A second group received this treatment in conjunction with relaxation training. At a 12-month follow-up the patients were classified as abstinent, improved (social drinking with marked improvement in general life adjustment), and relapsed. With aversion therapy alone only 23 percent were totally abstinent, but a further 27 percent were improved for a total of 50 percent; 27 percent had relapsed, and 23 percent could not be followed. When relaxation was combined with aversion, the figures were 46 percent abstinent and 13 percent improved, totaling 59 percent; 30 percent relapsed, and 11 percent could not be followed.

The low percentage of abstinence after electrical aversion alone reported by Blake, together with the clinical failures reported by MacCulloch et al. [36] who noted no improvement in four alcoholics treated with electrical aversion, does nothing to generate enthusiasm for the replacement of chemical aversion with electrical aversion.

VERBAL AVERSION.   One of the newer developments in the treatment of alcoholism is the use of descriptions of noxious images as the aversive stimulus, in a procedure that Cautela calls covert sensitization. Typically, scenes leading up to drinking are vividly described. These are detailed descriptions of events or thoughts leading to drinking, details of the setting in which drinking occurs, descriptions of drinking companions, and of the typical beverages imbibed. At every approach point aversive scenes are introduced so that aversion is connected not only to the actual drinking but to all aspects of behavior leading up to drinking (e.g., walking into the bar, sitting down, ordering a drink). Alternated randomly are scenes where the patient begins the chain of behavior but decides to avoid it and feels relieved and relaxed for having done so. Ten to 20 scenes are presented during each session, and Cautela recommends bi-weekly sessions for several months. An emphasis is placed on the use of the procedure to strengthen self-control; thus, patients are instructed to practice their scenes between sessions and to use them to dampen any urges to drink that might occur.

Miller [42] combined hypnosis with aversive scenes that sometimes produced vomiting in the office. In some cases only one session was administered. He reports 83 percent of 24 patients completely abstinent at a 9-month follow-up. In the one controlled study testing the effects of covert sensitization in the treatment of alcoholism, Ashem and Donner [3] administered six sessions of covert sensitization in which a total of 35 scenes were presented. At a 6-month follow-up, 6 out of 15, or 40 percent of the treated subjects, were abstinent, while none of eight no-contact, control subjects were abstinent. The findings indicate a clear effect from treatment, but the percentage remaining abstinent is modest.

IMPLICATIONS OF DATA. Due to the low remission rate of alcoholism, percentage of success, when described in a firm and verifiable manner such as total abstinence, can be meaningful. This is further buttressed by the few reports of "spontaneous" abstinence in untreated alcoholics over a period of time. Of 62 untreated alcoholics followed for a mean of 6.7 years by Kendell and Staton [25], only 1 became abstinent. Thus, the 60 percent 1-year abstinence rate reported by Lemere and Voegtlin with chemical aversion and the higher rate (95 percent) reported when patients participated in two or more booster sessions are impressive. The high abstinence rate of 83 percent reported by Miller with covert sensitization also arouses interest in this approach, although his series was smaller and was followed for a shorter time. When one considers the hypothetical guidelines for choosing an aversive stimulus mentioned in the introduction, it is significant that emesis and images of nausea and vomiting are both in the same sensory modality as the undesirable behavior. This may facilitate the acquisition of conditioned aversion and enable the patient to use the aversion to enhance self-control after treatment. Chemical aversion, particularly recent refinements of the procedure, and covert sensitization are deserving of more extensive clinical usage and further research.

ROLE OF OTHER FACTORS. It is unlikely, however, that the treatment of alcoholism will be complete when the means for establishing a perfect conditioned response are found. While aversion therapy will probably play a major role in treatment, close attention will also have to be paid to relieving environmental stress, identifying social reinforcers that maintain drinking behavior, and strengthening alternative behaviors to drinking. This notion is supported when one examines the social and environmental factors that predict treatment success in aversion therapy. In Lemere and Voegtlin's extensive series 71 percent of patients with stable employ ment records remained abstinent; the rate was 21 percent for those who were unemployed or only sporadically employed. Abstinence, however, did not vary with the type of work. Continued association with "drinking buddies" was also a major cause for relapse. Of those who formed new friendships by joining abstinence clubs, 87 percent remained abstinent, while only 40 percent of those who refused to join remained abstinent. This point is dramatically illustrated in several reports of patients who would force down the first several drinks despite the presence of the conditioned response of nausea and vomiting. For these patients the reinforcing value of relief from life stresses was prepotent over a strong conditioned aversion to alcohol.

WITH ANTABUSE. Finally, the relationship between the use of Antabuse and aversion therapy must be considered. Theoretically, Antabuse is an aversion treatment since drinking is suppressed by the threat of the Antabuse reaction. The major differences between aversion therapy and treatment by Antabuse, however, lie in the attitude of the patient. After successful aversion therapy the patient is no longer attracted to alcohol, although some weak temptations may come up and become progressively stronger if no booster sessions are used. With Antabuse treatment alcohol is just as attractive to the patient, but he is restrained from drinking. Thus, aversion therapy and Antabuse might be effectively combined so that the attractiveness of alcohol would be neutralized by aversion therapy, and any weak temptation that arose suppressed by the feared effects of Antabuse. Under this condition patients might be more disposed to continue taking the Antabuse.

Sexual Deviation

With sexual deviation (as with alcoholism) chemical, electrical, and verbal aversive stimuli have been used. Unlike alcoholism, however, the most popular and seemingly most effective stimuli are electrical and verbal rather than chemical.

CLINICAL STUDIES. The extensive series of homosexuals treated by Freund [21] with chemical aversion in Czechoslovakia aroused interest in the application of aversive techniques to this population despite the relatively poor results obtained (40 percent heterosexual after treatment, dropping to 25 percent after 3 years). Since this report, several series of cases and some controlled research has been reported on the application of aversive techniques to homosexuality. Feldman and MacCulloch [18] administered electric shock in an avoidance conditioning paradigm in which patients could avoid some of the shocks by switching off a homosexual slide. In addition, an attempt was made to increase heterosexual responsiveness by flashing on a slide of a female when shock was turned off in an aversion relief paradigm. The results demonstrated that 58 percent of 43 homosexuals were exclusively heterosexual at the end of treatment and remained that way for at least 1 year. In the most ambitious study on aversion therapy to date, Feldman [17] compared his avoidance paradigm with classical conditioning and found no difference, with approximately 60 percent success in both paradigms. Since the avoidance paradigm contains classical conditioning features (that is, a pairing of shock with the sexually deviant stimulus with no response required on the part of the patient), it seems likely that the classical conditioning component is responsible for success. These two treatments were superior to a third condition consisting of psychotherapy, after which treatment only 20 percent of homosexuals changed their sexual preference.

PREDICTIVE FACTORS IN TREATMENT. Feldman and MacCulloch also looked for predictors of success in their treatment. Generally, they discovered age, personality, and previous heterosexual experience to be the most important predictors. Patients under 30 years of age responded more favorably than those over 30. In addition, prior heterosexual experience improved response to treatment. Those patients with no heterosexual experience responded poorly, a finding corroborated by Bancroft [4] and emphasizing again the importance of acquiring alternative behavior. Lastly, patients with passive, weak, and insecure personalities responded favorably, while other personality patterns, notably "attention seeking" or "hysterical personality," responded less favorably.

FURTHER STUDIES. In a pilot study on 10 homosexuals Bancroft [4] made shock contingent upon penile erection to homosexual slides in a punishment paradigm, and in 3 patients also shocked homosexual fantasies. A modified aversion relief paradigm to females was also employed. The results were less favorable than those of Feldman and MacCulloch. Seven patients showed changes in sexual interest as measured by an attitude scale, but only 3 maintained their gains over a 1- to 3-year follow-up. Procedural differences between this technique and that of Feldman and MacCulloch and some evidence of adaptation to the shock may account for the differing outcome.

VERBAL AVERSION. This technique has not been used frequently in the treatment of homosexuality. In one study of the mechanism of action of aversion therapy in homosexuality, Barlow, Leitenberg, and Agras [7] demonstrated that a verbal aversive stimulus was responsible for decreases in homosexual responsiveness. Within single cases of homosexuality and pedophilia, respectively, a sequential experiment was carried out in which noxious scenes were paired with the homosexual scene in the first phase, the sexual scenes presented alone in the second phase (while the patient was told to expect continued therapeutic improvement), and the noxious scenes reinstated in the third phase. Despite positive expectations on the part of the patients throughout the experiment, homosexual responsiveness declined only during the pairing, indicating that this factor was responsible for improvement.

Either electrical or verbal aversion appear to be the treatments of choice in the treatment of homosexuality. However, more research is needed on ways of increasing heterosexual responsiveness, which should form a part of the treatment of homosexuals.

Transvestism and Fetishism

PROCEDURE. The most effective procedure for treating these two related deviations was devised by Marks and Gelder [37]. Typically, the patient is treated intensively in hospital for 2 weeks and receives two 1-hour aversion therapy sessions per day. The aversive stimulus is electric shock to the arm or leg.

For the first few sessions the transvestite or fetishist is asked to imagine his cross-dressing or his fetishistic object. When the patient reports a clear image of this fantasy by raising his finger, one or two shocks are delivered to suppress the images. The patient is told that the purpose of the procedure is to ensure that the fantasies are not pleasurable. Next the patient is asked to carry out the deviant behavior, i.e., a transvestite would begin to cross-dress. At variable intervals a warning signal is given followed by from one to three shocks, which stop when the clothes are removed. Sometimes the patient can avoid shock completely by undressing quickly. For several months thereafter, booster sessions are held at gradually increasing intervals (from weekly to monthly).

Ten transvestites were treated with this regime [22], and nine were rated much improved by the end of treatment while a tenth was improved as indicated by lack of sexual arousal to the cross-dressing behavior and absence of urges to engage in the behavior. Of seven patients who could be followed for at least 6 months, six maintained their improvement. Of the two fetishists treated both showed marked improvement although one began a slow relapse after 6 months.

SPECIFICITY. The same workers [37] also demonstrated the specificity of aversion therapy in a single case experimental design. In a case of fetishism involving several articles of women's clothing, responses to each piece of clothing were treated one at a time with electric shock, while measures of sexual arousal and attitudes toward each article of clothing were recorded. After treatment for each successive article of clothing, arousal and the "attractiveness" would be eliminated for that article only. This study demonstrates that the shock was responsible for clinical success rather than nonspecific aspects of the therapeutic situation.

A seemingly important factor in this procedure is the ability of the therapists to reproduce the behavior in the treatment situation, as in cross-dressing, and deal with it directly, ensuring a greater degree of transfer outside the treatment situation than would be possible using slides or images.

Sadism and Masochism

The treatment of sadism and masochism with aversive therapy is described less frequently in the literature, although some interesting case studies exist. Davison [13] treated a patient with troublesome sadistic fantasies with covert sensitization and techniques designed to increase normal heterosexual interest. The patient was advised to masturbate in the presence of a picture or fantasy that moved from his sadistic fantasies to a picture of a pin-up girl. When he could successfully masturbate to the latter, he noticed an increase in heterosexual arousal but no diminution of his sadistic fantasies.

After inquiry an image of "a large bowl of steaming urine with reeking fecal boli floating on top" was found to be aversive. A scene described to the patient in which he viewed a young girl tied to a stake in the ground while drinking this "soup" succeeded in making him nauseous. After this one session the patient reported an inability to even conjure up the fantasy, and no further fantasies were reported. Normal heterosexual interests continued to increase.

An interesting factor of this case is the patient's report of a "decision" to return to his sadistic fantasies 6 months later for a period of 9 months and then to give it up once more, which he did, by taking the cure himself. This suggests that the procedure worked initially in a self-control fashion in which the patient could turn it off or turn it on at will and that little or no automatic conditioning took place. This case also illustrates the desirability of increasing appropriate alternative behaviors.

Marks et al. [38] treated a masochist with an associated shoe fetish who would slap his genitals with the shoe. As in the treatment of cross-dressing, fantasies were first shocked followed by the actual behavior. Both masochistic behavior and attraction to shoes disappeared. Additionally, sexual intercourse became more pleasurable. It should be noted here that the patient did not enjoy the shock in a masochistic fashion as some might expect, but found it aversive, suggesting that the type of pain that gives sexual pleasure to masochists is very specific and can be eliminated by aversive techniques.

Exhibitionism

Evans [15] reports the use of an avoidance paradigm in a series of ten exhibitionists who had been exhibiting themselves an average of 2.5 times per month. Cards with printed words on them signaling either an aspect of the patient's exhibitionistic behavior or normal sexual activities were randomly projected on a screen, and the patient was instructed to imagine the behavior that was being cued. During each session 20 exhibitionistic words and 40 "normal" words were shown. Each exhibitionistic word was followed by a shock that the patient could avoid by quickly advancing to the next slide. One session was administered a week for 10 weeks, followed by one session every 2 weeks for 2 months, and finally one session a month. By the end of 6 months all patients had reported a cessation of urges to exhibit as well as any exhibitionistic behavior.

A number of general procedural points concerning the treatment of sexual deviates with aversion therapy should be noted. Sexual deviation consists of a chain of behaviors culminating in the sexual act. It was noted earlier that Gelder and Marks, when dealing with transvestites and fetishists, treated both fantasies and behavior, thereby pairing aversion with several aspects of the chain of events leading to the sexually deviant act. Evans also apparently shocked fantasies of each event in the deviant chain. This may be particularly important in light of recent data from our laboratory that indicate that behavior early in the homosexual chain, such as meeting and gaining consent from a prospective partner while cruising, is *more* pleasurable than actually engaging in sex. This may account for the oft-noted promiscuity of some homosexuals who seek out several different partners a night rather than remain with the first partner.

In addition, as in alcoholics, the availability of alternative responses as the deviant behavior is being suppressed has been linked to the success of aversion therapy. While research continues into

further improving the success of aversion therapy with sexual deviation, close attention should be paid to instigating or strengthening
alternative sexual behavior.

CLINICAL APPLICATIONS: OTHER
CONSUMMATORY BEHAVIORS

Smoking

The uncontrolled results of aversive treatment for smoking appear encouraging, since smoking rates decline substantially. However, many treatments, including smoking clinics and even placebo
controls, also substantially reduce smoking, suggesting that factors
other than aversive control are at play. Furthermore, the attained
reduction is short-lived. One reason for this may be the ubiquity and
high frequency of heavy smoking. Smoking is associated with an in-
finite variety of activities during a typical day; thus, cues that
prompt smoking are numerous as contrasted to sexual deviation
where the behavior occurs infrequently and in specific circumstances. Additionally, a smoker is not typically overwhelmed by the
urge for a single cigarette, making smoking subject to self-control for
periods of days and giving many smokers the illusion that they can
stop anytime they desire. However, since smokers cannot avoid and
are constantly confronted with situations where smoking formerly
occurred, the probability of relapse is high.

Several studies [26, 28, 44, 57] have compared groups receiving
electrical or verbal aversion, either self-administered or therapist administered, to groups receiving other treatments or attention
placebo and noticed a decline in smoking across all groups.

With all techniques producing equal but transient effects, one
must look to common factors inherent in the differing treatments.
All smokers in the aforementioned experiments were required to
record carefully the number of cigarettes they smoked per day so
that these rates could be compared to those of other groups. McFall
[39] has recently demonstrated that this in itself reduces smoking

behavior. This, in addition to nonspecific expectancy effects, may account for most of the change.

Wagner and Bragg [56] controlled for placebo effects by comparing different treatments only after the initial drop in smoking due to self-monitoring and other attention-placebo effects. Under these conditions they were able to determine that a group after receiving covert sensitization plus systematic desensitization to cigarette deprivation situations was smoking less at a 3-month follow-up (approximately 35 percent of preexperiment smoking rate for nine smokers) than after either treatment alone or a counseling group, although all treatments had a similar immediate effect.

Another aversive treatment, more effective than control groups, is reported by Steffy et al. [50] who shocked images of smoking situations and active smoking behavior. This is reminiscent of Marks and Gelder's [37] successful treatment of transvestites. Elliott and Tighe [14] report an interesting technique based on response cost in which a sizable amount of money ($65) was placed in escrow, portions of which were paid back as the smoker completed various periods of abstinence. With this regime 84 percent of 25 subjects remained abstinent. Fifteen to 17 months after the completion of treatment, 5 of the 11 patients in the group still being followed continued to be abstinent. Unfortunately, no control group was provided. This technique has the disadvantage of requiring a participant observer such as a close relative or spouse to make sure that the patient is really not smoking.

What may be the most promising aversive technique for smoking was first suggested by Wilde [58]. In this treatment hot, smoky air is blown into the patient's face. This stimulus has the possible advantage of sharing the same sensory modality as the undesired behavior and magnifies some of the mildly aversive properties that are naturally present in the smoker's environment. Recently, a similar technique has been used on a large series of smokers by Lublin and Joslyn [35] and Lichtenstein [32]. Lublin's apparatus consisted of a pistol-type hair dryer enclosed in a box with a lighted cigarette burning near the air intake. While the smokers puffed on a cigarette every 3 seconds, as cued by a metronome, the blower was turned on until the situation was intolerable. At this point the smoker would extinguish the cigarette. Then a fan would blow a refreshing stream of mentholated or pine-scented air toward the patient. The patient was asked to pick up a cigarette as soon as possible after the trial (usually half an hour) and repeat the procedure. Lichtenstein reports that this technique produces significantly greater decrements in smoking at follow-up than an attention placebo group.

Many research reports on smoking have administered very few treatment sessions, often as few as one or two, and seldom more than 10. Prevention of relapse may depend on the consistent administration of treatment sessions beyond the point where the smoker stops smoking. More prolonged treatment and the combination of aversive techniques such as Lichtenstein's with behavioral contracts that set up both negative and positive consequences for smoking in the natural environment, in the manner of Elliot and Tighe [14], might well lead to greater success in the treatment of this condition.

Overeating

Overeating presents an even more difficult problem than smoking if one is considering the exclusive use of aversive techniques, since occasions for eating are almost as numerous as those for smoking and the goal of treatment is to reduce, not eliminate, eating. Like smoking, overeating has, on occasion, been successfully treated by a number of procedures, suggesting once again that placebo factors and "will power" or, more accurately, self-control techniques probably play a significant role. The treatment of overeating by aversion therapy has been reported only in a few case studies. Meyer and Crisp [40] treated two obese patients by placing tempting foods in a treatment room for increasing periods of time and shocking approaches to food in a punishment paradigm. One patient lost weight, but the other became depressed and started eating again.

Cautela [11] has successfully treated obesity by covert sensitization. Images of eating "undesirable" foods were paired with scenes of nausea and vomiting. Although the eating of undesirable foods was eliminated, regular meals were still enjoyable, pointing to the oft-noted specificity of aversive control. In addition, the patient reported using the noxious images in a self-control fashion to successfully control temptation. Ashem [2] used the smell of sulfureted potash to enhance aversive descriptions of rotten food, nausea, and vomiting. Since olfactory and taste sensations play a major role in making food pleasurable, this approach seems particularly appropriate.

Clinicians who have treated severe cases of obesity in a hospital setting have often observed a complete loss of appetite by the patient in his new surroundings and a concomitant loss of weight. Usually, however, the weight is quickly regained when the patient leaves the hospital. This phenomenon seemingly is an example of Schacter's [49] findings that environmental cues, such as the sight of tempting food or situations in which eating formerly occurred, determine eating in the obese. In treating obesity, therefore, as in the treating of smoking, it is imperative to take the treatment to the environment by developing self-control. Stuart [51] incorporated covert sensitization to specific tempting foods in the context of an overall self-control program based largely on original suggestions of Ferster et al. [19] that the patient alter his environment to make the probability of eating less likely. All eight patients in this program were successful in controlling their eating and had not regained the weight lost at a 12-month follow-up.

Self-Injurious Behavior

One of the most dramatic results of aversive techniques is in their application to the self-injurious behavior of mentally retarded or psychotic children. In an early example of the use of time-out Wolf et al. [60] treated head banging, face slapping, self-scratching, and hair pulling in a 3½-year-old child. These behaviors occurred in high-frequency tantrums causing the child to be bruised and bleeding. Sedation, tranquilizers, and restraints had been tried without success. The attendants were instructed to put the child in an isolation room when two or more of these behaviors occurred simultaneously until the behavior ceased. Later a minimum time of 10 minutes in isolation was established. Self-destructive behavior steadily diminished in severity and was eliminated after 4 months. A 6-month follow-up revealed no tantrums at home.

In another example of the application of aversive procedures to self-destructive behavior, Lovaas [34] describes the case of a 16-year-old retarded girl with psychotic features who, when removed from restraints, would bite her hands severely (one finger had previously been amputated), remove her nails by their roots with her teeth, and bang her head (her scalp was covered with scar tissue as a result of this). A total of five 1-second shocks contingent on these behaviors eliminated the problem. In Lovaas' experience generalization to other situations is not always complete, and the patient may have to be shocked in other situations; however, if the command "No" is paired with the shock, then the word itself often becomes sufficient to suppress further behavior. A remarkably consistent finding in such cases is the appearance of more desirable behavior such as smiling, playing, and not avoiding adults after the elimination of self-destructive behavior.

Tate and Baroff [52] describe a case where both time-out and shock were successfully used to suppress different self-destructive behaviors. The patient was a blind, mentally retarded 9-year-old boy whose self-injurious behavior began at age 4 and consisted of slapping or punching his face and head, hitting his head on floors and other hard objects, butting his shoulder with his chin, and kicking himself. These behaviors were severe enough to have resulted in detached retinas. When left free, the patient hit himself approximately twice a minute; thus, most of the time he was restrained in bed. It was also noted that physical contact seemed quite pleasurable to the patient.

During daily 20-minute sessions two therapists walked with the patient, each holding one hand, allowing chin-to-shoulder hits which were ignored. After five sessions the therapists withdrew their hands whenever he hit himself. Hits were reduced from six per minute to zero. During a five-session control period when physical contact was not withdrawn, hits returned, only to be suppressed again by reinstatement of the punishment procedure. This suggests that the punishment procedure was responsible for the declines in this behavior.

This procedure could not be used on head banging since it would take too long, possibly endangering the child. Thus, the child was instructed that if he continued to hit himself he would be shocked and that the shock would hurt. Self-injurious behavior was then punished by a portable shocker, which quickly decreased the behavior. The patient was allowed freedom for increasing periods of time and was given attention by the attendant during periods when he did not hurt himself. Punishment was continued, and after 6 months no self-injurious behavior had occurred for 20 days. In addition, appropriate social behavior and smiling emerged, and recreational activities and occupational therapy became possible.

A dramatic study by Lang and Melamed [27] describes a 9-month-old infant who began vomiting (at the age of 5 months) following meals. The vomiting and rumination had worsened so that food was regurgitated within 10 to 15 minutes, and small amounts were brought up continually. All medical and dietary approaches had failed, and the child's life was considered in danger. Sessions were held immediately after eating, and lasted about one hour. Electro myogram recordings and observation determined the beginning of regurgitation. Shock was administered through electrodes placed on the infant's calf until vomiting stopped. The infant reacted to the shock by crying or cessation of vomiting. After two sessions very few shocks were needed. By the sixth session vomiting was eliminated during the sessions. Sessions were held at different times of the day and under different conditions, such as lying in bed or being held, to ensure transfer of effects. Several days after the sessions were discontinued, a brief relapse occurred, and treatment was resumed for three more sessions. Other more normal social behaviors increased along with weight, and a 1-year follow-up revealed a perfectly healthy child.

The experimental manipulation reported in some of the studies mentioned [34, 52] demonstrates that the aversive stimulus is responsible for treatment success. The rapidity with which electric shock eliminates self-destructive behavior supports the use of this stimulus since less aversive procedures may allow irrevocable injury to occur before the behavior is suppressed. However, since most of the patients described in the preceding section and some of the patients to be described in the following section cannot voluntarily leave the treatment setting, the aversive stimulus must be applied under carefully specified conditions. First, the inappropriate behavior must be clearly defined so that the occasion for the aversive stimulus is clear; every occurrence of the behavior should be punished, and the procedure, if carried out by an aide or parent, should be closely supervised. If no improvement is noted after two or three sessions, the procedure should be reassessed, with changes in the aversive stimulus or termination of punishment as possible alternatives. It also seems important to reinforce alternative behaviors during treatment to help ensure the continued absence of self-destructive behaviors, particularly if social attention was maintaining the self-destructive behavior in the first place.

Socially Disruptive Behavior

Most socially disruptive behavior referred for consultation occurs in nonvolutary patients such as psychotic adults or children. The referring agents are usually the nursing personnel on a psychiatric ward who cannot manage the patient, or the parents of an unruly child. By contrast, the socially disruptive behavior of nonpsychotic adults is usually handled through legal rather than medical channels.

Tyler and Brown [54] report the use of time-out procedures to control disruptive behaviors in 15 delinquent boys during recreational periods in a training school. Misbehavior around a pool table, such as throwing the balls, striking someone with the cues, or breaking the rules of the game, resulted in placement in isolation for 15 minutes. No warnings were given and the procedure was carried out very matter-of-factly. Under these conditions disruptive behavior was nearly eliminated. To test if this procedure was in fact responsible for the success, it was removed and the staff returned to their old methods of warning and reprimanding the boys contingent on disruptive behavior. The behavior quickly returned to a high rate. A further reinstatement of the punishment condition reduced the behavior once again.

As in the treatment of self-destructive behavior, the aversive stimuli are applied in the environment where the disruptive behavior occurs and initially are successful only when in effect (i.e., removal of the stimulus leads to recovery of the disruptive behavior). To permanently decrease disruptive behavior it will often be necessary to remove positive reinforcers which may have been maintaining the behavior, build up alternative behaviors during the time of behavioral suppression, or do both in combination.

Disruptive behavior in adults has also been treated with aversive therapy. In institutions, persistent yelling, alone or in combination with aggressive behavior, is responsive to time-out procedures, usually brief isolation.

In the majority of cases aversive techniques have been applied to adult disruptive behavior in institutionalized nonvoluntary patients. There are, however, some cases where patients have sought treatment to gain control of their disruptive behavior. Agras [1] reports the case of a 25-year-old schizophrenic who was participating in a rehabilitation program but suffered from occasional episodes of glass breaking that would necessitate physical restraints and recommitment to a state hospital. This behavior had a long history that included breaking over 30 pairs of spectacles. The patient was asked to imagine himself breaking a pane of glass. When he signaled a clear image, electric shock was administered. Sessions lasted 45 minutes. After 3 sessions the patient had difficulty in obtaining a clear image, and after 20 sessions he reported that he had lost all urges to break glass and "could not think of doing so." Following his release from the hospital, 12 sessions were held on a diminishing basis for 9 months. At an 18-month follow-up one brief glass-breaking episode had occurred for which the patient immediately apologized, and he had not broken his spectacles.

In another example Kellam [24] treated a 48-year-old housewife who was threatening suicide after her tenth apprehension for shoplifting over a 16-year period. There was no economic motive for her behavior since she could readily buy any of the items; however, as in the last case, an irresistible urge was subjectively reported. In this case electrical aversion to imagination of the sequence was not effective, nor was a situation in which she was shocked for lifting articles off a table. A realistic film was then made of the patient entering a store and engaging in shoplifting. After each item was lifted, shots of disapproving faces were inserted. For 5 weeks the patient watched the film 40 times, and shock was administered to coincide with the disapproving faces on an intermittent basis. At this point the patient reported a fear of shops and a sensation of being watched whenever she entered one. After three months she had not stolen, but reported several urges to steal at which point faces would loom before her eyes and she would feel that everyone in the store was watching her. The urge then quickly disappeared. The aversive stimulus of social disapproval is a very appropriate one for shoplifting since it is a natural consequence of the behavior in the environment.

AVERSIVE PROCEDURES: OVERVIEW

The preceding descriptions of behavior disorders in which aversive techniques have been used are by no means complete. Aversive therapies have also been used to treat drug addiction [31, 46, 53], speech dysfunctions such as stuttering [9, 20, 41], tics [61], and writer's cramp [33]. Others have applied the techniques to gambling [6] and hallucinations [10]. Thus, there is a wide potential application for these procedures.

Effectiveness Outside Treatment Situation

One of the most puzzling aspects of aversive control is why it is effective outside the treatment situation where the aversive stimulus is no longer present. This problem and the solutions that have been proposed illustrate a case where evidence from animal experiments can be misleading when applied to human behavior. Based on work

with animals, many investigators proposed that an avoidance paradigm should be employed in treatment since this leads to greater
resistance to extinction or, in other words, to longer-lasting effects.
The notion here was that the organism would continue to avoid the
stimulus or the undesired behavior long after learning trials were
over because he would not reality test, or take a chance on receiving
shock by performing the undesired behavior. This does not apply to
patients in a therapeutic setting, however, who are well aware of the
presence or absence of electrodes or emetic drugs. Thus, the active
learning paradigm in aversive control, as Rachman and Teasdale
[45] note, seems most often to be punishment, classical fear conditioning, or, as is usually the case in therapeutic situations, a combination of the two. This conclusion leaves the question of permanency of effect unanswered.

Persistence of Effects

Permanency of effect, however, does not occur in all patients. A
notable exception is in the case of nonvoluntary patients, e.g., psychotic adults and children. In several case studies involving this
population it has been noted that therapeutic effects did not generalize outside the treatment situation and had to be reapplied in
each new setting. However, voluntary patients, such as alcoholics or
sexual deviates, often report transfer of therapeutic effects from the
treatment setting to the environment, even after as little as one session. This discrepancy may be due to the motivation of the patient.
A voluntary patient is usually motivated to eliminate his behavior.
Thus, when he perceives that a technique is capable of suppressing
his undesirable behavior in a treatment setting, he uses it himself
outside treatment to achieve self-control.

Our research suggests that telling some patients that an aversive
technique is therapy and will help them results in improvement,
while telling them it will not help them leads to no improvement.
Patients later say that under positive instruction they were using the
procedure in a self-control fashion. It seems unlikely, however, that
a patient will be able to use the technique to control his own behav-

ior unless a strong conditioned aversion is first established for him to use.

Concluding Considerations

A second point to reemphasize is the necessity of building up viable alternative behaviors, whether these be new ways to deal with stress or new ways to achieve gratification or positive reinforcement from the environment. Evidence supporting the importance of this concept is found in both voluntary and nonvoluntary patients. The results of aversive therapy in alcoholism correlate directly with the presence of social and occupational skills. In homosexuality results correlate directly with the presence of heterosexual responsiveness. Disruptive behavior in psychotic adults and children is more easily eliminated if alternative social behaviors are available. The implication is that aversive techniques should seldom be used in the absence of procedures designed to instigate alternative behaviors.

Lastly, it should be noted that behavior usually occurs in a chain with a beginning and an end. Administering aversive techniques to the final behavior in the chain, such as the sexual act in homosexuality or tasting whiskey in alcoholism, may not be adequate. As noted earlier, evidence from our research in homosexuality indicates that behavior early in the homosexual chain, such as meeting and gaining consent from a prospective partner while cruising, may be *more* pleasurable than engaging in sex. Similarly, drug addicts, when deprived of drugs, will sometimes inject themselves with tap water to derive the acquired pleasure from the act of injecting. If aversion is applied only to the end of the chain, then the performance of preliminary behavior outside of treatment may rapidly set the occasion for recurrence of the undesirable behavior. Some of the more successful aversive procedures (e.g., Marks and Gelder [37]), in response to this phenomenon, administer aversion to all aspects of behavior including the initial fantasies or urges that are presumably the beginning of the chain.

Further research should continue to explore the application of aversive techniques to intransigent psychiatric problems. An important goal at this time, however, is to discover how aversive control works so that clinicians can minimize the aversiveness, increase the effectiveness, and move a step closer to the day when aversive techniques, either singly or in combination with other procedures, can be prescribed for specific clinical problems.

REFERENCES

1. Agras, W. S.   Behavior therapy in the management of chronic schizophrenia. *American Journal of Psychiatry* 124:240, 1967.
2. Ashem, B.   The use of covert sensitization in the treatment of overeating. Paper presented at the Association for the Advancement of Behavior Therapy, Miami, 1970.
3. Ashem, B., and Donner, L.   Covert sensitization with alcoholics: A controlled replication. *Behaviour Research and Therapy* 6:7, 1968.
4. Bancroft, J.   Aversion therapy of homosexuality. *British Journal of Psychiatry* 115:1417, 1969.
5. Bandura, A., and Walters, R. H.   *Social Learning and Personality Development.* New York: Holt, Rinehart & Winston, 1963.
6. Barker, J. C., and Miller, M. E.   Aversion therapy for compulsive gambling. *Journal of Nervous and Mental Disease* 146:285, 1968.
7. Barlow, D. H., Leitenberg, H., and Agras, W. S.   Experimental control of sexual deviation through manipulation of the noxious scene in covert sensitization. *Journal of Abnormal Psychology* 74:596, 1969.
8. Blake, B. G.   The application of behaviour therapy to the treatment of alcoholism. *Behaviour Research and Therapy* 3:75, 1965.
9. Brady, J. P.   A behavioral approach to the treatment of stuttering. *American Journal of Psychiatry* 125:155, 1968.
10. Bucher, B., and Fabricatore, J.   Use of patient-administered shock to suppress hallucinations. *Behavior Therapy* 1:382, 1970.
11. Cautela, J. R.   Treatment of compulsive behavior by covert sensitization. *Psychological Record* 16:33, 1966.
12. Clancy, J., Vanderhoof, E., and Campbell, P.   Evaluation of an aversive technique as a treatment for alcoholism. *Quarterly Journal of Studies on Alcohol* 28:476, 1967.

13. Davison, G. C. Elimination of a sadistic fantasy by a client-controlled counterconditioning technique: A case study. *Journal of Abnormal and Social Psychology* 73:84, 1968.

14. Elliott, R., and Tighe, T. Breaking the cigarette habit: Effects of a technique involving threatened loss of money. *Psychological Record* 18:503, 1968.

15. Evans, D. R. An exploratory study into the treatment of exhibitionism by means of emotive imagery and aversive conditioning. *Canadian Psychologist* 8:162, 1967.

16. Farrar, C. H., Powell, B. J., and Martin, L. K. Punishment of alcohol consumption by apneic paralysis. *Behaviour Research and Therapy* 6:13, 1968.

17. Feldman, M. P. Personal communication, 1970.

18. Feldman, M. P., and MacCulloch, M. J. The application of anticipatory avoidance learning to the treatment of homosexuality: I. Theory, technique, and preliminary results. *Behaviour Research and Therapy* 2:165, 1965.

19. Ferster, C. B., Nurnberger, J. I., and Levitt, E. B. The Control of Eating. In F. P. Robinson (Ed.), *Effective Study*. New York: Harper & Brothers, 1946.

20. Flanagan, B., Goldiamond, I., and Azrin, N. Operant stuttering: The control of stuttering behavior through response-contingent consequences. *Journal of the Experimental Analysis of Behavior* 1:173, 1958.

21. Freund, K. Some Problems in the Treatment of Homosexuality. In H. J. Eysenck (Ed.), *Behaviour Therapy and the Neuroses*. New York: Pergamon, 1960.

22. Gelder, M. G., and Marks, I. M. Aversion Treatment in Transvestism and Transsexualism. In R. Green (Ed.), *Transsexualism and Sex Reassignment*. Baltimore: Johns Hopkins Press, 1969.

23. Kantorovich, N. V. An attempt of curing alcoholism by associated reflexes. *Novoye v Refleksologii i Fiziologii Nervnoy Sistemy* 3:436, 1929. Cited by Razran, G. H. S. Conditioned withdrawal responses with shock as the conditioning stimulus in adult human subjects. *Psychological Bulletin* 31:111, 1934.

24. Kellam, M. P. Shop lifting treated by aversion to a film. *Behaviour Research and Therapy* 7:125, 1969.

25. Kendell, R. E., and Staton, M. C. The fate of untreated alcoholics. *Quarterly Journal of Studies on Alcohol* 26:685, 1965.

26. Koenig, K. P., and Masters, J. Experimental treatment of habitual smoking. *Behaviour Research and Therapy* 3:235, 1965.

27. Lang, P. J., and Melamed, B. G. Avoidance conditioning ther-

apy of an infant with chronic ruminative vomiting: Case report. *Journal of Abnormal Psychology* 74:1, 1969.

28. Lawson, D. M., and May, R. B. Three procedures for the extinction of smoking behavior. *The Psychological Record* 20:151, 1970.

29. Lemere, F., and Voegtlin, W. An evaluation of the aversion treatment of alcoholism. *Quarterly Journal of Studies on Alcohol* 11:199, 1950.

30. Lemere, F., Voegtlin, W. L., Broz, W. R., O'Hollaren, P., and Tupper, W. E. Conditioned reflex treatment of chronic alcoholism: VII. Technic. *Diseases of the Nervous System* 3:243, 1942.

31. Liberman, R. Aversive conditioning of drug addicts: A pilot study. *Behaviour Research and Therapy* 6:229, 1968.

32. Lichtenstein, E. How to quit smoking. *Psychology Today* 4:42, (Jan.) 1971.

33. Liversedge, L. A., and Sylvester, J. D. Conditioning techniques in treatment of writer's cramp. *Lancet* 1:1147, 1955.

34. Lovaas, O. I., and Simmons, J. Q. Manipulation of self-destruction in three retarded children. *Journal of Applied Behavior Analysis* 2:143, 1969.

35. Lublin, I., and Joslyn, L. Aversive conditioning of cigarette addiction. Paper read at the annual meeting of the American Psychological Association, San Francisco, 1968.

36. MacCulloch, M. J., Feldman, M. P., Oxford, J. F., and MacCulloch, M. L. Anticipatory avoidance learning in the treatment of alcoholism: A record of therapeutic failure. *Behaviour Research and Therapy* 4:187, 1966.

37. Marks, I. M., and Gelder, M. C. Transvestism and fetishism: Clinical and psychological changes during faradic aversion. *British Journal of Psychiatry* 113:711, 1967.

38. Marks, I. M., Rachman, S., and Gelder, M. G. Methods for assessment of aversion treatment in fetishism with masochism. *Behaviour Research and Therapy* 3:253, 1965.

39. McFall, R. M. Effects of self-monitoring on normal smoking behavior. *Journal of Consulting and Clinical Psychology* 35:135, 1970.

40. Meyer, V., and Crisp, A. H. Aversion therapy in two cases of obesity. *Behaviour Research and Therapy* 2:143, 1964.

41. Meyer, V., and Mair, J. M. M. A new technique to control stammering: A preliminary report. *Behaviour Research and Therapy* 1:251, 1963.

42. Miller, M. M. Treatment of chronic alcoholism by hypnotic aversion. *Journal of the American Medical Association* 171:1492, 1959.

43. Miller, E. C., Dvorak, A., and Turner, D. W. A method of creating aversion to alcohol by reflex conditioning in a group setting. *Quarterly Journal of Studies on Alcohol* 21:424, 1960.

44. Ober, D. C. Modification of smoking behavior. *Journal of Consulting and Clinical Psychology* 32:543, 1963.

45. Rachman, S., and Teasdale, J. *Aversion Therapy and Behaviour Disorders: An Analysis.* Coral Gables: University of Miami Press, 1969.

46. Raymond, M. J. The treatment of addiction by aversion conditioning with apomorphine. *Behaviour Research and Therapy* 1:287, 1964.

47. Risley, T. R. The effects and side-effects of punishing the autistic behaviors of a deviant child. *Journal of Applied Behavior Analysis* 1:21, 1968.

48. Sajwaj, T. E., and Hedges, D. Functions of parental attention in an oppositional, retarded boy. Paper submitted to be read at the annual meeting of the American Psychological Association in Washington, D.C., 1971.

49. Schachter, S. Obesity and eating. *Science* 161:751, 1968.

50. Steffy, R. A., Meichenbaum, D., and Best, J. A. Aversive and cognitive factors in the modification of smoking behaviour. *Behaviour Research and Therapy* 8:115, 1969.

51. Stuart, R. B. Behavioral control of overeating. *Behaviour Research and Therapy* 5:357, 1967.

52. Tate, B. G., and Baroff, G. S. Aversive control of self-injurious behavior in a psychotic boy. *Behaviour Research and Therapy* 4:281, 1966.

53. Thomason, I. G., and Rathod, N. H. Aversion therapy for heroin dependence. *Lancet* 2:382, 1968.

54. Tyler, J., and Brown, G. The use of swift, brief isolation as a control device for delinquents. *Behaviour Research and Therapy* 5:1, 1967.

55. Voegtlin, W. L., Lemere, F., Broz, W. R., and O'Hollaren, P. Conditioned reflex therapy of alcoholic addiction: Follow-up report of 1042 cases. *American Journal of Medical Science* 203:525, 1942.

56. Wagner, M. K., and Bragg, R. A. Comparing behavior modification approaches to habit decrement—smoking. *Journal of Consulting and Clinical Psychology* 34:258, 1970.

57. Whitman, T. L. Modification of chronic smoking behavior: A comparison of three approaches. *Behaviour Research and Therapy* 7:257, 1969.
58. Wilde, G. J. S. Behaviour therapy for addicted cigarette smokers: A preliminary investigation. *Behaviour Research and Therapy* 2:107, 1964.
59. Wilson, G. T., and Davison, G. C. Aversion techniques in behavior therapy: Some theoretical and metatheoretical considerations. *Journal of Consulting and Clinical Psychology* 33:327, 1969.
60. Wolf, M. M., Risley, T., and Mees, H. Application of operant conditioning procedures to the behavior problems of an autistic child. *Behaviour Research and Therapy* 1:305, 1964.
61. Yates, A. J. The application of learning theory to the treatment of tics. *Journal of Abnormal and Social Psychology* 56:175, 1958.
62. Zvonikov, M. Z. A modification of the technique of conducting conditioned reflex apomorphine and suggestive therapy of alcoholism. *Zhurnal Nevropatologii i Psikhiatrii* 68:596, 1968.

5

Systematic Desensitization

JOHN PAUL BRADY

EDITOR'S INTRODUCTION

As Brady points out, systematic desensitization is probably the single most used behavior therapy. When first described, it offered a new theoretic and practical approach to the treatment of neurotic disorders and with the techniques based upon operant conditioning stimulated the development of the behavioral therapies. The basic hypothesis underlying desensitization is that much neurotic behavior, including interpersonal problems, is anxiety based. In the case of phobia, for example, a neutral environmental event comes to elicit anxiety which leads to avoidance of the event. Like the therapies already discussed, desensitization is based on animal experiment and has led to much research.

In his original animal experiments Wolpe produced "neurotic" behavior in cats by applying strong electric shocks. The animals exhibited attempts to avoid being placed in the cage in which the shocks had been applied. Feeding the cats in a series of situations approximating the one in which the animal had been punished led to disappearance of maladaptive behavior. In the application of this demonstration to humans Wolpe took a great conceptual leap and equated imaginary with real exposure, and relaxation with feeding.

In the treatment procedure the patient imagines approaching the feared object or situation while deeply relaxed (see pp. 136–138). As a first step, the environmental stimuli that evoke anxiety are elicited by interviewing the patient, often using a fear inventory [2]. The feared events are then arranged according to class, e.g., fear of heights, fear of being criticized, and so on; and each class arranged in a hierarchy (see p. 135) from situations which evoke little anxiety to those evoking maximal anxiety, in 10 or 20 steps. Deep muscle relaxation is then taught (pp. 133–135), and once a satisfactory level is achieved, the patient visualizes each item of the hierarchy in order. When one scene no longer evokes a feeling of anxiety, the patient visualizes the next. The therapist often suggests that the patient confront his feared situation in reality; this facilitates transfer of the therapeutic effect to the real world, an important step since progress in reality has been noted to lag behind progress in imagination. Many clinicians also use methohexital sodium (Brevital) intravenously (pp. 146–147) to enhance relaxation, a procedure that increases the efficacy of desensitization.

Desensitization has been shown to be more effective than non-treatment or verbal psychotherapy in controlled outcome studies, although most of these studies have been of patients with phobic disorders. The treatment method is probably useful in a variety of other conditions including anxiety states, obsessive compulsive neurosis, interpersonal anxieties, frigidity, and some cases of homosexuality. Whether it will prove more effective than more traditional methods in these disorders remains to be seen.

The mechanism by which desensitization works is not entirely clear. Although Wolpe considered the mechanism to be counterconditioning, that is, replacing an anxiety response with relaxation, recent animal studies [1] suggest that the variable involved in overcoming avoidance behavior is neither counterconditioning nor graduated approach, but exposure to the feared situation. It may be that desensitization works by motivating the patient to expose himself to the feared situation, allowing anxiety and avoidance behavior to extinguish. This subject will be considered further in the next chapter.

W.S.A.

REFERENCES

1. Nelson, F.   Effects of two counterconditioning procedures on the extinction of fear. *Journal of Comparative and Physiological Psychology* 62:208, 1966.
2. Wolpe, J., and Lang, P. J.   A fear survey schedule for use in behaviour therapy. *Behaviour Research and Therapy* 2:27, 1964.

Systematic desensitization is probably the single most used behavior therapy. It has been extensively studied in both laboratory and clinic, and countless patients have been treated with it. This discussion of systematic desensitization includes the following: its basis in experimental psychology, a description of the procedure itself, a review of clinical studies, areas of application of systematic desensitization, and innovations in the basic procedure.

THEORETIC AND EXPERIMENTAL BASIS

Experimental Paradigms

It has been known for many years that if an experimental animal is exposed to a neutral stimulus such as a 5-second tone that is paired with an aversive stimulus like an electric shock (unconditioned stimulus), after a number of such pairings the tone alone will elicit a strong emotional response in the animal (conditioned response). This is an example of classical or Pavlovian conditioning. The psychophysiologic state elicited by the tone (conditioned stimulus) resembles fear or anxiety and is generally called conditioned fear. If the tone is then repeatedly sounded without the pairing of additional shocks, the intensity of the conditioned fear will gradually decrease to zero. This is called extinction.

Interest may be added to the experiment by giving the animal a way to avoid the shock. This can be done by placing a lever in the cage wired so that pressing it within five seconds of the onset of the tone turns the tone off and prevents shock from occurring on that trial. Most experimental animals quickly learn this response: when the tone comes on, signaling that shock is imminent, the animal promptly presses the lever, which terminates the tone and results in successful avoidance of shock. This is an example of avoidance learning; lever pressing is reinforced and maintained by avoidance of the aversive stimulus and by termination of the tone (which is associated with relief from the fear generated by the tone's onset).

In contrast to simple conditioned fear, conditioned avoidance is very resistant to extinction. Thus, if the apparatus is set so that no further shocks can be given, the animal will continue to press the lever in response to the tone alone for hundreds or thousands of trials. The reason for this is that the animal has no way of knowing that lever pressing is no longer necessary to avoid shocks. In other words, the animal cannot reality test, preventing extinction of the avoidance behavior (lever pressing) and the autonomic component (fear).

Relationship of Paradigms to Maladaptive Behavior

The similarity of these experimental paradigms to clinical phobias, phobiclike neurotic disorders, and obsessive compulsive neurosis is readily apparent. It has been observed from antiquity that harmless objects and innocuous situations (like the tone) may come to elicit anxiety if they are associated with single or repeated traumas. A common example is the intense anxiety experienced by some persons in an automobile after being in or witnessing a serious and terrifying accident. The automatic, involuntary, and "irrational" nature of this emotional response is apparent in that some persons so traumatized will experience anxiety even if they are induced to sit in a parked car in a garage and are reassured that the car will not move. However, if the person goes ahead and rides in automobiles again, the excessive (and maladaptive) uneasiness usually subsides in a short time. This is analogous to the extinction of conditioned fear. Depending on various factors, however, some persons will assiduously *avoid* riding in automobiles after such an experience. This often leads to a car-riding phobia that may persist for many years. The fear conditioned by the traumatic experience cannot undergo extinction since the behavior of avoiding automobile riding is being reinforced, and hence maintained, by anxiety reduction.

This mechanism is seen even more clearly in a very common phobia—fear of heights. The acrophobic patient typically avoids occasions that would put him in his feared situation at full intensity. Often, however, he will report abortive efforts to do so. This was illustrated by an acrophobic patient of mine who reported an attempt to shop on an upper floor of a tall department store. She experienced uneasiness as she rode the escalator from the second to the third floor. As she went higher and higher, her tension and anxiety mounted. When only halfway to her destination, she "gave in" to her phobia and crossed to the down side of the escalator. As she descended, her anxiety abated; relief from anxiety is very reinforcing. The behavior being reinforced in this case was phobic in nature; avoidance of heights. This is quite analogous to the animal with experimentally produced conditioned avoidance. The patient terminated the conditioned stimulus (approaching the height) by an avoidance response (retreating from the height) and hence strengthened her conditioned avoidance (the acrophobia).

Of course, a history of specific trauma is not obtained in the case of most clinical phobias. Some phobic objects are probably symbolic of other sources of real or imagined danger (e.g., Freud's "Little Hans'" fear of horses may indeed have derived from fear of retaliation by his father). The point is, however, that clinical phobias are similar to conditioned avoidance responses and it is therapeutically useful to regard them in this manner.

Removal of Maladaptive Behavior

The question that this analysis raises is how such maladaptive conditioned avoidance responses may be removed. One method in the experimental paradigm described earlier is to make the lever inoperative. In other words, when the tone sounds the animal attempts to press the lever but it is fixed in position. The tone continues for a full 5 seconds, but no shock is delivered. In this kind of forced reality testing the animal may first display intense fright, but the conditioned fear and its associated conditioned avoidance usually extinguish in a short time. The animal learns that it is no longer necessary to make the avoidance response since no real danger exists. The behavioral treatments corresponding to this experimental procedure are implosive therapy, flooding, response prevention, and in a less forced way, reinforced practice. Implosion and flooding are discussed in detail in Chapter 6 of this volume; reinforced practice is discussed in Chapter 2 (see pp. 43–44).

Systematic desensitization is based on another way of removing conditioned avoidance. A feared and avoided goal may be reached successfully if it is approached in a series of very small steps and if a psychophysiologic state inhibitory of anxiety is induced at each step. This general psychotherapeutic principle was termed *reciprocal inhibition* by Wolpe and described by him as follows: "If a response inhibitory to anxiety can be made to occur in the presence of anxiety-evoking stimuli, it will weaken the connection between these stimuli and the anxiety responses" [27, 29]. This principle is also referred to as *counterconditioning.*

The operation of this principle is seen in experiments performed by Wolpe in which cats were given electric shocks in a particular cage [27]. The animals displayed intense fear at the sight and smell of the cage (conditioned stimuli). To decondition a particular cat Wolpe brought the animal to a position sufficiently far from the fear-provoking cage that only a small amount of uneasiness was apparent. At this location the hungry animal was fed, with the expectation that the psychophysiologic responses induced by feeding would inhibit or countercondition the anxiety present. The animal was then moved a step closer and again fed and so forth. The last step on this *anxiety hierarchy* was being inside the cage itself. This proved to be an efficient way to eliminate the previous conditioned fear and conditioned avoidance in the cats.

In the treatment of phobic disorders with desensitization it is not necessary for the patient to approach the actual feared object or situation. Indeed, this would be impractical or impossible in many cases. Instead, the patient imagines a series of scenes having to do with the theme of his phobia that are arranged hierarchically from the least to the most anxiety arousing. Rather than use eating to induce a state inhibitory of anxiety, deep muscular relaxation is most commonly employed.

THE PROCEDURE OF DESENSITIZATION

Treatment by systematic desensitization involves three steps: training in progressive relaxation, construction of anxiety hierarchies, and the systematic combination of these in the desensitization process itself. Experienced behavior therapists may differ from each other in some details of technique, but the basic procedure is the same. What follows is a description of the way this author conducts the treatment.

Training in Progressive Relaxation

This method of inducing deep muscular relaxation is a modified and shortened version of a technique originally described by Jacobson [13]. In this procedure the patient learns to relax one gross-muscle group at a time by first tensing the muscles of that group and then releasing their tension. Relaxation is carried out with the patient in a comfortable reclining chair or couch; it is essential that he not have to exert any effort to maintain posture. The room is quiet, the lights are dimmed, and he is asked to close his eyes. Typical instructions during the first session follow. I begin with relaxing the right upper extremity.

1. "I am going to teach you to relax very deeply. To do this I will ask you to concentrate on and relax one group of muscles at a time. We will start with your right hand, forearm, and arm, i.e., your right upper extremity. Now you will find it easier to relax these muscles completely if you first tense them. To do this, make a tight fist, flex your hand and forearm and tense all the muscles of the limb

as much as you can." (If the patient is not clear what to do, I passively move the limb into the correct position or demonstrate the position to him.) "Now tense the muscles until you can feel the limb tremble. When I say 'relax' in a few seconds, simply release all the tension, let the muscles go and relax completely."

After about 5 seconds of tension I tell the patient: "Relax. Release all the tension in the muscles. Feel the tension drain out of your limb. Keep on letting go until the limb is completely limp." After about 25 seconds of relaxation this tension-release exercise is repeated once or twice more or until the limb is indeed deeply relaxed. This is ascertained by questioning the patient and by direct examination of the limb (passively moving and palpating the limb). I then proceed to have the patient relax each of several other grossmuscle groups in an analogous manner, using similar verbalizations and having the patient repeat each tension-release cycle once or twice as needed. These other groups are as follows:

2. Left upper extremity.

3. Upper portion of face. Here I have the patient strenuously frown, which tenses the muscles of the scalp, forehead, and around the eyes.

4. Lower portion of face. The patient is instructed to draw back the corners of his mouth in a wide grin, which tenses the lower facial muscles and some muscles of the jaw and neck.

5. Upper portion of trunk. The patient takes a very deep breath and slowly exhales.

6. Lower portion of trunk. Tightening the abdominal muscles as though anticipating a blow is used here.

7. Right lower extremity. I have the patient extend the leg and dorsiflex the foot to tense these muscles.

8. Left lower extremity.

When the preceding is completed, I give some general relaxation instructions and some suggestions in a monotonous tone that are similar to those used in hypnotic induction. However, actual hypnosis is rarely inadvertently induced in this procedure. (The explicit and intentional induction of hypnosis in systematic desensitization therapy is discussed later in this chapter.) Typically, I will say to the patient: "Now relax all the muscles of your body—let them all go limp. Let the last vestiges of tension drain out of your body. A pleasant heavy feeling may come over your body, and you may seem to be sinking deeper into the reclining chair. You may notice a pleasant, warm sensation in your abdomen as you relax more and more completely." And so on. It is important at this point to ask the patient if in fact he feels completely relaxed. If he reports some residual tension in some part of his body, additional tension-release exercises or suggestions of relaxation should be directed at the problem area. It is also useful at times to have the patient vividly imagine a scene or situation he finds especially relaxing, such as watching clouds drifting by overhead, floating in a pool of warm water, or lying on the warm sand at the shore.

Usually a portion of the first three or four treatment sessions is devoted to relaxation training. In addition, the patient is instructed to practice progressive relaxation at home at least 20 minutes daily between sessions. The time required for the patient to attain a deeply relaxed state should become shorter with practice. The preliminary tensing of muscles before relaxing them can usually be omitted after the first few weeks of training.

Construction of Anxiety Hierarchies

This is a crucial step in the treatment. By careful questioning the therapist determines all the stimulus situations that provoke inappropriate anxiety in the patient. These are then grouped into *themes*. Sometimes there is only one theme as in a monosymptomatic phobia. More often, however, several distinct themes emerge. For example, a patient might report inappropriate, maladaptive anxiety to being in high places, being in crowds, and to being criticized by others. A second and related task of the therapist is to identify the dimensions of each theme along which the intensity of the anxiety varies. For example, the intensity of anxiety provoked by crowds might vary with the number of persons in the crowd, their age, or some aspect of their attitude toward the patient. With this information the therapist devises 10 to 20 *scenes* or specific imaginal situations having to do with a given theme that can be arranged hierarchically, from one which elicits minimal anxiety to one which elicits intense anxiety. The acrophobic patient mentioned earlier was monosymptomatic, and the hierarchy used in her treatment was as follows:

1. On the 3rd floor of a tall building near no window.
2. On the 3rd floor near an open window.
3. On the 4th floor near no window.
4. On the 4th floor near an open window.
5. On the 6th floor near no window.
6. On the 6th floor near an open window.
7. On the 6th floor looking out an open window.
8. On the 8th floor near an open window.
9. On the 8th floor looking out an open window.
10. On the 10th (top) floor near an open window.
11. On the top floor looking out an open window.
12. On the top floor leaning head out of an open window.

Hierarchy construction usually requires a portion of two or three sessions. It is important during this period to ascertain that the patient is capable of vividly imagining scenes on command. This is best done using scenes the patient finds emotionally neutral or restful, such as lying on the grass and watching clouds overhead. Most patients are capable of obtaining quite vivid visual images with a little practice. The ability to obtain vivid anxiety-arousing images of hierarchy scenes is essential for conducting the desensitization proper, since anxiety must be elicited in order to be counterconditioned.

Desensitization Proper

Usually by the third or fourth session, desensitization proper can be started. If there is more than one hierarchy, i.e., if there is more than one fear-evoking theme, the most distressing of these is treated first and then the others in order. After the patient successfully enters a deeply relaxed state in the manner he has learned, he is instructed to imagine vividly the first or least anxiety-provoking scene of the hierarchy. He is told that if he experiences more than minimal anxiety and tension while visualizing this scene he is to indicate this to the therapist by lifting his index finger. If no anxiety is apparent from the patient's appearance and his failure to signal it, he is allowed to visualize the scene for about 5 seconds and then instructed to stop. After a rest period of 10 to 15 seconds, during which it is helpful to give additional relaxation suggestions, the same scene is presented once or twice more, gradually increasing the duration of scene presentation to about 10 seconds. If anxiety continues to be absent, it can be assumed that the anxiety associated with this scene has been successfully counterconditioned, and the therapist goes on to the next scene of the hierarchy and so forth. If anxiety is elicited by a scene, the presentation is immediately stopped and the patient is given further relaxation suggestions. The scene is then repeated a number of times, at first for shorter durations if necessary, until the scene no longer elicits anxiety for a full 10-second presentation. When this is accomplished, the therapist goes on to the next scene and so forth. Usually two or three scenes are used in each desensitization session.

Sometimes a scene will continue to evoke anxiety even with brief presentations. If this occurs, some other action is necessary depending on which of two main problems is responsible. First, the interval between the previous, successfully deconditioned scene and the present one may be too great. In this case one or more intermediate scenes need to be devised to make the steps in the hierarchy smaller. A second possibility is that the patient has become aroused and tense by some other event, e.g., a chance association between something said and some source of anxiety. The remedy for this is to help the patient relax more completely again by the use of further relaxation suggestions, restful scenes, or progressive relaxation exercises, singly or in combination. Experience with the technique helps to determine which of these is the problem; however, a certain amount of trial and error is often necessary. Finally, desensitization requires concentration; most patients become fatigued after a 20- or

25-minute session. The rest of the therapeutic hour can be spent in reviewing progress and discussing related problems.

The patient is not encouraged to enter the phobic situation at full strength during the treatment process. A "heroic" effort to do so may generate intense anxiety and result in a loss of some of the progress he has made. However, he *is* encouraged to enter situations that correspond to those of the hierarchy that have been successfully covered, if they in fact no longer provoke significant anxiety. Typically, this can be done because scenes desensitized in treatment tend to cause little difficulty in the corresponding real-life situations, although there may be some lag in transfer to the real-life situation [1]. This has several purposes. First, it tends to consolidate the gains the patient has made, and, as noted in Chapter 2, graded practice in the feared situation is beneficial in its own right. In terms of learning theory, exposure to the feared situation facilitates extinction and prevents the *spontaneous recovery* or return of recently extinguished conditioned avoidance responses. Second, it provides feedback to the patient that he is indeed overcoming his phobia (see pp. 41–42). Finally, it provides more accurate information to the therapist as to the progress of treatment.

Other Aspects of the Treatment

A number of authors have suggested that some of the improvement seen in patients treated by desensitization may be due to mechanisms other than the counterconditioning of anxiety. For example, when the patient reports progress in successfully entering more and more situations that correspond to his hierarchy, the therapist responds with approval; this approval by a person important to the patient may act as a powerful reinforcer to approach his feared situation, facilitating further progress [2]. In addition, suggestion, the therapist's expectations and enthusiasm, and other nonspecific therapeutic factors inherent in the treatment situation also play a role [17, 21]. Some of these potentially beneficial factors can be maximized by the skillful clinician and enhance the effectiveness of desensitization. However, it is unlikely that these factors alone account for the efficacy of the procedure. A number of experimental studies indicate that the major contribution to improvement comes from the systematic pairing of deep muscle relaxation with progressively more anxiety-provoking scenes related to the patient's neurotic difficulties [30].

EFFICACY OF DESENSITIZATION

The efficacy of desensitization therapy will be discussed under three headings: the results of experimental (analogue) studies, uncontrolled clinical studies, and controlled clinical trials.

Analogue Studies

These are controlled experiments on the amelioration or removal of specific irrational fears in human subjects. The term *analogue* is used since the participants are not patients in the usual sense of persons who seek professional help for a problem, but are persons, usually college students, who volunteer for an experiment. However, in most of these studies the subjects have been intensely fearful in the relevant area.

Perhaps the most elegant of these investigations is that of Dr. Gordon Paul of the University of Illinois [22]. Paul chose as subjects 96 college students who reported severe anxiety in public speaking situations. (The institutional requirement of a public speaking course for graduation made these subjects especially apprehensive.) Following psychologic and psychometric assessment and objective measures of their anxiety in a public speaking situation, the subjects were randomly assigned to four groups. The first of these was treated by systematic desensitization and the second by insight-oriented psychotherapy for the same number of sessions. The third group was treated by an attention-placebo procedure to control for the nonspecific, placebo effects of the psychotherapeutic relationship. Subjects in this group received attention from an interested therapist, but care was taken to avoid discussion of personal problems or other presumably specific aspects of the other two treatment modalities. The fourth group was a no-treatment, waiting-list control group. Finally, there was a no-contact control group who were never contacted individually for assessment of their problem-speaking anxiety, and who were in fact unaware of their inclusion in the study. These subjects had reported public speaking anxiety, however, and thus could be compared with the no-treatment waiting-list control group for the possible effects of the preliminary assessment procedures. Each of five therapists treated three randomly assigned subjects in each of the three treatment groups. All five therapists had extensive experience with insight-oriented psychotherapy, and all were dynamically oriented. However, all therapists underwent intensive training in the conduct of the systematic desensitization and the attention-placebo procedure before beginning those treatments.

The principal finding of the study was that the group treated by desensitization showed greater reduction in anxiety in a realistic test situation by cognitive (self-report), physiologic, and behavioral criteria than any other group. Insight-oriented psychotherapy and the attention-placebo procedure came next in efficacy, and both were superior to the no-treatment and no-contact control procedures. The latter two groups performed about the same. The superiority of the desensitization procedure was apparent also at follow-up assessments at 6 weeks and 2 years. There was no evidence of symptom substitution in any of the subjects who improved by any procedure.

Similar experimental studies have been carried out on subjects selected for fears of harmless snakes or rats, and disrupting anxiety in academic test situations [23]. From these studies it is clear that systematic desensitization is an efficient and effective means of ameliorating or removing such specific sources of anxiety and is generally superior to nonbehavioral treatment procedures with which it has been compared. The one limitation of these investigations is that the subjects were not patients seeking treatment but volunteers, and it can be argued that a clinical population might have responded differently. However, many of the symptoms treated in these analogue studies were in fact disabling to varying degrees.

Uncontrolled Clinical Studies

Wolpe, the originator of desensitization therapy, has treated several hundred patients with phobias and phobialike disorders by the procedure. Excluding patients who terminated treatment before a "fair trial" of desensitization, Wolpe reports success rates between 88 and 92 percent in several reports [27, 28, 30]. Meaningful comparisons of outcome with phobic patients treated by other means is difficult because of differences in assessment, criteria for improvement, equivalence of patients, and so forth. Nevertheless, Wolpe's success rate is impressive indeed. Other behavior therapists also report high success rates (in the 70 to 85 percent range) in the treatment of neurotic disorders with desensitization (e.g., 12, 15, 24).

Controlled Clinical Studies

Marks, Gelder, and their colleagues at the Maudsley Hospital in London have conducted a number of interrelated investigations on the indications and efficacy of systematic desensitization therapy [18]. Although some of these studies are imperfectly controlled (e.g., some studies are retrospective, in others treatments being compared were administered for different durations), some conclusions can reasonably be drawn from this work. First, it seems clear that systematic desensitization is more effective than individual or group (reeducative) psychotherapy for the treatment of most phobias. The severe agoraphobics in these studies did poorly with either systematic desensitization or psychotherapy. However, this probably reflects the poor prognosis of the highly disabled agoraphobics included in these investigations. Other therapists have reported better results in the treatment of agoraphobia with desensitization (e.g., [20]). A noteworthy feature of the Maudsley studies is the thorough assessment of multiple aspects of the patients' adjustment before and after treatment as well as at follow-up evaluations. A consistent finding is that symptom substitution is not a problem in patients who improve substantially with behavior therapy.

A number of other studies attest to the superiority of desensitization in the treatment of phobic disorders over various forms of interpretative psychotherapy [23]. In one of these Lazarus [16] randomly assigned patients with similar phobias to one of two treatments: systematic desensitization conducted in groups of three to five, or groups of the same size treated by interpretative psychotherapy. Group desensitization was found to be more effective than group psychotherapy.

INDICATIONS AND LIMITATIONS

A classic, monosymptomatic phobia is the indication par excellence for systematic desensitization therapy. However, a common misconception among clinicians whose primary orientation is not behavioral is that simple phobias are the only indication. As mentioned earlier, phobias usually occur in clusters, and two or more distinct themes may be found in a given patient. In such cases each phobic theme has to be desensitized in turn to achieve adequate clinical improvement. Further, treatment by desensitization is not limited to phobias. In general, desensitization is applicable when one can identify the specific stimulus antecedents of the patient's anxiety that in turn mediate the patient's maladaptive behavioral or physiologic responses. Thus, desensitization has been successfully applied to such seemingly disparate disorders as obsessive-compulsive neurosis, certain sexual disorder, and psychophysiologic reactions. Some examples will be helpful.

A careful questioning of a patient who complains of distressing obsessions and compulsions sometimes reveals that these occur in response to anxiety generated by particular events. For example, Wolpe [30] describes an interesting case of a man with an incapacitating washing compulsion that was based on a specific and intense fear of contamination by urine. Thus, after urinating his anxiety was quelled only by spending up to 45 minutes washing his genitalia and an additional 2 hours washing his hands. He was treated mainly by desensitization in which the fear hierarchy involved exposure to increasing concentrations of urine. Of course, in many obsessive-compulsive neuroses such specific anxiety-generating stimuli cannot be identified, and other behavioral methods are indicated (see Chapter 4 on aversive procedures).

No doubt many social-psychologic factors contribute to the development of a homosexual life style in some men. Clinicians of different theoretic orientation agree that one of the most frequent and powerful of these is heterosexual anxiety, i.e., fear of sexual contact with women. Thus, the homosexuality of some men may be mainly a defense against, reaction to, or compensation for heterosexual contacts since the latter generate anxiety. In such cases a rational approach involves the deconditioning of heterosexual anxiety. Male homosexuals have been successfully treated in this manner where the fear-provoking hierarchy consists of scenes of heterosexual contacts and activities (e.g., [14]). Certain cases of sexual frigidity and impotence have been treated in an analogous manner [3, 9].

Bronchial asthma is an example of a psychophysiologic disorder that is sometimes amenable to desensitization therapy. Thus, Sergeant and Yorkston [26] describe the treatment of a woman with late-onset asthma that was refractory to corticosteroid treatment. The scenes of her anxiety hierarchy consisted of the limited circumstances that precipitated her asthmatic attacks and descriptions of the asthmatic attacks themselves. Following desensitization these situations no longer precipitated attacks, and she remained symptom-free for the 5-year follow-up period reported.

One general limitation of desensitization therapy needs to be mentioned. This is the situation in which the maladaptive behavior persists not only because of its anxiety-reducing property (recall the conditioned avoidance paradigm) but also because it is reinforced in other ways as well. This is well illustrated by some cases of chronic, severe agoraphobia in women—the "house-bound housewife" syndrome. Initially, the patient may avoid going far from her house alone because to do so generates anxiety. As the agoraphobia persists, however, her family and especially her husband may "adapt" to her limitations by carrying out many of the duties and chores normally fulfilled by a wife and mother. Depending on the patient's personality, e.g., if passivity and dependency are prominent traits, this may be very gratifying. Thus, the symptom may be maintained in part by these very reinforcing social consequences. This is sometimes called secondary gain. Treating this patient by desensitization alone may not be sufficient. It may be necessary also to deal with the family's unwitting reinforcement of the maladaptive behavior using, for example, an extinction procedure (see pp. 45–47).

Some clinicians who use desensitization extensively in the treatment of neurotic disorders eschew its application to psychotic individuals. Systematic desensitization has proved useful, however, in improving the adjustment of hospitalized schizophrenics, the procedure being used to remove specific distressing symptoms such as intensive interpersonal anxiety in certain situations or anxiety-laden obsessional thoughts. There is no evidence that these applications influence the underlying or coexistent psychotic disorder, nor is there any evidence that they bring about symptom substitution.

PROCEDURAL VARIATIONS

A number of innovations in desensitization therapy have been developed. Some of these were born of problems or obstacles in conducting classic systematic desensitization in particular patients, and others were suggested by developments in behavioral pharmacology and related fields.

In Vivo Desensitization

Also called *practical retraining,* in vivo desensitization entails the patient actually entering the anxiety-provoking situations of his fear hierarchy rather than merely imagining them. Since relaxation responses are not used in this procedure, the emotional state induced by the psychotherapeutic relationship is assumed to act as the counterconditioning agent. For this reason the therapist accompanies the patient as he proceeds from one hierarchy item to the next, so that the patient feels safe, secure, and protected in the presence of anxiety cues.

The procedure is well illustrated by a celebrated case of cat phobia reported by Freeman and Kendrick [10].

The patient was a 37-year-old housewife whose lifelong intense fear of cats had intensified over the years to the point of being disabling. For example, she was afraid to go into her own garden alone for fear of encountering a cat, and washdays, which required her using the courtyard, were a torment to her. She experienced intense anxiety on touching any catlike fur and even felt uneasy sitting next to anyone wearing a fur coat on public transport (stimulus generalization). The therapist constructed an anxiety hierarchy which began with cloth which had the texture but not the appearance of cat fur. The hierarchy proceeded through a series of materials which resembled cat fur more and more in texture and color. Following in vivo deconditioning to these materials the patient was exposed to catlike toys, a series of pictures of cats, and finally brief exposure to a kitten of placid disposition. The final items on the hierarchy involved exposures to a full-grown cat. Desensitization to the entire hierarchy was completed in 10 weeks, and the patient remained symptom free.

A limitation of in vivo desensitization is that it is often impractical for the therapist to accompany the patient in his encounters with many kinds of phobic objects and situations. An advantage of the procedure, however, is that relaxation training is not necessary. Also it is applicable to patients who are unable to attain the deeply relaxed state required for desensitization in imagination.

Use of Hypnosis

Usually progressive relaxation training is preferred to hypnosis as a means of inducing relaxation for desensitization therapy. Indeed, there is some experimental support for this preference: Paul [25] has shown that progressive relaxation training is more effective than hypnotic suggestion in reducing subjective tension and physiologic arousal (heart rate, respiratory rate, tonic muscle tension, and skin conductance). However, an occasional patient may prove to be more amenable to hypnotically induced relaxation, and some persons can obtain more vivid visual images with hypnosis.

Of course, it is possible to combine progressive relaxation and hypnosis. This may prove useful for a patient who is refractory to either technique of inducing relaxation used alone. Another alternative for the patient who has difficulty relaxing is the preliminary administration of drugs with sedative, antianxiety, or muscle-relaxant properties. Oral doses of barbiturates (e.g., 30 mg. amobarbital) or minor tranquilizers (e.g., 25 mg. chlordiazepoxide, 5 mg. diazepam) given one-half hour before each relaxation training session have been used for this purpose.

Brevital-Aided Desensitization

The use of subanesthetic doses of intravenous methohexital sodium (Brevital) in desensitization therapy is a special technique of great promise. The procedure was first introduced by Friedman [11] in 1966 and has now been used by many clinicians for a wide variety of neurotic disorders [8]. The principal advantages of the use of this ultra-rapid-acting barbiturate are that preliminary training in relaxation is usually unnecessary and the anxiety-inhibition afforded by Brevital is both powerful and reliable. The counterconditioning of anxiety responses appears to proceed more rapidly. Mawson [19] recently reported a controlled (crossover) comparison of the treatment of 12 phobic patients with Brevital-aided desensitization versus desensitization with progressive muscular relaxation. The drug-aided desensitization was 50 percent more effective in terms of the time required for improvement. I have discussed the probable modus operandi of Brevital-aided desensitization extensively elsewhere [7]. In brief it appears that Brevital facilitates the deconditioning of anxiety not merely by enhancing relaxation but by inhibiting anxiety sui generis, the emotional calm induced by the drug counterconditioning the anxiety aroused by hierarchy scenes.

Some clinicians report dissatisfaction with Brevital-aided desensitization, citing such problems as inadequate relaxation and the complaints of some patients that the procedure is unpleasant. These and other problems can be largely obviated if a number of procedural details are carefully followed [3]. A brief description of the procedure I use follows. First, it is important that the total setting be conducive to physical and psychologic relaxation. Thus, the patient should be comfortably reclined in a chair or couch, the room should be quiet and not too brightly lighted, and so on. I explain to the patient that the drug will facilitate his relaxing, but that he must "work along with it." This greatly reduces the likelihood of paradoxical excitement being induced by the intravenous barbiturate and emphasizes the active role played by the patient in the treatment. Suggestions of relaxation, calm, and the like are made throughout the treatment. The venipuncture is made with a sharp, small gauge needle (#22) to minimize discomfort, and initially 1 to 1½ ml. of a 1 percent solution of Brevital are given over a 2- to 3-minute period. This amount of the drug is usually sufficient to induce a deeply relaxed and tranquil state without producing a degree of drowsiness that would impede the vivid visualization of hierarchy scenes. Scenes from the hierarchy, which has been constructed in the usual manner, are presented as in conducting systematic desensitization without Brevital. During the course of the 20- to 30-minute desensitization session, up to an additional 4 ml. (i.e., 40 mg.) of Brevital may be given in divided doses to maintain the deeply relaxed, tranquil state necessary to countercondition anxiety. (The needle is left in the vein throughout this period so that additional venipunctures are not necessary.) Because of the very rapid metabolism of the drug, the patient is usually fully alert and able to leave the therapist's office 10 to 15 minutes after the last Brevital is injected. As desensitization progresses, less and less of the drug is required to maintain adequate relaxation in each treatment session. Commonly, no drug is needed in the last few desensitization sessions.

I have found this procedure to be both effective and safe in the treatment of over 60 patients with a variety of disorders mediated by maladaptive anxiety [3, 5, 6, 9]. In general, the indications for Brevital-aided desensitization are the same as systematic desensitization without the drug. Contraindications include patients who might not tolerate the drug well (liver impairment, a history of drug addiction, and so forth) and the occasional patient with an inordinate fear of venipuncture or fear of drug-induced feelings of loss of self-control.

Supportive and Reeducative Psychotherapy

Systematic desensitization is conducted in the context of a psychotherapeutic relationship. Elements of supportive and reeducative psychotherapy often evolve quite naturally during the course of treatment. There is no reason to exclude arbitrarily the explicit use of these potentially powerful therapeutic forces from the total treatment of the patient, and indeed they often complement specific behavioral procedure very nicely [6].

REFERENCES

1. Agras, W. S. Transfer during systematic desensitization therapy. *Behaviour Research and Therapy* 5:193, 1967.
2. Agras, W. S., Leitenberg, H., and Barlow, D. H. Social reinforcement in the modification of agoraphobia. *Archives of General Psychiatry* 19:423, 1968.
3. Brady, J. P. Brevital-relaxation treatment of frigidity. *Behaviour Research and Therapy* 4:71, 1966.
4. Brady, J. P. Comments on methohexitone-aided systematic desensitization. *Behaviour Research and Therapy* 5:259, 1967.
5. Brady, J. P. A behavioral approach to the treatment of stuttering. *American Journal of Psychiatry* 125:843, 1968.
6. Brady, J. P. Psychotherapy by a combined behavioral and dynamic approach. *Comprehensive Psychiatry* 9:536, 1968.
7. Brady, J. P. Drugs in Behavior Therapy. In D. H. Efron (Ed.), *Psychopharmacology: A Review of Progress, 1957–1967*. Public Health Service Publication No. 1836. Washington, D.C., 1968.
8. Brady, J. P. Behaviour Therapy. In J. H. Price (Ed.), *Modern Trends in Psychological Medicine*, Vol. II. London: Butterworth, 1970.
9. Brady, J. P. Brevital-aided Systematic Desensitization. In R. D. Rubin, H. Fensterheim, A. A. Lazarus, and C. M. Franks (Eds.), *Advances in Behavior Therapy, 1969*. New York: Academic, 1971.
10. Freeman, H. L., and Kendrick, D. C. A case of cat phobia. *British Medical Journal* 2:497, 1960.
11. Friedman, D. A new technique for the systematic desensitiza-

tion of phobic symptoms. *Behaviour Research and Therapy* 4:139, 1966.

12. Hain, J. D., Butcher, R. H. G., and Stevenson, I. Systematic desensitization therapy: An analysis of results in twenty-seven patients. *British Journal of Psychiatry* 112:295, 1966.

13. Jacobson, E. *Progressive Relaxation*. Chicago: University of Chicago Press, 1938.

14. Kraft, T. Systematic desensitization in the treatment of homosexuality. *Behaviour Research and Therapy* 8:319, 1970.

15. Kraft, T. A short note on forty patients treated by systematic desensitization. *Behaviour Research and Therapy* 8:219, 1970.

16. Lazarus, A. A. Group therapy of phobic disorders by systematic desensitization. *Journal of Abnormal and Social Psychology* 63: 504, 1961.

17. Leitenberg, H., Agras, W. S., Barlow, D. H., and Oliveau, D. C. Contribution of selective positive reinforcement and therapeutic instructions to systematic desensitization therapy. *Journal of Abnormal Psychology* 74:113, 1969.

18. Marks, I. M. *Fears and Phobias*. London: William Heinemann, 1969.

19. Mawson, A. B. Methohexitone-assisted desensitization in treatment of phobias. *Lancet* 1:1084, 1970.

20. McConaghy, N. Results of systematic desensitization with phobias re-examined. *British Journal of Psychiatry* 117:89, 1970.

21. Oliveau, D. C., Agras, W. S., Leitenberg, H., Moore, R. C., and Wright, D. E. Systematic desensitization, therapeutically oriented instructions, and selective positive reinforcement. *Behaviour Research and Therapy* 7:27, 1969.

22. Paul, G. L. *Insight Versus Desensitization in Psychotherapy*. Stanford: Stanford University Press, 1965.

23. Paul, G. L. Outcome of Systematic Desensitization: II. Controlled Investigations of Individual Treatment, Technique Variations, and Current Status. In C. M. Franks (Ed.), *Behavior Therapy*. New York: McGraw-Hill, 1969.

24. Paul, G. L. Outcome of Systematic Desensitization: I. Background, Procedures, and Uncontrolled Reports of Individual Treatment. In C. M. Franks (Ed.), *Behavior Therapy*. New York: McGraw-Hill, 1969.

25. Paul, G. L. Physiological effects of relaxation training and hypnotic suggestion. *Journal of Abnormal Psychology* 74:425, 1969.

26. Sergeant, H. G. S., and Yorkston, N. J.   Verbal desensitization in the treatment of bronchial asthma. *Lancet* 2:1321, 1969.
27. Wolpe, J.   *Psychotherapy by Reciprocal Inhibition.* Stanford: Stanford University Press, 1958.
28. Wolpe, J.   The systematic desensitization treatment of neuroses. *Journal of Nervous and Mental Disease* 132:189, 1961.
29. Wolpe, J.   The Experimental Foundations of Some New Psychotherapeutic Methods. In A. J. Bachrach (Ed.), *Experimental Foundations of Clinical Psychology.* New York: Basic Books, 1962, p. 562.
30. Wolpe, J.   *The Practice of Behavior Therapy.* New York: Pergamon, 1969.

6

Flooding (Implosion) and Allied Treatments

ISAAC M. MARKS

EDITOR'S INTRODUCTION

Flooding comprises a range of procedures sharing the common element of exposing patients to their feared situation. Systematic desensitization is the most gradual way to do this, followed by implosion in which the patient imagines intense fear-provoking scenes, and then by flooding itself which confronts the patient with his feared situation in reality, either alone, with an encouraging therapist present, or with a therapist modeling approach to the feared situation. Related techniques are shaping (reinforced practice), paradoxical intention, and apotrepic therapy (a form of response prevention). These procedures are useful in the treatment of phobia, obsessive-compulsive neurosis, anxiety neurosis, and perhaps depression.

Implosion (flooding in imagination) (pp. 181–184) consists of having the patient confront his feared situation in imagination, deliberately provoking high levels of anxiety through vivid descriptions of the ultimate fear encounter. Therapy is preceded, as in the case of desensitization, by a careful elicitation of the environmental stimuli that provoke anxiety and avoidance. Unlike desensitization, strong anxiety-provoking scenes are used from the beginning. Some therapists use psychodynamic cues hypothesized to be related to the feared situation.

In flooding (in reality) (pp. 196–198) the patient is persuaded to confront his actual feared situation. The procedure essentially con-

sists of very rapidly shaping the patient to confront feared objects or situations and, as noted earlier, may include demonstration by the therapist of nonfearful approach behavior. Some evidence suggests that prolonged exposure, up to 3 or 4 hours at a time, may be most effective. This technique is similar to that of shaping approach to the phobic situation using social reinforcement (pp. 31–34), except that it may be faster and therefore more economical of the therapist's time.

Paradoxical intention (p. 179) is derived from existential therapy but effectively exposes the patient to his feared situation by asking him deliberately to try to bring on the feared consequences of his behavior instead of avoiding situations. Thus, the agoraphobic with a fear that she will faint if she walks alone is told to try and faint. She finds she cannot and is enabled to confront her phobic situation. The final technique in this group is response prevention, which was introduced by Meyer (pp. 199–203). In this procedure the compulsive patient is prevented from carrying out his rituals, thus exposing him to the feared situation that he has avoided by ritualistic behavior. Rituals must be totally stopped for a week or more. The remarkable success of this technique in a series of 10 cases of severe obsessive-compulsive neurosis suggests that this may prove to be a most effective approach to this difficult clinical problem.

The efficacy of some of these procedures has been investigated both in analogue studies and in clinical series. Marks makes a good case (see Table 1, p. 168) that the effectiveness of implosion in analogue studies is enhanced by longer exposure in imagination and by having a therapist rather than a tape recording present. These two variables may be similar in their effect, in that a therapist might well motivate the subject to imagine his feared situation more extensively than would a tape-recorded description. Anologue studies with desensitization suggest that graded presentation of the feared scenes is no more effective than random presentation. Pairing relaxation with the imagined scenes does not appear to be critical in either analogue studies (p. 172) or in the treatment of phobics [1]. Desensitization may then simply be a way to expose the patient to his feared situation in imagination.

The same theme continues when the results of controlled clinical studies are examined. *Implosion is more effective than desensitization in the treatment of phobics*—perhaps because it more effectively exposes the patient to his feared situation in imagination. *Shaping is more effective than either desensitization or implosion in the treatment of phobics,* and a recent clinical series suggests that flooding in the form of prolonged exposure will be even more effective. Whether flooding or shaping will be the most effective in the treatment of phobic disorders remains to be seen. *In obsessive-compulsive neurosis direct exposure to feared stimuli is more effective than a placebo treatment,* whether exposure is by flooding or with modeling.

One must conclude that for anxiety-based neurotic disorders direct exposure to the feared situation in reality is the best approach. It may be that all therapies—desensitization, shaping, implosion, and flooding with or without modeling—work to the extent that the patient faces his phobic situation. This presumably allows anxiety and avoidance behavior to extinguish. If it is not possible to arrange for direct exposure in reality, then exposure in imagination should be tried, using either implosion or desensitization, perhaps depending on the preferences of the patient. Implosion is more effective than desensitization, but because it is anxiety-provoking may not be tolerated well by some patients.

The conclusion that the best therapy consists of changing behavior in the environment in which it occurs echoes the theme of earlier chapters where it is demonstrated that a therapeutic environment is one in which the patient is motivated to practice adaptive and drop maladaptive behaviors. The token economy ward and the classroom are environments of this type, while the family is an example of an actual environment in which therapy can be arranged. Techniques such as role playing and modeling also allow the acquisition of skills within an interpersonal relationship and may come to form an important part of the future development of the behavioral therapies.

W.S.A.

REFERENCE

1. Agras, W. S., Leitenberg, H., Barlow, D. H., Curtis, N., Edwards, J., and Wright, D. The role of relaxation in systematic desensitization. *Archives of General Psychiatry,* 25:511, 1971.

Flooding is a method to relieve psychological distress by confrontation of the patient with the situation that provokes that distress. This confrontation can produce intense emotion, and some forms of flooding emphasize the importance of intense affect rather than the confrontation itself.

Flooding is not a fixed technique but comprises a range of procedures that merge into one another. Flooding is at one end of a continuum of approach to distressing situations, at the opposite end of which is desensitization. The difference between the two is largely one of degree. The more sudden the confrontation, the more it is prolonged, and the greater the emotion that accompanies it, the more apt is the label *flooding* for that procedure. Even flooding uses some gradation of approach, but much less than desensitization. When exposure to a phobic situation is slow, graduated, and brief, with but minimum tension, then the term *desensitization* is more appropriate. In much of the work to be reviewed the approach is somewhere between the two extremes, and choice of the terms *flooding* or *desensitization* is then rather arbitrary. In these instances the term *exposure* is preferable. The phrase *systematic desensitization* has come to imply the use of a very gradual approach to the phobic object combined with some soothing or distracting activity such as relaxation which is said to "reciprocally inhibit" or "countercondition" the anxiety. This combined procedure (see Chapter 5) will only be alluded to briefly where it is directly relevant to flooding.

Flooding treatment can be given in many ways, some of which are so different as to bring into question the similarity between them. For example, the confrontation may occur in imagination or in real life, individually or in groups, by tape recording or a live therapist, for shorter or longer durations, for intermittent or continuous periods, with escape allowed or curtailed, with anxiety minimized or deliberately provoked, with less or more elaboration of the distressing situation, and with varying therapeutic expectancies and instructions. It is unlikely that such a plethora of variants would all work in precisely the same fashion. To the extent that they share a common element they may operate through similar mechanisms, with other components added in varying degrees. The common elements in most forms of flooding are rapid confrontation of the patient with the stimuli that distress him until he gets used to them, the evocation of intense emotion during treatment, or both in combination.

Like many good ideas, flooding has a mongrel pedigree. This is evident from the varied applications of flooding procedures, which have been used on a common-sense basis since time immemorial. Pertinent ideas are derived from sources as diverse as meditation, psychoanalysis, existentialism, anthropology, and experimental psychology. Only recently has flooding become an area of special interest to workers who employ the language of learning theories. This phase has marked the beginning of systematic inquiry into the theoretic aspects of flooding. Such inquiry is facilitated by experiments in animals and in human volunteers. Following a review of terminology used in flooding, these experiments will be discussed. Past anecdotal material will then be reviewed to fill in the background essential for adequate perspective. Recent applications to patients will be surveyed in detail, and finally an overview will be made.

TERMINOLOGY

Implosion denotes the bursting inward of a vessel from external pressure. It has been used in disciplines like phonetics and astronomy and is employed by Stampfl [88] and others to describe a form of confrontation in which the patient vividly imagines his fears. Implosion "depicts the onslaught of phobic cues and the subsequent intense anxiety reaction which is followed by collapse of the symp-

toms because of extinction of the anxiety which supports them"
[38]. In this chapter implosion will be called flooding in fantasy (or
flooding in imagination).

High intensity stimulation is a phrase used by De Moor [21] and
by Rachman [77] to describe the techniques of implosion in man
and of flooding in animals. Nevertheless, Rachman made a plea in
his article to retain the word *flooding* to describe methods of this
kind.

Counterphobic treatment [92] denoted a method of flooding in
real life (synonyms: *in practice* or *in vivo*) in which snake phobic
subjects were pressured into holding a live snake for two 6-minute
periods without the benefit of successive approximation. Watson et
al. [94] called a similar method *prolonged exposure*. The essence of
this was continuous contact of the phobic patient with the real
phobic object for up to $2\frac{1}{2}$ hours.

Exposure of a graduated kind has been given various names—*participation, participant modeling,* and *contact desensitization* [2, 56,
79, 80]. These refer to subjects watching a model gradually coming
into contact with the real phobic situation and then following suit
himself. Graduated reexposure to real-life situations is also sometimes called *practical retraining* or simply *practice* [50]. Graduated
exposure that is accompanied by contingent reinforcement is termed
shaping, operant conditioning, or *reinforced practice* [14].

Reactive inhibition was Calef and Maclean's [13] term to describe presentations to the patient of imaginal phobic stimuli from a
hierarchy for 30 seconds at a time with the instruction to subjects to
attend to their sensations accompanying the anxiety. D'Zurilla et al.
[22] called a similar procedure *prolonged imagery*. Phobic scenes
from a hierarchy were imagined for up to 8 minutes at a time with
instructions to experience their feelings naturally. A related process
employed by Melamed [67] was called *catharsis*. Snake phobic subjects were required to view motion pictures of snakes for 15 seconds
at a time and to imagine they were really participating in and experiencing the events on the screen.

Deconditioning was the description given by Rudolf [81] for the
reduction of anxiety in soldiers in hospital who were subjected to

repeated air raids close by. The soldiers were moved in stages from the more protected ground floor to the first and then the second floor of the hospital.

Massed practice refers to repeated practicing of any behavior without much rest between trials. In discussion flooding is sometimes described as a special form of massed practice.

Arugamama [47] is a Japanese word for exposure to the real phobic situation without avoidance. Arugamama forms an aspect of Morita psychotherapy. An example is given in which a man who is frightened at the top of a high board accepts that his fear is inevitable and natural and dives into the pool despite his feeling nervous and timid. The fear is not escaped or avoided but is fully experienced while the original intention to dive is carried out.

Paradoxical intention [27] indicates treatment in which the patient is asked to exaggerate his fears deliberately.

With *induced anxiety* [72, 86] patients are relaxed under hypnosis and encouraged systematically to experience anxiety and other affects to the full, meanwhile associating these with past events. The process continues until emotion subsides or, if time does not permit this, is terminated by suggestions to relax. The method seems a special form of catharsis or abreaction.

ANIMAL EXPERIMENTS RELEVANT TO FLOODING

Flooding has been used in man mainly for the reduction of unpleasant affects. In animals the usual paradigm of such affects is fearful behavior. Many elegant ways of producing "fear states" in animals have been devised. These involve escape, avoidance, or freezing responses or suppression of ongoing behavior.

In animal experiments flooding denotes confrontation of animals with a stimulus that they have been conditioned to escape or avoid, or that provokes freezing or other signs of fear. Other terms to describe this are *forced exposure, forced reality testing* [6], or *environmental press* [63]. One way to produce confrontation is by prevention of the avoidance response in the presence of the conditioned stimulus, so some workers have used the term *response prevention* [6] or *detainment* [95] as synonymous with flooding.

Masserman [63], a pioneer worker with flooding in animals, produced "experimental neurosis" in cats, including strong avoidance to food. This was overcome by environmental press. He employed a movable barrier in the cage "to force the neurotic animal, at the height of its hunger, ever closer to the open food box as it became filled with delectable pellets of salmon seasoned with catnip. As the animal was thus slowly but inexorably brought nearer to the locus and psychological nidus of its conflict, its anxiety and attempts to escape at first increased in intensity; finally however, the maximally reinforced hunger drive explosively broke through its counterpoised inhibitions, and furtive, hurried gulping of food occurred. Once the motivational impasse was disrupted the feeding behavior soon became more natural and other neurotic manifestations rapidly diminished in intensity." Masserman noted that social example also helped, e.g., if another cat with active feeding responses was placed with the neurotic animal. This is an example of modeling. Other methods that helped the cats lose their avoidance included careful petting with gentle hand-feeding, and what he called "working through," namely training the animals to manipulate a switch that controlled their feeding signals and automatic deposition of food in the box.

Since that time thousands of experiments have been published about fear reduction in animals. Such animal behavior is, of course, but a poor mimic at best of abnormal behavior in psychiatric patients. Despite this reservation animal experiments still provide fertile ideas for treatment strategies and experiments in human volunteers and in the psychiatric clinic.

Acquisition of Fear

Seminal writings in this area include those of Bolles [10], Herrnstein [33], Baum [6], Shearman [83], and Katzev [45]. Bolles pointed out the enormous variation in speed with which different avoidance responses are acquired in different animal experiments and species. He proposed that animals have innate species-specific defense reactions such as fleeing, freezing, and fighting. The more the avoidance response to be learned resembles such an innate reaction, the more rapidly it is acquired. Running in a running wheel is close to the natural tendency of a rat to run away from a noxious stimulus and is acquired rapidly as an avoidance response. In contrast, bar-pressing, which is far removed from a rat's innate repertoire, is acquired slowly as an avoidance response, and its acquisition is said to begin by the innate response of freezing on the bar. The variables that are important in acquisition of the avoidance response depend largely upon the speed with which that avoidance response is acquired. Rapidly learned avoidance is said to occur through suppression of nonavoidance behavior by the successful avoidance response. With avoidance responses that are acquired relatively slowly, e.g., jumping into the safe side of a shuttle box, an additional variable becomes important for acquisition—whether the avoidance response successfully terminates the conditioned stimulus (CS) such as a tone. If the CS is immediately terminated by the avoidance response, then the acquisition of avoidance will be quicker. However, avoidance responses can be acquired even without any obvious conditioned stimulus at all. A rat can learn to depress a bar, a response far removed from its innate repertoire, simply in order to lower the frequency of shocks, not in order to escape any CS [33]. Under these conditions learning is extremely slow and takes thousands of trials, whereas in the running wheel or shuttle box situations stable avoidance is acquired within a few hundred trials [10].

Extinction of Fear

In the extinction of avoidance the precise nature of the situation is again important. Figure 4A shows the typical situation in which a rat learns to avoid a conditioned stimulus in a shuttle box. A tone (CS) sounds and is followed a few seconds later by a shock (UCS).

Both stop when the rat escapes by jumping into the other side of the box shortly after the tone begins. The animal soon learns to jump before the shock starts (Fig. 4B). The avoidance response (CAR) is now established.

In many experiments to extinguish such an avoidance response, the shock was switched off and the tone was sounded until the ani-

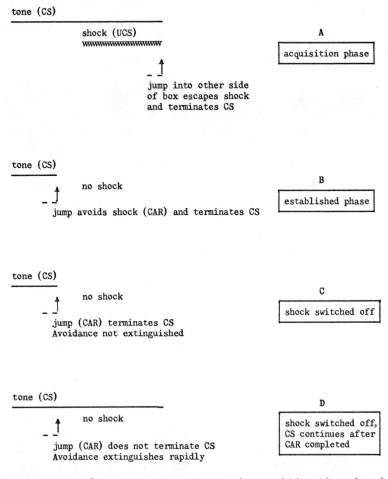

FIGURE 4. *Schematic representations of the acquisition (A) and maintenance (B and C) of avoidance responses in animals, together with an experimental paradigm for extinction (D).*

mal jumped into the other side of the box. This jump terminated the tone (Fig. 4C). From the animal's viewpoint the experimenter's switching off the shock did not change the situation (Figure 4C remains the same as Figure 4B). The animal never stayed put long enough to learn that the shock had been switched off, and continued to jump even after the tone had sounded hundreds of times without shock being programmed to follow.

Several experimenters [45, 83, 95] found that a small change in the experimental situation would lead to rapid extinction of avoidance in the shuttle box. The change was to allow the CS to continue for up to 10 seconds or longer after the avoidance response was completed (Fig. 4D) instead of allowing the CAR to terminate the CS. Katzev [45] found that the longer the tone was sounded after the rats had jumped, the more rapidly the rats ceased to avoid the tone. Prolongation of the CS beyond the CAR introduced a discernible change into the situation that the rats could detect (Figure 4D is different from 4C). The rats heard the tone before, during, and after the jump and thus had the opportunity to learn that the tone was no longer followed by shock.

EXPERIMENTS OF BAUM. Baum [6] used an experimental situation other than the shuttle box. His rats were placed on a grid at the bottom of a cage and a few seconds later received a shock from the grid floor unless they jumped onto a ledge halfway up the side of the cage (Fig. 5A). They soon learned to jump onto the safety ledge immediately after they were placed on the grid floor, before the shocks were delivered (Fig. 5B). When the shock was turned off, they never stayed sufficiently long on the floor to find this out, but continued to jump automatically onto the ledge straight after being placed on the grid floor (Fig. 5C). If the safety ledge was now removed, a rat which was placed on the grid floor showed initially intense attempts to jump onto a nonexistent shelf. These jumps rapidly diminished, and within a few minutes the rat behaved placidly on the floor of the cage (Fig. 5D). Baum called this form of extinction *response prevention* or *forced reality testing*. In his experiments the conditioned stimulus was contact with the grid floor of the cage,

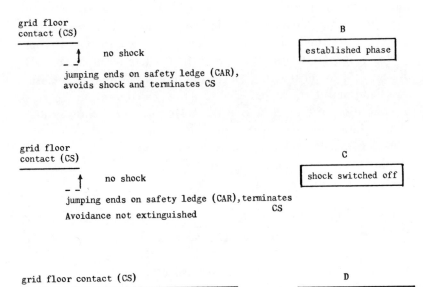

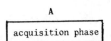

FIGURE 5. *Schematic representation of Baum's experiment in which avoidance responding (jumping) was acquired (A), maintained (B and C), and extinguished (D).*

not a sound or light as in Katzev's and Shearman's experiments. The complete avoidance response was not permitted by Baum as the ledge was removed from the cage. However, it could be argued that the rats' continuing initial jumps in the cage were abortive avoidance responses that were not prevented and that the active ingredient was forced contact with or exposure to the conditioned stimulus (the grid floor) in the absence of shock.

PARAMETERS INFLUENCING RATE OF EXTINCTION. Baum systematically explored some parameters governing the speed with which his procedure extinguished avoidance responses in rats. An important factor was the duration of response prevention (or exposure to the CS). One minute of response prevention had no effect, but 3- and 5-minute periods were highly effective where rats had been trained to avoid low levels of shock. An even longer duration of 30 minutes response prevention was necessary to extinguish avoidance that had been learned in relation to strong shocks. In addition, if rats had simply received random shocks prior to the avoidance training, they too subsequently required longer periods of response prevention to extinguish their avoidance behavior. The presence in the cage of nonfearful rats shortened the period of response prevention necessary to produce extinction. Extinction was also facilitated by forcing the rats to move around and explore the cage, either by direct handling or by using a loud buzzer. Whether the avoidance had been acquired in massed or distributed fashion did not affect the duration of response prevention necessary to extinguish it.

EFFECT OF DRUGS. Baum reviewed evidence that drugs usually have no lasting effect on extinction of avoidance responses in animals. Chlorpromazine [71] and amobarbital sodium [44] were not effective in extinguishing avoidance responses. Bindra et al. [9] showed that conditioned fear learned in a nondrug state and extinguished under a subanesthetic dose of phenobarbital recovers its strength in a nondrug state. The same finding was reported by Barry et al. [5]; i.e., drugs decrease the efficacy of response prevention. However, Sherman [84] showed that gradual withdrawal of sedatives may hasten extinction. Drug dissociation is a complex phenomenon [73], and the rules governing the process have yet to be delineated.

Relevance of Animal Work to Patients

There are many problems in comparing animal with human behavior because they differ in so many ways. The resemblance is perhaps closest between conditioned avoidance and escape responses in animals and phobic avoidance in humans, although even here there are many differences [17]. The paradigm is more remote for obsessive-compulsive neurosis or depression. It is often hard to define precisely what the conditioned stimulus is in a phobia or an obsession; the assumption that the noxious qualities of the stimulus have in fact been conditioned often lacks confirmatory evidence. It is similarly unclear what the unconditioned stimuli are. When one shocks a rat, this is obvious; but in a human phobic or obsessive, what is the equivalent of the shock? Is anxiety the unconditioned stimulus, the conditioned stimulus, the conditioned response, or the unconditioned response? In different situations it could be any or none of these, so that an alternative terminology appears to be desirable. Though we may be able to define some innate species-specific defense reactions in certain animal species, what are these in humans? Finally, much anxiety in humans occurs internally at a symbolic level without necessarily being accompanied by motor or autonomic signs, so it becomes difficult to follow operationally. Ideational avoidance and escape responses may operate according to rules different from those governing overt responses.

Baum and Poser [7] drew attention to further differences between flooding in animals and in man. Animals are forced physically to be exposed to the feared situation, while in patients exposure is at least partially voluntary, though encouragement and social pressure may be exerted by the therapist to persuade the patient to undergo flooding. Ethical considerations dictate that the patient has to agree to the treatment, or it cannot be used. Second, animals usually confront the feared situation alone, while most flooding of patients is in the presence of a therapist. In rats the presence of other nonfearful rats during the flooding procedure enhances extinction of avoidance behavior. The presence of a therapist might similarly influence the efficacy of flooding in patients. Third, in animal experiments there is usually a single conditioned stimulus used in the experimental situation. Clinically, however, a variety of objects or situations usually trigger the patient's distress. Unlike the situation with most experimental animals, patients' fears are not usually traceable to a particular learning experience. The causal antecedents have to be inferred from what patients say and do. Such inference can be as much a projection of the therapist's fantasies as a reflection of reality.

FLOODING IN VOLUNTEERS

The controlled study of flooding in humans began in 1965, after which time a growing spate of Ph.D. dissertations and other reports has appeared on the subject. By the time this chapter appears many more will have been published, some of which may modify present conclusions. Most studies on volunteers have been of psychology students, especially women, who appear to be the "white rats" of clinical psychology. A few have concerned other volunteers, but most studies were of a small section of the general population, i.e., intelligent, middle class, young, mainly white students. This naturally limits the conclusions that can be drawn. Volunteers who happen to have a fear but are not sufficiently distressed by it to seek treatment until sought out by a keen experimenter differ in important aspects from psychiatric patients with severe phobias or obsessions. The fears of volunteers are usually less intense and less extensive [61]. They are not associated with other psychiatric symptoms, and the personalities of volunteers may be more stable. Granted these caveats it is worthwhile reviewing volunteer studies in detail for the light they might shed on psychiatric problems.

Experimental Designs

Most volunteer studies follow a similar plan. Normal students or other adults are invited to participate in research. Those who agree are given a screening questionnaire such as the Fear Survey Schedule

(FSS). Subjects who show particular fears on these questionnaires are then given an avoidance test in which they are asked to approach as near as they can to the phobic object, usually a snake or a rat. Those who fail to touch the phobic object are generally accepted into the research design and are told that treatment is designed to reduce their fear. Other measures used in addition to the avoidance test and its variants include ratings of subjective anxiety during the avoidance test (e.g., the so-called fear thermometer); ratings of general anxiety (subjective, overt, or both); and various questionnaires. Subjects are then assigned at random to flooding and to contrasting control procedures. After the end of "treatment" (often but a few minutes later) the subjects are given a repeat avoidance test and other measures. Most studies have a brief follow-up period of several weeks or more, after which they are retested.

A recurrent weakness in many designs is a failure to measure sufficient aspects of fear behavior. Sophisticated physiologic measures are rarely used. Many studies rely excessively on avoidance tests, even when measures of other aspects of fear may reveal different trends. Undue reliance on any one measure of fear may be misleading, and an avoidance test in an experimental situation can be but a poor guide to performance in the natural situation.

Change on avoidance tests can occur without active treatment. In several studies control subjects who were simply given an avoidance test, sometimes followed by procedures such as listening to music, were able to touch the phobic object after having previously failed to do so [18]. Up to one quarter did this in the studies of Fazio [23], 6 out of 23; Layne [49], 6 out of 24; and Barrett [4], 3 out of 12. Change in controls at times occurred in other measures of fear; for example, in the study by Willis and Edwards [98] controls who were "treated" by vague discussion showed improvement on self-report by follow-up, at which time they were not significantly different from the experimental groups treated by flooding and by desensitization. This emphasizes the importance of adequate measures of fear both at the end of treatment and at follow-up. Confidence in experimental results in this area can only be placed where there is a consistent pattern of change across measures and across time.

Results of Studies

In spite of this, consistent results, summarized in Table 1, are emerging. All the studies except one were of flooding in fantasy in volunteers; the exception is that of Strahley [92], which was in practice. Investigations where flooding proved of some value are separated from those where flooding was ineffective. In those studies where flooding in fantasy had a significant effect, there was a longer duration of treatment sessions, a longer total duration of flooding in fantasy taken over all sessions together, and a rather longer duration of scenes within sessions. Treatment was by a therapist rather than a tape recorder in seven of the nine successful studies in fantasy, but in only two of the eight unsuccessful studies. The ineffective study of the longest duration was that of Layne [49] in which flooding for 60 minutes was delivered by tape recorder. In successful studies with short sessions [21, 102] treatment was given personally by a therapist and not by a tape recorder.

Important Variables

DURATION. Taken together, the pattern is for longer durations of flooding to be associated with better results, especially when treatment is given personally by a therapist. In some studies where flooding was ineffective [49, 66, 98] subjects nevertheless became less anxious as treatment sessions went on. However, at the time the experiment was terminated this improvement had not generalized to overt behavior in an avoidance test. Lott and Carrera [58] found that 25 minutes of flooding in fantasy by tape recorder had little effect, but 125 minutes did lessen avoidance.

Thus, there is evidence that, as in animals, duration of flooding is an important variable, though the relationship between treatment duration and improvement is complex and linked to other variables, e.g., whether treatment is in fantasy or in real life. In Strahley's [92] study two 6-minute periods of holding a live snake had a marked therapeutic effect. The importance of exposure in real life as opposed to fantasy is also evident in patients and will be discussed

TABLE 1. *Controlled volunteer studies on flooding*

Author	Subjects	Phobia	No. Flooded	Scene Duration (minutes)
	A. *VOLUNTEER STUDIES IN WHICH*			
Strahley [92]	FS	snakes	16	6
Wolpin & Raines [102]	FI	snakes	2	2–30
Kirchner & Hogan [46]	FS	rats	16	40
Hogan & Kirchner [38]	FS	rats	21	40
Hogan & Kirchner [39]	FS	snakes	10	60
Barrett [4]	FS & MS + public	snakes	12	35–145 ($\bar{x}$ 75)
De Moor [21]	MS	snakes	9	20
Calef & MacLean [13]	FS & MS	stagefright	10	½
Lott & Carrera [58]	FS & MS	snakes	14	25
Dzurilla, Wilson & Nelson [22]	FS	dead animals	9	8
		Mean =		32
	B. *VOLUNTEER STUDIES IN WHICH*			
Rachman [78]	FS	snakes	3	2
Mealiea [66]	FS	snakes	10	1–4
Willis & Edwards [98]	FS	mice	16	10–30
Hodgson & Rachman [35]	FS	snakes	10	40
Hodgson et al. [36]	FS	snakes	8	40
Fazio [24]	FS	cockroaches	6	29
Lott & Carrera [58]	?	snakes	10	25
Layne [49]	FS	rats	36	60
		Mean =		26

a All flooding in fantasy except for Strahley [92].

KEY: FS = female students; FI = female inpatients; MS = male students; $\bar{x}$ = mean.

Session Duration (minutes)	Total Duration (minutes)	Treatment by Tape-recorder	Follow-up Duration (months)	Comments
FLOODING WAS EFFECTIVE [a]				
12	12	no	0	Flooding = exposure in real life
?30	?90	no	1	Scenes emphasized contact, not·anxiety
40	40	yes	0	
40	40	no	0	
60	60	no	0	
35–145 ($\bar{x}$ 75)	150	no	6	
20	80	no	6	Scenes emphasized contact, not anxiety
60	300	no	0	Very brief scenes
125	125	yes	1	
60	240	no	0	Very brief scenes
56	125	2/9 taped		
FLOODING WAS INEFFECTIVE [a]				
20	200	no	3	
30	150	yes	1	Every 1–4 minutes students told to open eyes and see there was nothing to fear. Students became less anxious
10–30 ($\bar{x}$ 17)	55	no	2	Students improved; at follow-up not significantly different from desensitization or controls
40	40	yes	0	
40	40	yes	0	
29	87	yes	2	
25	25	yes	1	
60	60	yes	0	Students became less anxious. Suggestion had no significant effect
32	82	6/8 taped		

further later. Shorter periods of flooding may be necessary for treatment in real life compared with treatment in fantasy.

COVERT ESCAPE. Another variable affecting the duration necessary for improvement may be whether covert escape responses are permitted. In Mealiea's [66] study, where flooding was ineffective, subjects were told to open their eyes every 1 to 4 minutes to see that they had nothing to fear. This could be construed as encouraging covert escape, which might decrease the efficacy of flooding. Similarly, in the study of Rachman [76] duration of flooding scenes within sessions was only 2 minutes per presentation. The end of each scene presentation again might be regarded as a form of escape. However, this alone may not be a crucial variable since several successful studies employed not dissimilar procedures. The implosion tape of Hogan and Kirchner [38] contained instructions like Mealiea's about eye opening. In Wolpin and Raines' [102] study two subjects were successfully flooded with scene durations varying from 2 to 30 minutes; in De Moor's successful flooding the scene duration was 20 minutes; and in Calef and MacLean's [13] study scene presentation lasted only 30 seconds.

An interactional model could reconcile these differences. The duration of flooding necessary to reduce fear might be increased when treatment is in fantasy rather than in real life, by tape recorder rather than by a therapist, and intermittent rather than continuous. The shortest effective duration would then be associated with the combination of exposure in real life by a therapist who confronts the volunteer continuously with the phobic object.

Mechanism of Action

HABITUATION. The therapeutic ingredient of these studies could be construed as habituation of the subject to the fear-evoking stimuli. Extinction could describe the process equally well except that it assumes that the fear-evoking stimuli were originally acquired through conditioning mechanisms, an assumption for which there is only occasional evidence in patients. Some of the successful studies with flooding in volunteers are reminiscent of the animal work of Baum, Katzev, and Shearman in that subjects continued to experience the fear-evoking stimuli despite the anxiety these produced, i.e., continued exposure to the CS produced habituation. Forced response prevention was not employed in any study, but most subjects were under social constraint not to escape. This might be just as effective as the physical restraints in animal situations.

SUGGESTION AND EXPECTANCY. A recurrent problem in therapeutic work is the role of suggestion and expectancy; thus, Larsen [48] found that simple, posthypnotic suggestions not to be afraid produced short-term improvement in snake phobics although this gain was not maintained at follow-up. Whether suggestion and expectancy can act without any exposure of the subject either in fantasy or reality has not been tested. Indeed, it would be difficult to devise an experiment that would exclude the latter factors completely. Marcia et al. [60] found that snake-phobic subjects given a high expectancy of improvement improved more in their ability to touch a snake than did untreated controls or subjects given a low expectancy of change. The subjects were not exposed to phobic situations during "treatment" that involved looking at blank cards through a tachistoscope. The possibility remains, however, that these subjects were in fact imagining contact with snakes during treatment. Wilson [99] has suggested that the type of responses being rehearsed could have a positive or a negative effect depending upon the set of the patient. The subjects who improved in Wolpin and Raines' [102] study were told: "Practice in your imagination doing the thing you are afraid of, i.e., picking up a snake, the one you saw in the office." These subjects rehearsed accomplishment of the final criteria of fear reduction, while Rachman's [76] subjects who did not improve were rehearsing fear responses to these situations. However, the factor of *what* is rehearsed cannot alone be overriding, since successful studies such as those of Barrett [4] did employ rehearsal of fear responses. In some cases suggestion appears to work by encouraging subjects to rehearse contact with a phobic situation in their imagination, thus allowing habituation to occur. In other cases cognitive factors may work differently. A subject who is frightened but wills himself to undergo exposure to a test will improve more than somebody who is equally frightened but cannot be motivated to undergo the necessary exposure. Suggestion can act by making the subject more cooperative in carrying out the full treatment maneuvers necessary before he will improve. Improvement, however, is not due to the suggestion itself, but rather to the way in which suggestion enables treatment to be completed.

Comparison of Flooding with Desensitization

If flooding works through exposure of the subject to the phobic fantasy or object, then the procedure differs from desensitization only in degree, since desensitization consists of graduated, slow exposure to phobic images and objects with a simultaneously contrasting procedure. Desensitization is then, like flooding, a special form of treatment by exposure. Wolpe [100] suggested that desensitization acted by reciprocal inhibition or counterconditioning. According to this principle the anxiety of exposure is inhibited by muscular relaxation or some other maneuver, and emphasis is laid on the subject's not experiencing undue anxiety during treatment. Earlier evidence supported the idea of reciprocal inhibition [20, 76], but increasing evidence against this is beginning to appear. Wolpin and Raines [102], Schubot [82], Perloff [75], Crowder and Thornton [18], Benjamin [8], and Mathews [64] all produced evidence that desensitization combined with muscular relaxation was not superior to an identical procedure that omitted relaxation; i.e., simple exposure to phobic scenes in fantasy reduced fear without deliberate counterconditioning. Even the idea of *graduated* exposure has now been brought into question by such workers as Welch and Krapfl [96] who showed that desensitization can work equally effectively whether the scenes are presented going up, down, or randomly across the hierarchy.

EXPERIMENTAL STUDIES.   Comparisons of flooding with desensitization are thus essentially comparisons of two different forms of exposure—flooding being exposure near the top of the hierarchy and desensitization gradually moving up from the bottom. Three volunteer studies found flooding to be quicker in action than desensitization. Barrett [4] found that flooding in fantasy achieved a given criterion of improvement 55 percent more quickly than desensitization, and Strahley [92] found that 12 minutes of flooding in real life was superior to more than 200 minutes of desensitization in fantasy (of which 30 minutes was spent in presentation of phobic scenes). D'Zurilla et al. [22] found that flooding in fantasy tended to produce more behavioral improvement than desensitization.

Other workers have found desensitization and flooding to be equally effective [13, 21], while in three studies desensitization was found to be better than flooding. In one of these [94], however, the duration of desensitization treatment was on average 2½ times longer than that of flooding [97, p. 92], so that the comparison was biased against flooding. In the other two studies [66, 76] desensitization and flooding were given for equal durations, but the flooding scenes were interrupted every 1 to 4 minutes, a variable that might be important.

In several studies phobic scenes have been imagined for a few seconds at a time, with instructions either to remain calm or to relive the emotion. The imagining of these brief phobic scenes in a calm state was superior to that in a cathartic state [47, 67].

ROLE OF ANXIETY. Whether intense anxiety actually speeds improvement with exposure of a few minutes or longer is an open question. This is an important point, especially for psychiatrists who would naturally like to make flooding as pleasant a treatment as possible. Most proponents of implosion concentrate on production of the maximum possible anxiety. However, flooding in fantasy has been effective where the scenes emphasized contact with the phobic object rather than the experience of anxiety [13, 21, 102].

PRACTICE. That exposure to the phobic object is important is supported by studies in which graduated exposure produced improvement without deliberate attempts at counterconditioning or reciprocal inhibition. Callahan and Leitenberg [14] found that height phobics who were simply encouraged to climb a fire escape as high as they could, being praised for each point of progress, improved more than a control group that was not treated. They called their procedure *reinforced practice.* The same procedure has been therapeutic in other patients [1]. Even practice alone without reinforcement can benefit phobic and obsessive patients [50].

GRADUATED EXPOSURE. Ritter [80] showed the value of graduated exposure combined with modeling. She studied 44 children with fears of snakes who were assigned to one of three treatment conditions: (1) *vicarious desensitization:* children observed models engage in gradually bolder interactions with a tame snake over two sessions; (2) *contact desensitization:* children not only observed the models but themselves were brought into gradual physical contact with the snake itself; (3) *control:* children had no treatment. Both desensitization groups showed significantly less avoidance than untreated controls, but contact desensitization yielded significantly greater reduction of avoidance than vicarious desensitization alone. Contact desensitization of Ritter is graduated exposure in real life while following a model. Bandura [3], Litvak [56], and Rimm and Mahoney [79] called the same procedure *participant modeling* and showed its efficacy in adult volunteers with snake phobias.

When exposure is slowly graduated along a hierarchy with or without modeling, then little anxiety is evoked. This procedure would not be called flooding. When exposure is at a forced pace, much anxiety ensues with a desire to escape. This procedure would appropriately be termed flooding, and it has produced rapid improvement in volunteers. The role of anxiety in this procedure, however, is moot. It is quite possible that anxiety is an unfortunate by-product of forced exposure rather than the therapeutic agent itself. This crucial question remains to be settled.

PAST APPLICATIONS OF FLOODING

Justice to the subject of flooding cannot be done simply by examining formal experiments of recent years. Despite their ingenuity, such studies have so far covered but a tiny segment of a rich area. A glimpse at allied techniques used in the past in different uncontrolled contexts is essential for perspective before we consider recent applications of flooding in psychiatric patients.

Studies of Jersild and Holmes

Parents have long taught their children to overcome fear by various forms of confrontation. Jersild and Holmes [43] interviewed parents about the methods they used to reduce fear in their children. One technique used was compulsion of the child to participate in the phobic situation by force or by ridicule. Though Jersild and Holmes commented that "such tactics seldom succeeded," several examples of successful application of flooding were presented; e.g., "parents compelled the child to go alone into a dark bedroom; according to the parents' report, the child in the end completely overcame his fear of the dark room" (p. 85). In another case the father repeatedly brought the child back to an enclosure in which there were horses that the child feared; after many such visits (in the company of his father) the child grew interested in the horses and appeared to lose his fear. In a third case a mother repeatedly and deliberately operated a feared vacuum cleaner in the child's presence (plus additional demonstration that the brother was not afraid of riding on the cleaner while the motor was running); here again, the child was reported to have overcome his fear. As a contributory method to other fear-reducing techniques, this kind of flooding was successful in 50 percent of cases. It was noted that ridicule or invidious comparisons never helped a child.

The authors felt that the most useful methods were those that increased the child's skills and competence in dealing with the feared situation. "By 'skills' and 'competence' were included all activities and techniques designed to bring the child into *direct active contact with* or *participation in* the situation that he feared or any feature of the thing that is feared with a view to helping the child, with such experience, to be able to cope with the situation and thus overcome his fear." They commented that the important thing was to bring the child into active experience with the thing he feared. An attractive stimulus was primarily useful not as a means of changing associative connotations of the feared event, but as an auxiliary means of luring the child into activities that would increase his knowledge and competence in dealing with the thing he fears.

Also dealing with children, Jacobsen [41] reviewed methods that helped school phobics return to school and concluded that one of the most important aspects of treatment was quickly to get these school phobics back into the school setting in spite of their fearful protestations. She stressed the importance of firmness in this regard. If need be, the mother might accompany the child for a while.

Senoi Dream Interpretation

Intriguing reports also suggest that flooding procedures have been an aspect of child rearing in some cultures [91]. In 1935 Stewart studied the Senoi, a small isolated tribe of jungle folk living in the remote rain forest of the central range of the Malay Peninsula. His report is fragmentary and anecdotal and idealizes the Senoi. However, it is so thought provoking as to deserve detailed summary despite its paucity of hard fact. The Senoi tribe appeared to have unusually little violent crime or intercommunal strife, and this was attributed to their methods of child rearing and healing. These centered around particular kinds of dream interpretation that were a feature of child education and common knowledge among adult Senoi. The average adult Senoi practiced dream interpretation of his family and associates as a regular feature of education and daily social intercourse. Breakfast in the Senoi house was like a dream clinic, with the father and elder brothers listening to and analyzing the dreams of all the children. At the end of the family clinic the male population gathered in the council, at which the dreams of the elder children and all the men in the community were reported, discussed, and analyzed.

Much of the Senoi dream interpretation emphasized flooding-type practices. An example is the handling of dreams that provoked anxiety or terror. The simplest of these were falling dreams.

When the Senoi child reports a falling dream, the adult answers with enthusiasm, "That is a wonderful dream, one of the best dreams a man can have. Where did you fall to, and what did you discover?" He makes the same comment when the child reports a climbing, traveling, flying, or soaring dream. The child at first answers, as he would in our society, that it did not seem so wonderful, and that he was so frightened that he awoke before he had fallen anywhere.

"That was a mistake," answers the adult-authority. "Everything you do in a dream has a purpose beyond your understanding while you are asleep. You must relax and enjoy yourself when you fall in a dream. Falling is the quickest way to get in contact with the powers of the spirit world, the powers laid open to you through your dreams. Soon, when you have a falling dream, you will remember what I am saying, and as you do you will feel that you are traveling to the source of the power which has caused you to fall. The falling spirits love you. They are attracting you to their land, and you have but to relax and remain asleep in order to come to grips with them. When you meet them you may be frightened of their terrific power, but go on. When you think you are dying in a dream, you are only receiving the powers of the other world, your own spiritual power which has been turned against you and which now wishes to become one with you if you will accept it."

Over a period of time, with this type of social interaction, praise, or criticism, imperatives, and advice, the dream that started out with fear of falling changed into the joy of flying.

The Senoi also believed and taught that the dreamer—the "I" of the dream—should always advance and attack in the teeth of danger, calling on the dream images of his fellows if necessary, but fighting by himself until they arrived. Dream characters were bad only as long as one was afraid and retreated from them, and would continue to seem bad and fearful as long as one refused to come to grips with them.

Use with Adults

In adults many workers of divergent theoretic hues have made sporadic use of flooding or related methods. Freud [28] himself stressed the importance of exposure to the phobic situation in real life for improvement to occur: "One can hardly ever master a phobia if one waits till the patient lets the analysis influence him to give it up. . . . one succeeds only when one can induce them through the influence of the analysis to . . . go about alone and struggle with the anxiety while they make the attempt." Ferenczi [26], one of Freud's most notable pupils, illustrated the use of this principle in a young woman with severe stage fright who had shown little improvement in previous analysis. He asked the patient to sing a song. After several hours encouragement she was able to move from a halting voice to singing clearly, and then was asked to get up and sing expressively like her sister. The patient enjoyed these performances. Ferenczi noted that improvement was followed by the evocation of many childhood memories.

Yet another psychoanalytic account of exposure was given by Ovesey [74], who stressed that agoraphobics must reenter the phobic situation repeatedly until the anxiety dissipates. He advocated a gradual approach, the therapist sometimes accompanying the patient, the patient being armed if need be with a little bottle of whiskey, sedative pills, and a certificate of safe conduct. Writings on learning also describe similar maneuvers; e.g., Guthrie [32] cited how a girl overcame her car phobia by being driven for hours through the streets of Washington, her anxiety during treatment having reached a great peak.

Among other workers who have independently recommended the use of exposure in real life for the treatment of phobias have been Herzberg [34], Levine [52], Leonhard [51], and Rudolf [81]. These workers advocated a graduated reentry into the phobic situation in real life, but without assistance of counterconditioning mechanisms.

Malleson [59] described treatment in which "the patient is helped to break the phobic cycle by having him make a deliberate effort to feel and to experience fully his fear without trying to escape from it." The patient was an Indian student with examination panic 48 hours before an examination. He had already failed a previous examination because of a similar attack of panic. "He was made to sit up in bed, and try to feel his fear. He was asked to tell of the awful consequences that he felt would follow his failure—derision from his colleagues in India, disappointment from his family, financial loss. . . . at first, as he followed the instructions, his sobbings increased. But soon his trembling ceased. As the effort needed to maintain a vivid imagination increased, the emotion he could summon began to ebb. Within half an hour he was calm." He was instructed to repeatedly experience his fears. "Everytime he felt a little wave of spontaneous alarm he was not to push it aside, but was to enhance it, to try to experience it . . . more vividly." The patient was intelligent and assiduous, practiced his exercises methodically, and became almost unable to feel frightened. He passed his examinations without difficulty.

Paradoxical Intention

Writers have also claimed an existential basis for techniques such as paradoxical intention that include flooding methods. Paradoxical intention (existentialist logotherapy) has been described by Frankl [27]. The patient is asked to cease fleeing or fighting his symptoms and instead is asked to bring them on deliberately or even exaggerate them. The technique depends upon observations that anticipatory anxiety brings about precisely what the patient had feared, while excessive intention or self-observation of one's own functioning may make this functioning impossible. Anxiety or compulsions may be increased by the endeavor to avoid or right them.

Gerz [30] illustrated the use of paradoxical intention in a man afraid that he might die of a heart attack: "When I asked the patient in my office to 'try as hard as possible' to make his heart beat fast and die of a heart attack 'right on the spot' he laughed and replied 'Doc, I'm trying hard but I can't do it.' Following Frankl's technique I instructed him to 'go ahead and try to die from a heart attack each time his anticipatory anxiety troubled him. As the patient started laughing about his neurotic symptoms, humor helped him to put distance between himself and his neurosis. The patient . . . [was] instructed to die at least three times a day of a heart attack, and instead of trying hard to go to sleep, try hard to remain awake. . . . In the moment he started laughing at his symptoms and when he became willing to produce them (paradoxically) intentionally, he changed his attitude toward his symptoms. . . . With this change in attitude, he . . . interrupted the vicious cycle and strangled the feedback mechanism."

The rationale and method of paradoxical intention bear certain resemblances to flooding. As the rationale for use of a flooding procedure, Malleson [59] suggested that "fear or panic is always integrally bound up with the wish to escape. So long as that wish persists, reciprocally the fear persists." This suggestion is reminiscent of John Hunter's rationale for his treatment of impotence in the eighteenth century; as long as a patient was afraid of failing with his mistress he failed miserably. As soon as he was told not to engage in intercourse his potency returned [40].

Relationship of Flooding to Oriental Techniques

Flooding methods are also incorporated into meditative techniques of Zen Buddhism. Describing the stages of training, Maupin [65] wrote: "There is an initial phase in which concentration, difficult at first, eventually becomes more successful. Relaxation and a kind of pleasant 'self-immersion' begin to follow. At this point internal distractions, often of an anxiety-arousing kind, come to the fore . . . the only way to render this disturbance inoperative is 'to look at it equally and at last grow weary of looking.' "

Morita psychotherapy in Japan uses similar methods. In patients with severe anxiety and fear of death, Kora [47] noted that "the patient will always entertain a premonitory fear that the seizure [of anxiety] might attack him any moment and his sphere of activity is usually very much limited because of this anxiety. . . . he should be told that it is important not to upset the regular pace of his life even if he had a premonitory fear that the seizure might attack him, by accepting such fear as it is calmly and passively. When he does not have the fit, the patient should be made to go out all by himself even if he has an anticipatory fear or is suffering from anxiety. He should ride the bus or the streetcar if that is necessary and should attempt to enlarge his sphere of activity in any way possible. If he takes advantage of his disease and leads a life like that of a patient by capitalizing on his condition, he will never be cured." Similarly, in the treatment of intrusive thoughts "the only solution is to accept the desultory thoughts as something inevitable and to keep on reading without repelling them but tolerating them as they are. If this state of self-resignation is achieved, there will no longer be any antagonistic ideas."

One of the principles of brief dynamic psychotherapy is that of confrontation of the patient with his problem. Sifneos [85] went so far as to describe his method as "anxiety-provoking psychotherapy."

The recent upsurge of interest in flooding in man was influenced by Stampfl, whose work began to be publicized from 1964 onward [57]. He wrote that his methods had a basis both in psychodynamic and in learning theory. Recent studies of flooding in patients require detailed examination and form the subject of the next section.

RECENT CLINICAL APPLICATIONS OF FLOODING

Work of Stampfl

Flooding in fantasy became publicized under the name of implosion by Stampfl [88, 89], who claimed that the method was useful for a wide range of problems including obsessive-compulsive and depressive disorders, schizophrenia, homosexuality, alcoholism, and stuttering. Detailed evidence was not presented on which an informed opinion could be reached about efficacy of the method in defined disorders. Improvement was claimed in 1 to 15 sessions.

Stampfl aimed to obtain an intense emotional reaction by presenting fantasies to the patient that concerned both fears that the patient had actually expressed and others that the therapist thought were present but repressed, e.g., concerning hostility, aggression, and sexual feelings. He gave an example of fantasies to be used with an obsessive-compulsive handwasher who avoided "dirty" waste paper baskets. "He is afraid of what might be in the waste paper basket and it is not clean. So he reaches in with his hand and what does he come out with? His hand is dripping with a combination of mucus, saliva, vomit and feces. [If there is evidence] that oral incorporative tendencies are present . . . the implosive therapist might well have the patient imagine that he is licking off the material into his mouth. [Following a hypothesis about anal material] one might then ask the patient to imagine being in a septic tank; he lives, eats, and sleeps there, he mushes around in there, and throws cocktail parties there. He lives for weeks and months in a variety of similar situations." Improvement in obsessives and compulsives was said to follow such treatment. "He who has lived in a septic tank need not fear the dirt found in a waste paper basket."

Work of Levis

More details about this form of flooding were given by Levis [53]. Two or three standard diagnostic interviews with the patient usually provided sufficient information to begin flooding, and as treatment progressed, further interviewing might be needed. After a few sessions patients frequently reported various memories that had previously evaded them. During treatment a patient was encouraged to "lose himself" in the part he was playing and to "live" the scenes with emotion.

> He is asked, much like an actor, to portray certain feelings and emotions and to experience them. . . . little or no attempt is made to secure any admission from the patient that the cues or hypotheses actually apply to him; at each stage an attempt is made by the therapist to attain a maximal level of anxiety evocation from the patient, which continues until signs of spontaneous reduction in the anxiety inducing value are indicated (extinction). The process is repeated with new variations until a significant diminution in anxiety has resulted. After a few repetitions of a particular scene, the patient is given an opportunity to act out the scene by himself. Between sessions the patient is instructed to reenact in his imagination the scenes that were presented during the treatment session. This homework provides additional extinction trials. It is hoped that at the termination of treatment the patient will be able to handle new anxiety provoking situations without the therapist's help.

The cues to be presented in implosion were graded, though much more steeply than in desensitization. Levis postulated an Avoidance Serial Cue Hierarchy and began with cues low on this hierarchy. Many of these were "symptom-contingent cues." In phobics these might be the sight of a tall building, the driving of a car, or being confined to a small enclosed space. An obsessive might be asked to imagine himself prevented from carrying out his ritual, or to visualize the acting out of his feared obsession. "Whether the symptom involves a compulsive ritual, an obsessive thought, a hysterical fit, or a conversion reaction, the strategy is . . . the identification of as much of the stimulus complex as possible surrounding the occurrence of the symptom." The therapist forces the patient to be exposed to some of the anxiety-provoking cues that he partially avoids outside of the treatment session whenever he performs his symptom. Therefore, with the avoidance response circumvented, greater exposure to the cues will occur, and subsequently greater extinction will be effected.

When "symptom-contingent cues" no longer evoked anxiety, Levis proceeded to "hypothesized sequential cues" assumed to be higher up on the hierarchy. Such cues concerned the expression of hostility and aggression toward parents, retaliatory bodily injury of the patient, and "experiences of rejection, deprivation, abandonment, helplessness, guilt, shame and sex. Oedipal, anal, oral, sibling rivalry, primal scene, and death wish impulse themes were also included." Although Levis referred to his style of flooding as an extinction procedure, it seems to contain extra elements such as catharsis, role playing, and assertive training.

The results of this form of flooding were examined by Hogan [37] and by Levis and Carrera [54]. Neither study permits firm conclusions because the populations treated were heterogeneous, and imprecise measures of change were employed. Hogan assigned 50 inpatient psychotics to either flooding in fantasy (n = 26) or to more traditional forms of psychotherapy (n = 24). Flooded subjects were significantly more improved on the Minnesota Multiphasic Personality Inventory (M.M.P.I.) at the end of treatment, and at follow-up 1 year later significantly more flooding subjects had been released from hospital. Levis and Carrera divided 40 "psychoneurotic" outpatients into four groups. It is not clear if assignment to these groups was randomized. Ten patients had flooding in fantasy for 10 hours. Another ten patients had insight and supportive psychotherapy for approximately 10 hours. The third group had psychotherapy for a mean of 37 sessions, and a fourth group consisted of untreated patients on a waiting list. The authors noted that only the flooded group "showed consistent trend to shift away from psychopathology on the M.M.P.I." Patients reported significant reduction of anxiety, depression, obsessive thoughts, compulsive behavior, and phobias.

A number of other workers [7, 24] have reported the successful use of flooding in individual phobic patients. However, Wolpe and Lazarus [101] described treatment of several adult cases with phobias and obsessions, but commented that several of their patients were made worse rather than better by the technique. They were therefore reluctant to recommend flooding.

Use in School Phobia

Very few reports have described formal flooding in fantasy with children. Smith and Sharpe [87] described treatment of a 13-year-old boy who had severe school phobia of 60 days' duration. He was treated by ten sessions of flooding in fantasy that evoked much anxiety. The patient returned to school after the first session and by the tenth session had apparently lost his anxiety at school. At 13 weeks follow-up his improvement was maintained. Barrett (personal communication) also treated a 10-year-old school-phobic girl successfully by flooding in fantasy.

Induced Anger

One way in which flooding might act is by catharsis; in this respect the therapeutic use of induced anger by Goldstein et al. [31] is of interest. Their report claimed that anger was used as a reciprocal inhibitor of fear. Their method also had an element of assertive training. When an agoraphobic patient felt phobic anxiety, he was asked to imagine being accosted on the street and screaming obscenities. During treatment he was encouraged to scream these obscenities out loud, to pound on a pillow, and to imagine attacking his accoster and shooting people who frightened him. After three sessions of 10 repetitions per session of scenes appropriate to his fears the patient improved greatly and traveled freely. He was well at a 6-month follow-up, and no hostile feeling took the place of fear. This technique was used in 10 patients, including some with anxiety states, neurotic depression, and phobias. In 6 patients the technique was successful. Results were poor if emotion was not felt or if the expression of anger produced guilt. Of the 4 patients who failed, 2 improved with subsequent flooding in fantasy. In successful cases anger was not necessarily concerned with the etiology of a patient's fear, e.g., one patient was asked to say "I am *not* afraid! I don't *want* to be afraid! It's stupid and unfair; I will not be afraid," and to punch a pillow placed on a chair in front of her.

Induced Anxiety

Also related to abreaction is Sipprelle's [86] method of *induced anxiety*. He relaxed a patient under hypnosis and instructed him "to turn his attention inward, to forget everything outside of himself and to feel a small feeling way down inside starting to grow. Continued suggestions of the feeling growing stronger and stronger were given." The therapist sat on a chair next to the patient's couch with one hand on his wrist and one hand on his upper arm, monitoring the patient's appearance and tension. When the patient contracted his muscles, the therapist said "good," "let it out," and so on. Gradually, intense affect would develop, with muscular tension, rapid breathing, anxiety, and sobbing, sometimes with intense anger, fear, and even laughter. The patient would remember past events eliciting the affect and be encouraged to associate to them. When time permitted, this continued until the affect subsided. If not, the patient was instructed to relax, to wake up refreshed, and to remember what had happened.

Sipprelle used his method as the main treatment in six patients and as a subsidiary method in five. He claimed that symptoms remitted in four to six sessions. Two of the patients were followed up for a year and found to be well. Unfortunately, few clinical details were supplied about the patient's problems that were relieved. One patient had paranoid schizophrenia with auditory hallucinations that were said to have come under control. Another was a woman with obsessive fantasies of killing her husband. She was relaxed while she had these thoughts in mind, upon which the thoughts disappeared. Improvement generalized to overt behavior at home.

Induced anxiety clearly has several components, including abreaction, relaxation, and in the obsessive patient, a technique reminiscent of thought-stopping [90]. Differences from Stampfl's method are first, the way in which a patient's emotions are allowed to emerge (instead of being entirely suggested by the therapist), and second, that instructions to relax are given. The initial instructions to introspect are reminiscent of meditational techniques [65].

CONTROLLED CLINICAL STUDIES OF FLOODING

Studies at Maudsley Hospital

In 1968 systematic research into the use of flooding in phobic patients began at the Maudsley Hospital. First was a pilot study of flooding in fantasy and in practice in four phobic patients [11]. As an example of treatment in fantasy a spider phobic had 2- to 3-hour sessions a week during which she sat in a comfortable chair and was asked to imagine as vividly as possible that she was alone in a room in which there were numerous black hairy spiders. These surrounded her on all sides and began to crawl up her legs and arms and bite her and entered her mouth and nose while she screamed uncontrollably and helplessly. The therapist maintained a running commentary on the scene she was to imagine for a full hour, aiming to produce maximum anxiety as long as possible.

The degree of phobic anxiety was judged by the patient's behavior—for example, by grimaces and clenching of fists—by the patient's own report, and by continuous monitoring on a polygraph of galvanic skin resistance and heart rate during the session. As soon as anxiety appeared to be diminishing, new variations of the phobic theme were introduced. At the end of the session the patient was asked to repeat to herself at home the fantasy experiences that had produced anxiety during the session. After a few sessions the patient lost her anxiety to the fantasy scenes and was then asked to reenter the phobic situation in real life, both by herself and in the presence of the therapist; for example, when the patient with a spider phobia was shown a spider by the therapist, she would be asked to touch it and was told that it was a dangerous creature that would bite her slowly and painfully. The patients received an average of 10 sessions of flooding in fantasy and 4 in practice, about two to three times weekly. They rated their phobic and other symptoms twice weekly on scales described by Gelder and Marks [29].

Three of the four patients improved and rated their main phobia as normal 12 weeks after treatment began. They maintained their gains to 1-year follow-up. One patient failed to improve after treatment began. Physiologic change paralleled clinical improvement and is seen in detail for one case in Figure 6A. Heart rate increased during the periods of phobic fantasy, which are indicated by the solid black line, as did spontaneous fluctuations and skin resistance. In contrast, there were no changes during visualization of a neutral fantasy (Fig. 6B). After six sessions of flooding the same phobic fan-

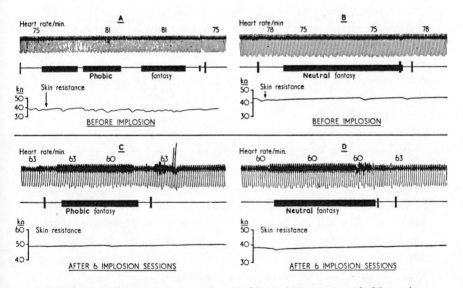

FIGURE 6. *Heart rate and galvanic skin resistance of a phobic patient during visualization of a phobic and neutral fantasy before and after six sessions of flooding in fantasy and in practice. (From Boulougouris and Marks,* Brit. Med. J. *2:721, 1969, by permission of editor.)*

tasy no longer produced any tachycardia or increase in fluctuations of galvanic skin resistance (Fig. 6C), while the neutral fantasy again produced no changes (Fig. 6D).

Flooding versus Desensitization

METHODS. The next study [12, 62] was a controlled comparison between flooding and desensitization in phobic disorders. Interest at this time focused on short-term effects, so a crossover design was employed. Sixteen patients with severe chronic phobias were treated. Eleven subjects were outpatients and 5 inpatients. Seven had specific phobias restricted to one situation, and 9 were agoraphobics, 4 with marked free-floating anxiety. There were 10 therapists, all novices to both desensitization and to flooding. The study was concerned with results that could be obtained in routine clinical practice with brief training of therapists. Each patient had all treatment sessions from the same therapist.

The patients were told that they would be given two different treatments, that both were probably effective but it was not known which was better. Both treatments involved their imagining phobic scenes, one method in a relaxed manner, the other in a very frightening way. They were free to withdraw at any stage if treatment proved unacceptable. All patients were taken off drugs during the trial, except for an epileptic patient on phenobarbital.

Patients were randomly allocated either to six 50-minute sessions of desensitization in fantasy followed by six sessions of flooding in fantasy, or vice versa. The fifth and sixth sessions of either treatment were followed immediately by 70 minutes of either desensitization or flooding in practice. Treatment was given two to three times weekly and average treatment time was 5 weeks. Clinical and physiologic assessments were made before the start of treatment and 2 days after the end of the sixth and twelfth sessions. Clinical ratings were continued at intervals to a year's follow-up.

All 16 patients received both treatments, 8 in one order and 8 in the other, equal therapeutic time being spent in both. All patients were accompanied by their therapists during the practice sessions, except for 3 patients who specifically asked to do their flooding in practice alone. All patients were asked to practice outside treatment the relaxation or flooding they had received during treatment.

ASSESSMENT. Clinical assessment was by patient, therapists, and an independent medical assessor on the scales of Gelder and Marks [29]. Clinical ratings of phobias were highly reliable between the three raters, correlations ranging from .78 to .94 between raters for main phobia and total phobia. Physiologic assessment was of heart rate, spontaneous fluctuations of skin conductance, and maximum deflection of skin conductance during phobic and neutral imagery presented in standardized fashion.

RESULTS. The data were analyzed by crossover design analyses of variance (Fig. 7). Flooding produced significantly more improvement for doctors' ratings of the main phobia and total phobias than did desensitization, although both treatments produced significant improvement in the ratings of the main phobia. Physiologic assessments showed similar results; flooding was followed by significantly more decrease in heart rate during the main phobic fantasy and in measures of spontaneous fluctuations of maximum deflection of skin conductance during phobic imagery. On no measure was desensitization superior to flooding. An unexpected finding was that although desensitization as usual produced greater improvement in specific phobias than in agoraphobia, the reverse was true for flooding. In line with this a good outcome with flooding was significantly associated with higher levels of anxiety before treatment; thus, improvement in conductance fluctuation during phobic imagery correlated +.53 with initial deflection of skin conductance during neutral imagery.

FURTHER TREATMENT. Ten patients had further treatment during early follow-up to consolidate their improvement. No patient who improved during treatment showed significant relapse during the follow-up period. Mean scores for the 16 patients on the 1 to 5 main phobia scale (patients' and doctors' ratings combined) were

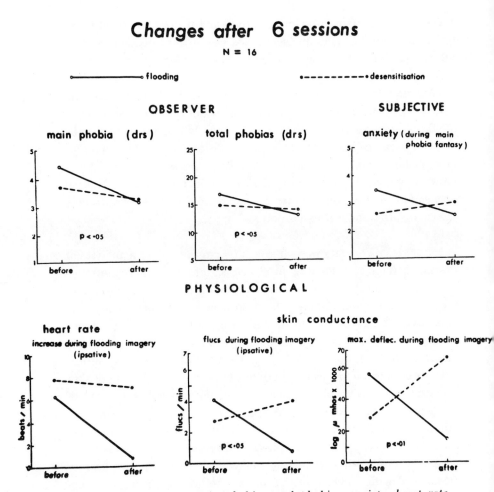

FIGURE 7. *Scores for main phobia, total phobias, anxiety, heart rate, and skin conductance, before and after treatment with either desensitization or flooding. Flooding was generally superior to desensitization. (From Marks, Boulougouris, and Marset,* Brit. J. Psychiat. *119:353, 1971, by permission of editor.)*

before treatment, 4.6; after 12 sessions, 3.1. At follow-up scores were after 1 month, 2.5; 3 months, 2.4; 6 months, 2.5; 9 months, 2.3; and at the end of 1 year, 2.3. Importance of follow-up lies in the fact that improvement in the group was lasting, not transient. The respective contributions of desensitization or of flooding to the end results are unknown since all patients had both treatments.

REACTION TO THERAPY. Flooding was a surprisingly acceptable treatment. Three patients even indicated a preference for flooding to desensitization because they felt it did more for them. Subsequent to this study other patients who were offered desensitization insisted that they wanted flooding. The fact that the treatment is anxiety-provoking does not necessarily make it unacceptable to patients. However, patients in this study had to be highly motivated before they were accepted into the trial. They had to commit themselves to attending at least 15 sessions (12 for treatment and 3 for assessment) before they could start and had to agree to listen to frightening descriptions of their fears during the treatment. Furthermore, they were told that if for any reason they stopped treatment prematurely during flooding, they might be made worse rather than better, hence the importance of completing treatment. There were two dropouts after flooding, while no patients dropped out of desensitization. One of the dropouts had previously dropped out of other forms of treatment.

DEGREE OF ANXIETY. Anxiety during treatment sessions varied greatly. Most patients were distressed during the first flooding sessions. Several showed no anxiety in the final sessions, and one actually fell asleep at that stage. Some patients seemed but slightly perturbed at any time, while others spent every session crying, grimacing, and clenching their hands. Subjective anxiety was not always maximum during the first session, which sometimes elicited only slight anxiety, anxiety reaching a peak in the second or third sessions. Usually, after the end of the flooding session anxiety dissipated quickly. However, one patient (a spider phobic) had nightmares for two nights after the first session. Another patient (severely agoraphobic) had mild mood swings that required no special treatment. A third patient (also agoraphobic) became depressed after the fifth flooding session. He had a history of two previous depressive episodes that had been treated by electroconvulsive therapy. He was readmitted at 6 months follow-up for treatment of his depression by electroconvulsive therapy after which he improved.

Several patients commented that they felt challenged by the treatment to perform well when confronted with their real phobic situations. Some commented that the reality of the real phobic situation never matched up to the horrors of the flooding fantasies. One patient noted that anxiety during treatment made her angry.

Relevant versus Irrelevant Fear Imagery

In this study [93] the question whether the content of flooding fantasies needs to be relevant to a patient's phobia to produce improvement in the phobia was investigated. Improvement could conceivably be produced by any frightening material, even if irrelevant, or perhaps by imagery that is not frightening but concerned with other intense emotions, e.g., anger or sexual arousal.

METHODS.   Sixteen patients with severe phobias were treated in a balanced crossover design. Eight patients had eight sessions of imaginal flooding concerned with their phobias followed by eight imaginal sessions concerned with normal fear situations, while another eight patients had the same treatments in reverse order. The order of treatment was allocated at random, and delay in crossing over from one treatment to the other was 4 to 8 days. Each session lasted 50 minutes, and treatment was given two to three times weekly.

Flooding in fantasy was given along the lines previously described by Boulougouris et al. [12], while in the case of irrelevant fear-arousing cues the therapist tried to maintain the patient's fear at maximum pitch by describing experiences that, if encountered in reality, would be accompanied by intense fear, pain, or other unpleasant emotions. In 12 patients the themes described being caught, mangled, and eaten by a tiger; in the other patients the themes dealt with being burned to death (3 cases) and drowning (1 case). Three to four themes were used in each session. It was almost always necessary to vary a theme to some extent on each repetition because patients habituated rapidly when identical words were repeated, and the aim was to elicit maximum fear for as long as possible. Patients were assessed clinically and physiologically just before treatment, 2 to 4 days after the eighth and sixteenth sessions, and at 3 and 6 months follow-up along lines similar to those of previous trials [12, 62]. Patients also completed attitude scales of semantic differential type from three dimensions—evaluation, anxiety, and danger. Concepts rated included the main phobic situation, a control fear situation (e.g., "tiger"), and a control pleasant concept. During treatment sessions the therapist rated the overt anxiety of the subject at the start and at 10-minute intervals during every session, while the patient rated his peak anxiety during a session as it ended.

RESULTS. Results showed that the combined effect of relevant and irrelevant fear was significant reduction of all clinical phobia ratings, of negative attitudes to phobic concepts, and of tachycardia and subjective anxiety during phobic imagery. Physiologic responses to control fear, or neutral imagery did not change. Throughout the trial attitudes remained consistently negative to the control fear and consistently positive to the control pleasant concept. Each of the two treatments alone produced significant improvement in clinical phobia scales. None of the clinical, attitudinal, or physiologic measures were significantly differently affected by the two procedures except for subjective anxiety during phobic imagery, which was reduced more by irrelevant than by relevant fear.

Anxiety in each treatment session was usually at its peak by 20 minutes and remained at that peak till the end of the session at about 50 minutes. As soon as the session ended anxiety usually dropped rapidly. Later sessions usually provoked less anxiety than earlier ones, especially with irrelevant fear. When given as first treatment, relevant and irrelevant fear generated similar amounts of anxiety during the sessions. However, in the second treatment block, relevant flooding was more anxiety-provoking than irrelevant fear. Irrelevant fear was more anxiety-provoking as first than as second treatment (Fig. 8). Flooding thus seemed to protect patients from

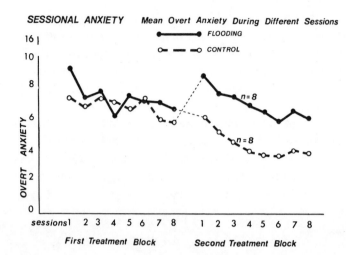

FIGURE 8. *Amount of overt anxiety provoked by imagining relevant fear scenes (flooding) or irrelevant fear scenes (control) in a crossover design. Although both procedures provoke similar amounts of anxiety when given as a first treatment, flooding provokes more as a second treatment than the control procedure.* (From Rachman, Hodgson, and Marks, Behav. Res. Ther. *9:237, 1971, by permission of editor.*)

anxiety during subsequent frightening experiences, but irrelevant fear did not, which is puzzling.

Though relevant and irrelevant fear produced similar therapeutic effects, they had significantly different prognostic correlates. As in the studies of Boulougouris et al. [12] and Marks et al. [62], flooding produced greater improvement in those patients who had shown more physiologic anxiety before treatment began. In contrast, irrelevant fear produced less improvement in patients who showed more subjective anxiety at initial assessment. In other words, the more anxious a patient became during imagery at initial assessment, the more likely he was to improve with relevant fear and the less likely he was to improve with irrelevant fear.

Another difference between the two treatments was that outcome to irrelevant fear was better in those patients who showed much anxiety *during* treatment sessions, while outcome to relevant flooding did not correlate with the amount of anxiety experienced during treatment. This goes against the idea that relevant flooding acts by abreaction, but suggests that abreaction may be an operative element in irrelevant fear.

Patients maintained their improvement over 6 months follow-up. At the start of treatment the mean rating for the main phobia on a 0 to 8 scale was 7.2 across raters. This became 4.2 after 16 sessions of treatment and 3.9 after 6 months follow-up. The overall improvement with flooding in this study was greater than in previous studies of desensitization [61]. However, it was less than that obtained with flooding by Boulougouris et al. [12] and Marks et al. [62], being 1.4 compared with 2.0 on an 8-point scale for the main phobia after 8 hours treatment. In that study 8 hours of flooding comprised 6 hour-long sessions in fantasy, the last two of which were followed immediately by an hour's practice. The overall effect of the present study was thought to be reduced by the absence of flooding in practice.

Patients were given the same expectancy for both procedures. They were told that they would be helped by treatment, that it would involve experiencing anxiety, but that it was not known which way of experiencing anxiety would be more helpful to them. Some patients became disillusioned with the treatment, particularly the irrelevant fear procedure, well before their sessions ended, appearing to share the authors' growing view with time that irrelevant fear was ineffective. Improvement with irrelevant fear therefore occurred despite some contrary expectancy.

Flooding versus Desensitization versus Shaping

The next study [19] compared the three most useful treatments of phobias available at the time it was planned—flooding, desensitization, and operant shaping. Fourteen phobic outpatients each received three treatments in a balanced design. Every patient had three preparatory interviews and then 12 sessions made up of 4 successive sessions of each technique. Flooding in fantasy followed the relevant flooding procedure of Watson and Marks [93]. Desensitization in fantasy was like that of Boulougouris et al. [12] but omitting the practice sessions, while operant shaping was the method of *reinforced practice* used by Callahan and Leitenberg [14].

Measures of change were the clinical scales of Gelder and Marks [29] and an avoidance test. Results on avoidance showed that shaping was significantly superior to desensitization, with flooding being in between and differing significantly from neither. On clinical scales shaping improved patients less than flooding or desensitization. Both flooding and desensitization improved untreated as well as treated phobias, whereas shaping had a more specific effect on treated phobias alone.

Overall therapeutic changes were smaller than in previous trials, perhaps because no single treatment had time to build up much effect before a new one was started. Four sessions were fewer than in previous controlled trials of this kind. The trend for flooding to be superior to desensitization was in line with earlier findings [12]. Both flooding and desensitization were in fantasy only, while shaping was given in practice. This factor probably explains the behavioral superiority of shaping.

Prolonged Exposure

The preceding experiments suggested that treatment in practice increased the efficacy of treatment in imagination; evidence also suggested that prolonged practice sessions might be more effective than shorter ones, particularly when they could be devoted continuously to overcoming avoidance of or escape from the phobic object or situation. Accordingly, a pilot study [94] was made of prolonged exposure in practice in 10 patients with severe specific phobias (e.g., of dogs, spiders, balloons) who could be attached to a polygraph while in the phobic situation. They were assessed by the same clinical and physiologic measures as were used in the previous two studies. Three patients had previously made but partial improvement in the trial of Watson and Marks [93]. Five patients had relevant flooding in fantasy first, to accustom them to the idea of confronting the real feared object. They were told the fantasy sessions were a preliminary to practice sessions. Two patients had treatment in practice only.

The aim was to encourage the patient to approach the feared object as closely and as quickly as he could, and to remain in contact with it until his anxiety diminished. Avoidance, including averting the head or eyes and drawing the hand away, was discouraged. Attempts to deliberately provoke anxiety were gradually abandoned, for patients seemed to overcome their phobic avoidance more quickly if the therapists did not add to the anxiety induced by the feared object. In later patients the sessions were conducted in as free and pleasant a way as possible. These patients were praised liberally each time they progressed. Modeling was also added where necessary. If a patient was unable to touch the phobic object, the therapist did it first, asking the patient to watch carefully and then follow suit. Later patients thus had real-life exposure facilitated by operant shaping and modeling.

As an example, one case received two 2-hour sessions of flooding in fantasy. She then said she could face real cats. After the assessment she was told that a black cat would be brought into the room. This was held on a table about 6 feet away from her; looking at the cat provoked intense tachycardia and subjective anxiety that subsided after about 5 minutes. Over the next 5 minutes the therapist gradually brought the cat nearer to her, and each change in the position of the cat produced a short-lived increase in tachycardia and subjective anxiety during which she was reassured and encouraged to keep looking at the cat. After 15 minutes she was able to touch the cat, and as the session proceeded she became able to stroke the cat and hold it on her lap. She spent the last 15 minutes of the 2-hour session cuddling the cat on her lap without anxiety.

All ten patients showed significant reduction of their phobia on the clinical scales after treatment. The main phobia was scored 7.3 before treatment, 5.7 after the fantasy sessions, and 2.4 after practice. Treatment in practice thus had more effect than treatment in fantasy. Attitude to phobic concepts on semantic differential scales improved correspondingly, as did tachycardia during phobic imagery. Before treatment heart rate increased about 21 beats per minute from rest to a period of phobic imagery, but at the end of treatment this increase was 7 beats per minute. Patients maintained improvement over follow-up during which they showed little residual fear or avoidance of their phobic objects.

All patients were greatly improved even though they were treated on only two to three afternoons for an average of 6 hours in all. They improved more rapidly as a group than did patients in previous trials. Their improvement after a mean of 6 hours treatment was greater than that usually obtained in 15 hours of desensitization in fantasy or in 8 hours of flooding in fantasy.

Flooding in Phobia: Summary

Studies of phobic patients suggest that flooding in fantasy and *especially* in real life effectively reduce phobic distress. Both specific phobics and agoraphobics respond to treatment, and the presence of free-floating anxiety does not militate against its success. Flooding in practice appears to be more effective than flooding in fantasy, but this has yet to be proved by experiments. Similarly, longer durations of flooding appear more effective than shorter ones, a point that also requires proof. Flooding can be successful when it simply concentrates on prolonged exposure to the phobic situation without emphasis on anxiety provocation, and is facilitated by the addition of generous praise for progress, and modeling by the therapist of what he wants the patient to do. The evocation of anxiety not connected with the phobia can also have therapeutic value, though the mechanism of action of this procedure appears different from flooding in which relevant fear cues are employed.

There may be no optimum duration for flooding, and the chief necessity might be continuation of a given session, for many hours if need be, until all aspects of anxiety have subsided, i.e., subjective, behavioral, and physiologic. For the moment, however, as a rough guideline, 1- to 2-hour sessions appear to be effective.

Flooding in Obsessive-Compulsive Neurosis

Few systematic studies of this subject are available. Meyer [68] reported treatment of obsessive-compulsive patients by *modification of expectations* in which compulsive rituals were interrupted while patients were brought into contact with the situations that triggered those rituals. Meyer and Levy [69, 70] reported encouraging success with this technique in 10 obsessive-compulsive patients.

APOTREPIC THERAPY. At this stage they called their procedure *apotrepic therapy* from the Greek "to turn away, deter, or dissuade." Treatment involved 24-hour supervision by nurses to prevent the patient carrying out any rituals. To stop these the patient was engaged in other activities, discussion, cajoling, and rarely, mild physical restraint with the patient's agreement. When total prevention of rituals was achieved, continuous supervision was continued for 1 to 4 weeks, during which the patient was gradually exposed to situations that previously evoked rituals (e.g., dust, lavatories) and was again prevented from carrying these out. Supervision was then gradually decreased until the patient was finally totally unsupervised but occasionally observed.

As an example [69], an obsessive-compulsive handwasher with fears of contamination from his family was instructed to bring into hospital several contaminated objects from his home. The patient's room and his belongings on the ward were contaminated by contact with these objects. He was supervised continuously by nurses, the water taps in his room were turned off, and his cleansing agents were limited. Appropriate routine washing was supervised to prevent excessive cleansing. During brief daily visits the therapist made the patient touch contaminated objects, which provoked strong anxiety and an urge to carry out rituals. "Persuasion, encouragement, reassurance and recreational activities were used whenever the patient reported experiencing anxiety and compulsive urges. Avoidance behavior was dealt with by making the patient perform the avoided acts." This continued for 9 days, during which time the patient visited his home. Supervision was withdrawn slowly, but observation continued and routine washing was supervised. The water taps were then turned on. The patient's family visited him in hospital and the patient then spent several nights at home. With each step 24-hour supervision was reinstated for 2 days and then gradually withdrawn. Ritualistic handwashing disappeared, and preoccupation with contamination gradually subsided. The patient remained well at 18-months follow-up.

Of 10 patients followed for a mean of 2 years [70], all except one showed a great decrease in obsessive-compulsive behavior that was maintained at follow-up except for slight relapse in two cases. Anxiety and depression improved concurrently.

Meyer and Levy speculated on the similarities between their approach and the structured situations in certain institutions that limit opportunity to engage in rituals. They noted Janet's [42] observations of 14 "accidental cures" of obsessive-compulsive neuroses during Military Service, and one patient who, when his term of service was over, took refuge in a seminary "in order to have chiefs once more and to be subject to discipline." Janet also commented that many cases remained well in convents. Lewis [55] described a severe case in which obsessions disappeared during war service but returned afterwards.

MAUDSLEY HOSPITAL STUDIES. At the Maudsley Hospital Rachman et al. [78] modified the technique of Meyer [68] in a controlled study in which flooding in vivo was compared with the effects of modeling in vivo and with relaxation. They selected 10 patients who were at least moderately incapacitated by an obsessive-compulsive disorder of at least 1 year's duration. Mean age of the treated patients was 35 years, and mean symptom duration 10 years. Seven patients had had depression at some stage, and in 6 the obsessive-compulsive illness created striking handicaps and repercussions in the family.

All patients were told that they would have new forms of treatment that would probably help them. They were admitted for a minimum of 7 weeks; the first week was devoted to evaluation, and the next 6 weeks to experimental treatment, with one session lasting 40 to 60 minutes every weekday. No supervision was provided between sessions. In the first 3 weeks all patients had 15 sessions of control relaxation treatment. Over the second 3 weeks patients were assigned at random to 15 sessions either of modeling or of flooding. After this 6-week experimental period patients were followed up and treatment was continued when necessary. All patients were taken off drugs throughout the experimental period, except for one who was continued on amitriptyline treatment that had been started many months before.

The relaxation control sessions began with general inquiries about the patient's health and mood. He was then given tape-recorded relaxation instructions followed by a request to think about one of his obsessive worries during the final 10 minutes of each session. During flooding in vivo the patient was encouraged and persuaded to enter the most disturbing obsessive situation first. The therapist did not act as a model for imitation but was calming and reassuring throughout the session, at the end of which the patient was encouraged to maintain any contamination and refrain from carrying out his rituals for increasing periods. As an example of flooding, in managing a patient who feared contamination from animals a hierarchy was constructed. During the first session the patient was encouraged to touch items from the top of her hierarchy (i.e., hamster and dog). The hamster was then set free to run around on her bed, towel, clothes, and personal belongings. It was placed in her handbag for a few minutes and also on her hair. This almost total contamination of her environment was accomplished during the first session and repeated daily. Several times throughout treatment she was encouraged to stroke a dog and then to contaminate her clothes, hair, and face.

MODELING. During modeling in vivo the patient and therapist again constructed a hierarchy of situations that caused distress and produced avoidance and compulsive rituals. The patient was then encouraged to enter gradually each of the provoking situations commencing with the least upsetting and graduating to increasingly disturbing ones. Each step was first demonstrated to the patient by a calm and reassuring therapist, and the patient then "shadowed" his therapist's actions. Every step was repeated until the patient completed the sequence without assistance. As an example of modeling treatment, in a patient with fear of contamination from hospitals the first session began with the lowest item from the hierarchy. The therapist repeatedly touched a bandage on his own clothes, hair, and face; the patient was then asked to imitate his action. Throughout the 3 weeks of modeling all items in the hierarchy were dealt with in the same way, e.g., toward the top of the hierarchy the patient watched the therapist walk up to the hospital entrance and touch an ambulance. She then copied the therapist's actions.

After the 3-week experimental period patients were discharged home if they had improved sufficiently. If further problems were reported at home, the therapist visited the home and gave appropriate further treatment.

RESULTS. Assessment measures were taken just before treatment, after 3 weeks of relaxation control treatment, after a further 3 weeks of either modeling or flooding, and after 6 months' follow-up. Ratings were on the clinical rating scales of Gelder and Marks [29], semantic differential-type attitude scales, an avoidance test, fear thermometer during the avoidance test, and the Leyton Inventory [16].

Results (Fig. 9) showed that modeling and flooding in vivo both produced significantly more improvement than did relaxation control treatment on clinical rating scales, the avoidance test, fear thermometer, and attitude scales on the evaluative factor. There were no significant differences between flooding and modeling in vivo. Improvement continued during follow-up, which is 9 months at the time of writing.

The two patients who responded most quickly—one to flooding and one to modeling—had the most circumscribed compulsions linked to highly specific situations. The more varied the rituals and their ramifications in the patients' lives, the more difficult it seemed to be to reduce them.

In several patients improvement in the hospital failed to generalize sufficiently to the home until treatment was carried into the

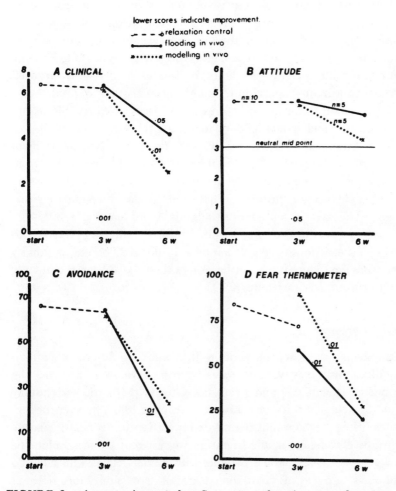

FIGURE 9. *A comparison of the effects of a relaxation procedure (control), flooding, and modeling in vivo, in the treatment of obsessive-compulsive neurosis. (From Rachman et al. [78], by permission of the editor.)*

home. Patients with extensive rituals did not seem worth treating in hospital unless home treatment was guaranteed later. Obsessions and compulsions can have major social repercussions, and these have to be dealt with by home supervision and support of the family.

Relatives have to be taught not to be involved in patients' rituals and how to respond to patients' demands on them. As patients stop their rituals, time becomes available for alternative constructive activities, and they need encouragement to develop a normal social life. It is possible that continuous supervision of certain patients may facilitate their improvement. One patient who failed to improve outside the study without continuous supervision improved under continuous supervision from Meyer in another hospital.

A common factor might be present in Meyer's [68] technique and in flooding and modeling in vivo. In all three techniques the patients are exposed in a therapist's presence to in vivo situations of discomfort and anxiety and are then discouraged or prevented from "undoing" the exposure. These common features suggest that improvement occurs through habituation to the discomfiting situations. The tacit prevention of rituals might also play a role.

Systematic studies on flooding of obsessive thoughts as opposed to compulsive actions have yet to appear. Prolonged flooding in fantasy of obsessive thoughts, e.g., of harming others, have been therapeutic in uncontrolled case studies (25).

Other Disorders

Systematic research on flooding in defined conditions other than phobias and obsessive-compulsive neurosis have yet to appear. The work of Hogan [37] and Levis and Carrera [54] with "psychotics" and "psychoneurotics" was reviewed on page 183. The vagueness of these categories does not permit extrapolation to defined diagnostic groups. References in the literature suggest that flooding might be of value in at least some patients with anxiety states who have no phobias, and may also help some forms of depression. More research is needed on this before recommendations can be made.

OVERVIEW

Flooding denotes a range of treatment procedures in which the patient is exposed to situations that provoke his distress until he tolerates them. Good evidence is available for the efficacy of flooding in phobic disorders, including those where free-floating anxiety is present, and in obsessive-compulsive neurosis. It may have potential application in other conditions such as anxiety states and certain forms of depression, but more work is needed here before any recommendations can be made.

Patients need to be well motivated and to understand what is required of them in flooding treatment; otherwise, they might terminate treatment prematurely and enhance future tendencies to escape. Their commitment to face unpleasantness in treatment has to be obtained beforehand. Treatment can be given both in fantasy and in practice, but acts quicker when given in practice. Treatment in fantasy may be indicated where treatment in practice is not feasible, or as a necessary preliminary before the patient will agree to treatment in real life. Treatment in fantasy can be given by tape recorder as well as by a live therapist. Longer flooding sessions appear more potent than shorter ones, but the optimum duration is unknown. Less than 15 minutes seems too short, but 1 to 2 hours is useful. It is possible that duration alone is a less satisfactory criterion than that of terminating the session only after the patient's distress has ceased and he has felt comfortable for several minutes.

Flooding is facilitated by selective praise of the patient for each step toward improvement. Real-life exposure can be further facilitated by the therapist modeling the maneuvers that will be necessary for the patient to carry out. On the other hand, it is not known whether the evocation of distress potentiates the effect of exposure. Both exposure itself and emotional arousal alone are therapeutic, but in different ways.

Flooding can act by specific extinction, i.e., by habituating a patient to the particular distressing situation he is exposed to. Extinction occurs of overt avoidance, of subjective anxiety, and of physiologic concomitants. It is not known whether blocking of avoidance (response prevention) is essential in its own right. Blocking does facilitate extinction by prolonging contact with the noxious situation, which allows greater opportunity for habituation to occur. Blocking of avoidance can occur both in fantasy, when a patient visualizes what he normally shrinks from, and in real life. In addition, flooding can act by habituating patients not only to specific fears but also to the experience of unpleasant feelings in general; e.g., exposure of a dog-phobic patient to a dog led to her losing not only her fear of dogs but also to loss of her inhibitions in previously frightening social relationships. Relevant flooding seems unlikely to act by abreaction because its outcome is unrelated to the amount of anxiety generated during flooding by scenes relevant to a patient's problem.

It is not known how important it is to tailor flooding themes to a patient's clinical picture, or to include hypothetical "repressed material." The more that flooding in fantasy is concerned with the patient's specific problem, the more the specific extinction which can be expected. The greater the emotional arousal, the larger the abreaction component that is involved, regardless of the relevance of the content. It should be recognized that flooding is a composite treatment, the constituents of which will vary according to the preference of the therapist and the problem to be treated. It is still too early to compile a precise cookbook of flooding recipes for different clinical problems.

REFERENCES

1. Agras, W. S., Leitenberg, H., Wincze, J. P., Butz, R. A., and Callahan, E. J. Comparison of effects of instructions and reinforcement in the treatment of a neurotic avoidance response: A single case experiment. *Journal of Behavior Therapy and Experimental Psychiatry* 1:53, 1970.
2. Bandura, A. *Principles of Behavior Modification.* New York: Holt, Rinehart & Winston, 1970.
3. Bandura, A. Modelling Approaches to the Modification of Phobic Disorders. In *The Role of Learning in Psychotherapy.* Ciba Foundation Symposium. London: Churchill, 1968.
4. Barrett, C. L. Systematic desensitization versus implosive therapy. *Journal of Abnormal Psychology* 74:587, 1969.
5. Barry, H., Etheredge, E. E., and Miller, N. E. Counterconditioning and extinction of fear fail to transfer from amobarbital to non-drug state. *Psychopharmacologia* 8:150, 1965.
6. Baum, M. Extinction of avoidance responding through re-

sponse prevention (flooding). *Psychological Bulletin* 74:276, 1970.

7. Baum, M., and Poser, E. G. Comparison of flooding procedures in animals and man. *Behaviour Research and Therapy*, in press.

8. Benjamin, S. M. Phil. dissertation, University of London, 1970.

9. Bindra, D., Nyman, K., and Wise, J. Barbiturate induced dissociation of acquisition and extinction: Role of movement-initiating processes. *Journal of Comparative and Physiological Psychology* 60:223, 1965.

10. Bolles, R. C. Species-specific defense reactions and avoidance learning. *Psychology Review* 77:32, 1970.

11. Boulougouris, J. C., and Marks, I. M. Implosion (flooding)— A new treatment for phobias. *British Medical Journal* 2:721, 1969.

12. Boulougouris, J. C., Mark, I. M., and Marset, P. Superiority of flooding (implosion) to desensitization for reducing pathological fear. *Behaviour Research and Therapy* 9:12, 1971.

13. Calef, R. A., and MacLean, G. D. A comparison of reciprocal inhibition and reactive inhibition therapies in the treatment of speech anxiety. *Behavior Therapy* 1:51, 1970.

14. Callahan, E. J., and Leitenberg, H. Reinforced practice as a treatment for acrophobia: A controlled outcome study. Paper presented at Annual Meeting of American Psychological Association, Miami, 1970.

15. Cooper, A., Furst, J. B., and Bridger, W. H. A brief commentary on the usefulness of studying fears of snakes. *Journal of Abnormal Psychology* 74:413, 1969.

16. Cooper, J. E. C. The Leyton obsessional inventory. *Psychological Medicine* 1:48, 1970.

17. Costello, C. G. Dissimilarities between conditioned avoidance responses and phobias. *Psychology Review* 77:250, 1970.

18. Crowder, J. E., and Thornton, D. W. Effects of systematic desensitization, programmed fantasy and bibliotherapy on a specific fear. *Behaviour Research and Therapy* 8:35, 1970.

19. Crowe, M., Marks, I. M., Agras, W. S., and Leitenberg, H. Operant shaping, flooding and desensitization in phobic patients. *Behaviour Research and Therapy*, Vol. 9, in press.

20. Davison, G. C. Systematic desensitization as a counterconditioning process. *Journal of Abnormal Psychology* 73:91, 1968.

21. De Moor, W. Systematic desensitization versus prolonged high intensity stimulation (flooding). *Journal of Behavior Therapy and Experimental Psychiatry* 1:45, 1970.

22. D'Zurilla, T. J., Wilson, G. T., and Nelson, R. A comparative

study of systematic desensitization, prolonged imagery and cognitive restructuring. Unpublished manuscript, 1971.

23. Fazio, A. F. Treatment components in implosive therapy. *Journal of Abnormal Psychology* 76:211, 1970.
24. Fazio, A. F. Implosive therapy in the treatment of a phobic disorder. *Psychotherapy: Theory, Research and Practice* 7:228, 1970.
25. Feather, B. W. A central fear hypothesis of phobias. Unpublished manuscript, Duke University, North Carolina, 1970.
26. Ferenczi, S. The Further Development of an Active Therapy in Psychoanalysis. In *Theory and Technique of Psychoanalysis,* 1952.
27. Frankl, V. E. Paradoxical Intention: A logotherapeutic technique. *American Journal of Psychotherapy* 14:520, 1960.
28. Freud, S. Turnings in the Ways of Psychoanalytic Therapy. In *Collected Papers,* Vol. 2. London: Hogarth Press and Institute of Psychoanalysis, 1919. P. 399.
29. Gelder, M. G., and Marks, I. M. Severe agoraphobia: A controlled prospective trial of behaviour therapy. *British Journal of Psychiatry* 112:309, 1966.
30. Gerz, H. O. The treatment of the phobic and the obsessive-compulsive patient using paradoxical intention sec. Victor E. Frankl. *Journal of Neuropsychiatry* 3:375, 1962.
31. Goldstein, A. J., Serber, M., and Piaget, G. Induced anger as a reciprocal inhibitor of fear. *Journal of Behavior Therapy and Experimental Psychiatry* 1:67, 1970.
32. Guthrie, E. R. *The Psychology of Human Learning.* New York: Harper, 1955.
33. Herrnstein, R. J. Method and theory in the study of evidence. *Psychological Review* 76:49, 1969.
34. Herzberg, A. Short treatment of neuroses by graduated tasks. *British Journal of Medical Psychology* 19:19, 1941.
35. Hodgson, R. J., and Rachman, S. An experimental investigation of the implosion technique. *Behaviour Research and Therapy,* 8:21, 1970.
36. Hodgson, R. J., Hallam, R., Miller, S., and Rachman, S. An experimental investigation of "implosion": Replication. Unpublished manuscript, 1971.
37. Hogan, R. A. Implosive therapy in the short-term therapy of psychotics. *Psychotherapy: Theory, Research and Practice* 3:25, 1966.
38. Hogan, R. A., and Kirchner, J. H. Preliminary report of the extinction of learned fears via short-term implosive therapy. *Journal of Abnormal Psychology* 72:106, 1967.

39. Hogan, R. A., and Kirchner, J. H.   Implosive, eclectic, verbal and bibliotherapy in the treatment of fears of snakes. *Behaviour Research and Therapy* 6:167, 1968.

40. Hunter, J.   Treatise on Venereal Disease (1786). In Hunter, R. and MacAlpine, J., *Three Hundred Years of British Psychiatry*. London: Oxford University Press, 1963.

41. Jacobsen, V.   Influential factors in the outcome of treatment of school phobia. *Smith College Study on Social Work* 18:181, 1948.

42. Janet, P.   *Psychological Healing*, Vol. II. New York: Macmillan, 1925.

43. Jersild, A. T., and Holmes, F. G.   Methods of overcoming childrens' fears. *Journal of Psychology* 1:75, 1935.

44. Kamano, D. K.   Joint effect of amobarbital and response prevention on CAR extinction. *Psychological Reports* 22:544, 1968.

45. Katzev, R.   Extinguishing avoidance responses as a function of delayed warning-signal termination. *Journal of Experimental Psychology* 75:339, 1967.

46. Kirchner, J. H., and Hogan, R. A.   The therapist variable in the implosion of phobias. *Psychotherapy: Theory, Research and Practice* 3:102, 1966.

47. Kora, T.   A method of instruction in psychotherapy. *Jikeikai Medical Journal* 15:315, 1968.

48. Larsen, S. R.   Strategies for reducing phobic behavior. Ph.D. dissertation, Stanford University, California, 1965.

49. Layne, C. C.   The effect of suggestion in implosive therapy for fear of rats. Ph.D. dissertation, Southern Illinois University, 1970.

50. Leitenberg, H., Agras, S., Edwards, J. A., Thomson, L. E., and Wincze, J. P.   Practice as a psychotherapeutic variable: An experimental analysis within single cases. *Journal of Psychiatric Research* 7:215, 1970.

51. Leonhard, K.   *Individual therapie der Neurosen*. Jena: Gustav Fischer Verlag., 1963.

52. Levine, M.   *Psychotherapy in Medical Practice*. New York: Macmillan, 1942.

53. Levis, D. J.   Implosive Therapy: Part II. The Subhuman Analogue, the Strategy and the Technique. In S. G. Armitage (Ed.), *Behavior Modification Techniques in the Treatment of Emotional Disorders*. Battle Creek, VA Publication, 1967. P. 22.

54. Levis, D. J., and Carrera, R. M.   Effects of 10 hours of implosive therapy in the treatment of outpatients. *Journal of Abnormal Psychology* 6:504, 1967.

55. Lewis, A. J.   Problems of obsessional illness. *Proceedings of the Royal Society of Medicine* 29:325, 1936.
56. Litvak, S. B.   A comparison of two brief group behavior therapy techniques on the reduction of avoidance behavior. *Psychological Record* 19:329, 1969.
57. London, P.   *The Modes and Morals of Psychotherapy*. New York: Holt, Rinehart & Winston, 1964.
58. Lott, D. R., and Carrera, R. N.   The effect of group implosive therapy on snake phobias. Unpublished manuscript, 1971.
59. Malleson, N.   Panic and phobia: Possible method of treatment. *Lancet* 1:225, 1959.
60. Marcia, J. E., Rubin, B. M., and Efran, J. S.   Systematic desensitization: Expectancy change or counterconditioning. *Journal of Abnormal Psychology* 74:382, 1969.
61. Marks, I. M.   *Fears and Phobias*. London: William Heinemann, and New York: Academic, 1969.
62. Marks, I. M., Boulougouris, J. C., and Marset, P.   Flooding versus desensitization in the treatment of phobic patients: A cross-over study. *British Journal of Psychiatry* 119:353, 1971.
63. Masserman, J. H.   *Behavior and Neurosis*. Chicago: University of Chicago Press, 1943.
64. Mathews, A. M.   Paper to Conference on Behavioural Engineering, Dublin, September 1969.
65. Maupin, E. W.   Zen Buddhism: A psychological review. *Journal of Consulting Psychology* 26:362, 1962.
66. Mealiea, W. M., Jr.   The comparative effectiveness of systematic desensitization with implosive therapy in the elimination of snake phobia. Ph.D. dissertation, University of Missouri, Columbia, 1967.
67. Melamed, B. G.   The habituation of psychophysiological response to tones, and to filmed fear stimuli under varying conditions of instructional set. Ph.D. dissertation, University of Wisconsin, 1969.
68. Meyer, V.   Modification of expectations in cases with obsessional rituals. *Behaviour Research and Therapy* 4:273, 1966.
69. Meyer, V., and Levy, R.   Behavioural treatment of a homosexual with compulsive rituals. *British Journal of Medical Psychology* 43:63, 1970.
70. Meyer, V., and Levy, R.   Treatment of obsessive-compulsive neurosis. *Proceedings of the Royal Society of Medicine* 1971, 64:1117, 1971.
71. Nelson, F.   Effects of chlorpromazine on fear extinction. *Jour-*

nal of Comparative and Physiological Psychology 64:496, 1967.

72. Noonam, J. R. An obsessive-compulsive reaction treated by induced anxiety. *American Journal of Psychotherapy* 25:293, 1971.

73. Overton, D. A. Dissociated learning in drug states (state dependent learning). In D. H. Efron et al. (Ed.), *Psychopharmacology: A Review of Progress 1957–67*. U. S. Public Health Service Publication No. 1836, 1968. Pp. 918–930.

74. Ovesey, L. The Phobic Reaction: A Psychodynamic Basis for Classification and Treatment. In G. S. Goldman and D. Shapiro (Eds.), *Developments in Psychoanalysis at Columbia University*. New York: Hafner, 1966.

75. Perloff, B. Influence of muscular relaxation and positive imagery on extinction of avoidance behavior through systematic desensitization. Ph.D. dissertation, Stanford University, 1970.

76. Rachman, S. Studies in desensitization: II. Flooding. *Behaviour Research and Therapy* 4:1, 1966.

77. Rachman, S. Treatment by prolonged exposure to high intensity stimulation. *Behaviour Research and Therapy* 7:295, 1969.

78. Rachman, S., Hodgson, R., and Marks, I. M. Treatment of chronic obsessive-compulsive neurosis. *Behaviour Research and Therapy* 9:237, 1971.

79. Rimm, D. C., and Mahoney, M. J. The application of reinforcement and participant modelling procedures in the treatment of snake-phobic behaviour. *Behaviour Research and Therapy* 7:369, 1969.

80. Ritter, B. The group desensitization of childrens' snake phobias using vicarious and contact desensitization procedures. *Behaviour Research and Therapy* 6:1, 1968.

81. Rudolf, G. Deconditioning and time therapy. *Journal of Mental Science* 107:1097, 1961.

82. Schubot, E. D. The influence of hypnotic and muscular relaxation in systematic desensitization of phobias. Ph.D. dissertation, Stanford, August, 1966.

83. Shearman, R. W. Response-contingent CS termination in the extinction of avoidance learning. *Behaviour Research and Therapy* 8:227, 1970.

84. Sherman, A. R. Therapy of maladaptive fear-motivated behaviour in the rat by the systematic gradual withdrawal of a fear-reducing drug. *Behaviour Research and Therapy* 5:121, 1967.

85. Sifneos, P. E.   Learning to Solve Emotional Problems: A Controlled Study of Short-Term Anxiety-Provoking Psychotherapy. In R. Porter (Ed.), *The Role of Learning in Psychotherapy*. Ciba Foundation Symposium. London: Churchill, 1968.

86. Sipprelle, C. N.   Induced anxiety. *Psychotherapy: Theory, Research and Practice* 4:36, 1967.

87. Smith, R. E., and Sharpe, T. M.   Treatment of a school phobia with implosive therapy. *Journal of Consulting and Clinical Psychology* 35:239, 1970.

88. Stampfl, T. G.   Implosive Therapy: The Theory, the Subhuman Analogue, the Strategy and the Technique: Part I. The Theory. In S. G. Armitage (Ed.), *Behavior Modification Techniques in the Treatment of Emotional Disorders*. Battle Creek: V.A. Publication, 1967. Pp. 22–37.

89. Stampfl, T. G., and Levis, D. J.   Essentials of implosive therapy: A learning-theory-based psychodynamic behavioral therapy. *Journal of Abnormal Psychology* 72:496, 1967.

90. Stern, R.   Treatment of a case of obsessional neurosis using thought-stopping technique. *British Journal of Psychiatry* 117:441, 1970.

91. Stewart, K.   Dream Theory in Malaya. In C. Tart (Ed.), *Altered States of Consciousness*. New York: John Wiley, 1969. Chap. 9.

92. Strahley, D. F.   Systematic desensitization and counterphobic treatment of an irrational fear of snakes. Ph.D. dissertation, University of Tennessee, University Microfilms No. 66-5366, 1965.

93. Watson, J. P., and Marks, I. M.   Relevant and irrelevant fear in flooding—A crossover study of phobic patients. *Behavior Therapy* 2:275, 1971.

94. Watson, J. P., Gaind, R., and Marks, I. M.   Prolonged exposure: A rapid treatment for phobias. *British Medical Journal* 1:13, 1971.

95. Weinberger, N. M.   Effect of detainment on extinction of avoidance responses. *Journal of Comparative and Physiological Psychology* 60:135, 1965.

96. Welch, H. J., and Krapfl, J. E.   Order of stimulus presentation in desensitization. Paper to Annual Convention of Midwest Psychological Association, Cincinnati, May, 1970.

97. Willis, R. W.   A study of the comparative effectiveness of systematic desensitization and implosive therapy. Ph.D. dissertation, University of Tennessee, University Microfilms No. 69-7189, 1968.

98. Willis, R. W., and Edwards, J. A.   A study of the comparative

effectiveness of systematic desensitization and implosive therapy. *Behaviour Research and Therapy* 7:387, 1969.

99. Wilson, G. D.   Efficacy of "flooding" procedures in desensitization of fear: A theoretical note. *Behaviour Research and Therapy* 5:138, 1967.

100. Wolpe, J.   *Psychotherapy by Reciprocal Inhibition*. Stanford: Stanford University Press, 1958.

101. Wolpe, J., and Lazarus, A. A.   *Behavior Therapy Techniques*. New York: Pergamon, 1966.

102. Wolpin, M., and Raines, J.   Visual imagery, expected roles and extinction as possible factors in reducing fear and avoidance behaviour. *Behaviour Research and Therapy* 4:25, 1966.

Annotated Therapeutic Index

The following are behaviors and disorders that have been effectively managed with behavior therapy techniques. If more than one technique has been found to be effective in dealing with a particular behavior or disorder, the additional techniques have been listed. Page numbers refer to descriptions of a technique applied to the specific problem. Where there is no number, refer to the subject index (e.g., Systematic desensitization, Positive reinforcement) for a general discussion of the procedure. Cross-references (e.g., Assertive Behavior [training in]. *See also* Blushing, Assertive training) apply to listings in the therapeutic index.

Alcoholism
  Aversion therapy
    Chemical aversion, 93–94, 99–101
    Covert sensitization (verbal aversion), 95, 102
    Shock, with or without aversion relief, 92
    Shock used in an operant avoidance paradigm, 101–102
    Note: Interpersonal anxiety and family problems also require attention, 103–104
Anorexia (in schizophrenic patients)
  Extinction, removal of attention for not eating, 67
Anorexia nervosa
  Shaping, reinforcement of eating behavior usually combined with extinction for all somatic complaints, 39–40, 49
  Systematic desensitization, of anxiety themes associated with eating
Aphonia (hysterical)
  Aversion therapy, shock (in Avoidance paradigm)
  Shaping, reinforcement of increasingly loud vocalization
  Systematic desensitization, of anxiety themes associated with speaking
Assertive behavior (training in). *See also* Blushing, Assertive training
  Behavior rehearsal (Role playing), includes Feedback and Shaping, often with Modeling
Astasia-abasia
  Shaping, of normal walking behavior

Asthma
  Systematic desensitization, with or without assertive training, 143
Attention-seeking behaviors
  Extinction, removal of social reinforcement for such behavior, 48–50
  Punishment, Time-out (with Positive reinforcement for appropriate behavior)
Autism (childhood)
  Shaping, of appropriate behavior, 79
  Modeling, combined with Positive reinforcement
  Shock, in Avoidance training or Punishment paradigm, combined with Positive
    reinforcement, 113–114

Bedtime disturbances
  Extinction, removal of social attention
Blindness (hysterical)
  Avoidance training or Shaping using a light as signal to allow avoidance of
    shock *or* access to reinforcement
Blushing
  Assertive training. This technique consists of a mixture of Role playing, Model-
    ing, and social Reinforcement aimed at teaching appropriate interpersonal
    assertiveness. Usually the therapist develops several situations in which the
    patient has failed to demonstrate the necessary assertive behavior. These
    situations are rehearsed with the therapist, who gives feedback as to the
    appropriateness of both verbal and nonverbal behavior for that situation.
    The therapist may also demonstrate more appropriate behavior to the
    patient, who then rehearses that behavioral sequence. Videotape replay may
    also be used to advantage in this procedure. Although this appears to be
    a very promising technique no controlled study of its efficacy has appeared
  Desensitization, of social anxiety themes
Bowel retention
  Operant conditioning, Shaping appropriate bowel behavior
Bruxism (teeth gnashing)
  Assertive training. *See* Blushing, Assertive training
  Relaxation training

Compulsive Behavior
  Response prevention (Apotrepic therapy), prevention of the compulsive ritual,
    199–200
  Flooding, exposure to fear-evoking stimuli in reality or in fantasy, with or with-
    out modeling, 181, 200–204
  Systematic desensitization, to anxiety themes maintaining the compulsive rituals,
    142–143
  Paradoxical intention, 179–180
  Aversion therapy, Punishment, shock contingent upon the compulsion

Deafness (hysterical)
  Avoidance training, tone used as discriminative stimulus for avoidance response,
    i.e., the patient can make use of sound to avoid a painful shock delivered
    10 seconds after a tone
Delinquent behavior
  Token economy, reinforcement of appropriate behaviors and punishment of
    inappropriate behavior by response cost or time-out, 80–81, 116

Aversion therapy, covert sensitization or shock (used most frequently with discrete behaviors, e.g., shoplifting), 117
Delusions (in schizophrenia)
    Extinction, removal of social attention for delusional utterances, combined with positive reinforcement of appropriate speech content, 47–48, 67
    Reinforcement of nondelusional speech (often in a token economy), 36–38, 67
Disruptive behavior (in children)
    At home
        Extinction, together with positive reinforcement of appropriate behavior
        Punishment, e.g., Time-out, noise, slaps, combined with positive reinforcement of appropriate behavior
    At school
        Extinction, used with positive reinforcement of adaptive behavior, 48, 80–81
        Time-out, 116–117
        Token economy, 80–81
Disruptive behavior (in adults)
    Aversion therapy, shock, 117
    Extinction, 47, 50
    Time-out, 117
Drug addiction
    Aversion therapy
        Shock (using portable shock apparatus) contingent on impulse to take drug
        Apomorphine in a classical conditioning paradigm (as in Alcoholism, 93–94, 101–102), may be combined with Desensitization of social anxiety themes, and Assertive training
Dysmenorrhea
    Systematic desensitization
Dyspareunia
    Systematic desensitization

Encopresis
    Shaping regular bowel habit
Enuresis
    Classical conditioning (most frequently the bell and blanket technique)

Frigidity
    Systematic desensitization, 143

Gambling
    Aversion therapy, shock in a Punishment paradigm
Gilles de la Tourette syndrome
    Negative practice. *See* Tics, Negative practice
    Time-out contingent upon deviant behavior
Gross stress reaction (combat)
    Flooding in fantasy (implosion)
    Systematic desensitization of fear themes

Hallucination
    Time-out contingent on hallucinating, if this behavior can clearly be defined by observation
Hemiparesis (hysterical)
    Avoidance training (or escape)

Hiccoughing
Aversion therapy, shock in a Punishment or Avoidance paradigm
Hoarding behavior (in schizophrenia)
Stimulus satiation, 68–69
Hyperactivity (in children)
Extinction, with reinforcement for appropriate behavior, 51
Shaping attentive and other incompatible behaviors using points or tokens

Impotence
Systematic desensitization of sexual anxiety-evoking themes
Insomnia
Systematic desensitization of anxiety themes
Isolate behavior (in children)
Extinction with positive reinforcemen for appropriate behavior (social approach), 48–49

Kleptomania
Aversion therapy
Shock in a punishment paradigm, 117
Covert sensitization

Masturbation (compulsive)
Aversion therapy, shock (to verbal cues)
Mutism (elective)
Shaping vocalization, 35

Nailbiting
Negative practice. *See* Tics, Negative practice
Neurodermatitis
Extinction, removing attention for scratching behavior, 48–49
Punishment, shock contingent on scratching
Nightmare
Systematic desensitization, of anxiety themes of the nightmare

Obesity
Aversion therapy
Covert sensitization, 112–113
Shock, in an avoidance or punishment paradigm, 112
Self-control procedures (based on operant conditioning principles), 113
Obsessional thoughts
Aversion therapy, shock in a Punishment paradigm or thought stopping
Systematic desensitization of phobic themes related to obsessional thoughts, 14£

Paralysis (hysterical)
Avoidance training, moves to avoid shock
Shaping movement
Pervasive anxiety (guilt feelings and feelings of devaluation)
Systematic desensitization of relevant guilt and anxiety themes
Phobias
Flooding (in imagination and reality), 181–184, 186–192, 196–198
Paradoxical intention, 179–180
Shaping, reinforced practice, 9–11, 32–34, 40–44, 195
Systematic desensitization, 133–138, 142–144

Premature ejaculation
  Systematic desensitization of sexual anxiety themes

Remedial education
  With low achievers
    Token economy, 80
  With retarded children
    Modeling
    Shaping, 80

Sadistic fantasy
  Aversion therapy
    Covert sensitization, 108
    Shock in a Punishment paradigm with positive counterconditioning (mastur-
      bation) to appropriate stimuli
Scratching
  Extinction, 48–49
Screaming
  Time-out
Self-care (training in)
  Modeling
  Shaping (token system), 73–74, 80
Self-control (training in)
  Application of Covert sensitization scenes by patients in order to control urges
    to perform deviant behaviors
  Self-reinforcement, 21
Self-injury
  Punishment using shock, 114–115
  Or contingent application of time-out, 113–114
Sexual Deviations. *Note:* Behavior rehearsal (Role playing), Assertive training, and
    Modeling are often used together with the aversive techniques to build
    socially appropriate behaviors replacing the deviant behavior weakened or
    removed by aversion techniques
  Exhibitionism
    Assertive training. *See* Blushing, Assertive training
    Punishment, shock contingent on fantasy of behavior, 109
    Systematic desensitization
  Fetishism
    Aversion therapy, shock contingent on fantasy and/or actual behavior, 106–
      108
    Systematic desensitization to sexual anxiety themes
  Homosexuality
    Assertive training
      Avoidance training or classical conditioning, 105–106
      Covert sensitization, 95, 106
    Systematic desensitization, of heterosexual anxiety themes, 143
  Masochism
    Aversion therapy, shock contingent on fantasies, 108
  Pedophilia
    Aversion therapy, shock contingent on fantasies of behavior and slides of
      erotic stimuli
    Covert sensitization

Sexual Deviations—*Continued*
  Sadism
    Aversive therapy, verbal aversion, 108
  Transvestism
    Aversion therapy, shock applied in a punishment paradigm both to cross-
      dressing and fantasies of the deviant behavior, 106–107
Smoking
  Aversion therapy
    Covert sensitization, 111
    Shock used in a punishment paradigm, 110
    Smoke used in a punishment paradigm, 111–112
  Contingency management. In this procedure patients learn to make reinforcers
    in their natural environment contingent upon behavior which they wish
    to strengthen [3]. Thus a student with difficulty in studying might make
    pleasurable activities such as reading a novel, watching television, or going
    out, contingent upon a certain amount of studying. Although a number of
    clinical examples of the use of this technique have been published [4, 5] no
    controlled examination of its effectiveness has appeared
  Contract management, 112
      This procedure is used mainly in the treatment of families as a mechanism
      by which contingencies can be applied to the behavior of a particular
      family member. A contract is drawn up between that person and other key
      family members which defines the contingencies for certain behaviors. Thus,
      an adolescent with unruly behavior and poor school attendance might con-
      tract to demonstrate cooperative behavior and perfect school attendance.
      For each day on which these behaviors are shown he might earn a money
      allowance, use of the family car, or other privileges which he desires. Ex-
      hibition of unruly behavior, which would be defined precisely, would lead
      to loss of all or part of these privileges for a particular time. Contracts
      often require reworking when first applied, but may prove a useful vehicle
      for a family to work out its problems in a concrete way
  Systematic desensitization, to cues or anxiety themes associated with smoking
Social interaction (training in)
  Assertive training
  Modeling
  Shaping, 32–34
  Token economy, 74–78
Somnambulism
  Assertive training
Speech (reinstatement or increase in rate)
  Shaping, 32–34, 35
  Token economy
Spelling
  Positive reinforcement for correct spellings with Extinction of incorrect at-
    tempts
Stealing. *See* Delinquent behavior
Stuttering
  Aversion therapy, using Avoidance training in which patient avoids noise by
    talking more fluently
  Shaping, normal speech

Tantrums
  Hair-pulling
    Aversion therapy, shock or time-out, 113–114
  Head-banging
    Aversion therapy, noise or shock, time-out, 113–114
  Screaming and/or crying
    Extinction, removal of social attention
    Aversion therapy, Time-out
  Self-injurious behavior (other than the preceding)
    Aversion therapy, shock, used in a punishment paradigm, 115
    Time-out
  Sulking
    Extinction, 50
Tics
  Aversion therapy, noise, used in a Punishment or Avoidance training paradigm
  Negative practice. This technique first described by Dunlap [2] has been used
    mainly in the treatment of tics [1, 2, 6]. The procedure consists of encour-
    aging the patient to reproduce the movement of the tic as exactly as pos-
    sible and repeating this movement many times in sessions of from half- to
    one-hour duration. Repeated practice of this kind has been shown to lessen
    the frequency of both the voluntary and involuntary occurrence of tics,
    and several successful case reports have been published [1, 2, 6]
Torticollis
  Aversion therapy, shock, in a passive avoidance paradigm
  Shaping, normal head movements
Truancy
  Shaping, in a token system with or without a punishment technique, such as
    response cost

Vaginismus
  Systematic desensitization of sexual anxiety themes
Vocal Nodules (resulting from continued hypertension of the laryngeal muscula-
    ture)
  Systematic desensitization
Vomiting
  Aversion therapy, shock, 115; or Time-out
  Extinction, removal of attention for vomiting, 49–50

Withdrawal
  Shaping, reinforcement of social interaction, 32–34

REFERENCES

1. Agras, W. S., and Marshall, C. The application of negative practice to spas-
   modic torticollis. *American Journal of Psychiatry* 122:579, 1965.
2. Dunlap, K. *Habits, Their Making and Unmaking.* New York: Liverwright,
   1932.
3. Homme, L. E. Perspectives in psychology: XXIV. Control of coverants, the
   operants of the mind. *Psychological Record* 15:501, 1965.
4. Johnson, W. G. Some applications of Homme's coverant control therapy: Two
   case reports. *Behavior Therapy* 2:240, 1971.

5. Mahoney, M. J.   The self management of covert behavior: A case study. *Behavior Therapy* 2:275, 1971.
6. Yates, A. J.   The application of learning theory to the treatment of tics. *Journal of Abnormal Social Psychology* 56:175, 1958.

Subject Index

Aggressive behavior, 47, 50, 80, 116, 117
Agoraphobia, 9–11, 40, 141, 143, 178, 189, 191
Alcoholism
  antabuse in, 104
  apomorphine therapy in, 99
  aversion therapy in, 5, 89, 99–104
  group therapy in, 100
  social factors in, 103
  succinylcholine in, 101
  verbal aversion in, 102
Analogue experiments, 139–140, 165–174
Anorexia
  nervosa, 39–40, 49
  in schizophrenia, 67
Antabuse, 104
Anxiety
  conditioned, 13–14, 129–131, 158–159
  drug effect on, 146, 163
  extinction of, 14, 159–163, 182
  habituation of, 170. See also Habituation
  heterosexual, 143
  hierarchy, 140
  induced, 157, 185
  neurotic, 178, 182
  role in flooding, 173
  systematic desensitization for, 127–128
Apomorphine, 14, 93, 99, 105
Apotrepic therapy, 199–204
Arugamama, 157
Assertive training, 216
Astasia-abasia, 41
Asthma, 143
Attention seeking behavior, 47, 48–50, 80–81, 105
Autistic children, 79, 113–115

Autonomic
  arousal, 129–130, 159, 173, 187, 190–191, 194, 197–198
  conditioning, 13–14, 18, 129–131, 158–159
Aversion relief, 92–93, 105, 106
Aversion therapy. See also Aversive stimuli
  clinical application, 99–118
  overview of, 87–90, 118–120
  paradigms for application of, 16–17, 87, 91–93
  permanence, 119–120
  side effects, 17, 97–99
  time-out, 50, 95–96, 113, 116, 117
Aversive stimuli
  chemical, 14, 93–94, 99, 101, 105
  choice of, 97
  electrical (shock), 4, 94, 101, 105, 106, 107, 109, 115–116, 117, 118
  ethical considerations, 88, 116
  noise, 96, 97
  side effects of, 97–99
  smell, 96, 113
  smoke, 111
  social, 88
  verbal, 95, 102, 106, 108, 111
Avoidance behavior, 22, 131, 159, 160, 162
  extinction of, 159–163
Avoidance training, 16, 87, 92, 129–131, 158–159

Behavioral analysis, 9, 31–32, 52, 59, 63–64, 73–75, 83
Behavioral contract. See Contract Management
Behavioral measurement, 10, 27, 31–33, 59, 64–66, 75, 88, 166, 195

Behavior modification
  aims, 9, 10, 30–32, 52, 60–61, 63–64,
    72–74, 83, 128, 153, 154, 205
  history, 3–6, 175–181
  principles, 13–22
  procedure, 9–11
Behavioral objectives, 9, 27, 31–32, 59,
    64, 72–73
Behavioral therapies. *See also specific
    type, e.g.,* Apotrepic therapy;
    Aversion therapy; Covert sensiti-
    zation; Desensitization; Flooding
    (Implosion); Modeling; Paradox-
    ical intention; Practice; Response
    prevention; Role playing; Shap-
    ing; *and* Behavior modification;
    *specific disorder in Therapeutic
    Index*
  definition of, 6–7
  development of, 2–6
  types, 1, 6–7
  vs. psychoanalysis, 7–13, 60, 63
  with psychotherapy, 148
Brevital, 146–147

Catharsis, 156, 173, 184
Chlorpromazine, 167
Classical conditioning. *See* Condition-
    ing, classical
Claustrophobia, 41–42
Cognitive control, 11, 18–23, 28, 95, 119,
    138, 171–172, 177, 179, 205
Compulsive behavior, 17, 32–34, 142–
    143, 179–180, 200–204. *See also*
    Obsessive-compulsive neurosis
Conditioning
  classical, 13–14, 87, 89, 91, 99, 101,
    105, 129
  operant, 6, 9–11, 14–18, 27, 30, 52, 59,
    64, 87, 91, 144
Confrontation, 177, 181
Contingency management, 111, 220
Contract management, 21, 61, 113, 220
Counterconditioning, 5–6, 128, 132–133,
    144, 147, 154, 172. *See also* Re-
    ciprocal inhibition
Counterphobic treatment, 156
Covert sensitization, 1, 7, 88, 95, 97,
    102, 106, 108, 111, 113
Cross-dressing, 106–107

Deconditioning, 156

Delinquent behavior, 80–81, 116
Delusions
  belief, 37
  speech, 36–38, 47–48, 67
Dermatitis, 48–49, 114
Desensitization
  analogue studies of, 139, 172–173
  Brevital in, 145
  contact, 156, 174
  controlled clinical studies, 141–142,
    172–173, 188–192, 195–196
  efficacy of, 111, 127, 139–142, 153
  hierarchy contruction in, 135–136
  indications, 142–144
  in vivo, 144
  mechanism, 6, 23, 128, 153
  procedure of, 5, 133–139, 154
  with psychotherapy, 148
  relaxation training in, 133–135
  theory of, 129–133
  uncontrolled studies, 141
  variations of, 144–148
  vicarious, 174
Discriminative learning, 17
Disruptive behavior, 47, 48, 50, 80–81,
    116–117
Drugs
  addiction, 118, 216
  apomorphine, 14, 87, 93, 99, 105
  behavioral effects, 72, 163
  Brevital, 146–147
  chlorpromazine, 163
  emetine, 93
  relaxation effects, 128, 150, 163
  sodium amytal, 163
  succinylcholine, 101
  sulfureted potash, 113

Emetine, 93
Ethics in aversive therapy, 88, 116
Exhibitionism, 109
Expectancy, 12, 19–20, 43, 110, 138,
    171–172, 203
Exposure
  graduated, 153, 156, 173–174
  prolonged, 167, 196
Extinction
  animal experiments, 45, 132, 159–164
  burst, 10–11, 16, 28, 33
  definition of, 14, 16, 28
  procedure, 14, 16, 45–46

therapeutic application, 29, 47–51
  for neuroses, 48–51
  for psychoses, 47–48

Fading, 17
Family
  problems, 29, 51, 61, 220
  as therapists, 29, 32, 51, 61, 153
Fear
  acquisition, 13–14, 129–131, 158–159
  darkness, 175
  dreams of, 176, 177
  extinction, 14, 127–128, 130, 159–163, 182
  height, 43–44, 131, 136, 173–174
  hierarchies, 135–136
  public speaking, 139
  rats, 140
  relevant vs. irrelevant imagery, 192–195
  snake, 140, 171–174
  spider, 187, 196
  survey schedule, 128, 165
  test, 140, 178
  vacuum cleaner, 175
Feedback, 20, 28, 41, 67, 138
Fetishism, 106–108
Flooding (Implosion), 151–206
  analogue studies of, 165–174
  controlled clinical studies of, 186–198, 200–204
  covert escape from, 170
  definition of, 1, 7, 23, 151, 154
  duration of, 167–169
  in fantasy, 167, 181–184, 192–195
  mechanism of, 170–171
  overview, 204–206
  practice in, 173–174
  psychodynamic cues in, 151, 181–182
  in reality, 166, 186, 188–189, 196–198, 201–203
  treatment of
    obsessive-compulsive neurosis, 199–204
    phobia, 181–198
Frigidity, 143

Gambling, 118
Glass breaking, 117
Graduated exposure, 174
Group therapy, 100

Habituation, 128, 135–136, 170–171
Halfway house, 61
Hierarchies, 132
High intensity stimulation, 156
Hoarding behavior, 68–69
Homosexual behavior, 104–106, 143
  aversion treatment of, 4, 95, 106–108
  fading in treatment of, 18
  social factors, 105
Homosexual fantasy, 108
Hypnosis, 19, 102, 134, 157

Imagery, prolonged, 156
Imitative learning. *See* Modeling
Implosive therapy. *See* Flooding (Implosion)
Induced anger, 184
Induced anxiety, 157, 185
Instructional control, 12, 19, 28, 34, 38, 138, 171
Instrumental conditioning. *See* Conditioning, operant

Kleptomania, 117

Masochism, 108
Massed practice, 157
Measurement, 10, 27, 31–33, 64–66, 75, 88, 166, 195
Meditation, 180
Mental Retardation, 6, 49, 80, 113–115
Methohexital sodium (Brevital), in systemic desensitization, 128
Modeling, 21–23, 144, 153, 156, 174, 200–202
Morita therapy, 180
Mutism, 35

Negative practice, 221
Negative reinforcement. *See* Reinforcement, negative
Negative reinforcers, 15, 87–88, 93–97
Neurosis. *See also* Agoraphobia; Anorexia, nervosa; Astasia-abasia; Claustrophobia; Compulsive behavior; Obsessive-compulsive neurosis; Phobia; School phobia
  anxiety, 14, 128, 139, 178, 179, 185
  experimental, 4, 127, 129–133, 157–163
  extinction, application to, 48–51
  reinforcement application, 38–45

Obesity, 112–113
Obsessive-compulsive neurosis, 17, 32–34, 142–143, 179–180, 200–204
  treatment of
    apotrepic therapy, 199
    desensitization, 142–143
    rituals, 152–199
    shaping, 32–34
Operant conditioning. *See* Conditioning, operant

Paradoxical intention, 157, 179–180
Pavlovian conditioning. *See* Conditioning, classical
Pedophilia, 106
Phobia, 9–11, 32–34, 40–44, 133–138, 142–144, 179–180, 181–184, 186–192, 196–198. *See also* Agoraphobia; Claustrophobia; Fear; School phobia
Positive reinforcement. *See* Reinforcement, positive
Positive reinforcers, 6, 15, 28, 31, 59, 67, 70–71, 74, 77
Practice, 9–10, 12, 28, 32–34, 40–44, 128, 173–174, 195–196
Premack principle, 70
Progressive relaxation, 133–135
Prolonged exposure, 196–198
Psychoanalysis, 4
Psychoanalytic psychotherapy
  aims, 4, 7–9, 52–53, 60, 63, 66
  population treated, 63
  results, 5, 128, 142
  similarities to behavior therapy, 11–13, 22, 177–178
Psychological testing, 64–66
Psychotherapy, supportive, 148, 178. *See also* Psychoanalytic psychotherapy
Punishment, 16, 81, 87, 91, 95, 106, 107, 109, 111, 114, 127
  side effects, 97–99

Reality testing, 46, 130, 157, 161, 164
Reciprocal inhibition, 6, 128, 132, 139, 154, 172
Reflex conditioning. *See* Conditioning, classical
Reinforced practice, 43–44, 144, 156, 195–196

Reinforcement
  negative, 16, 81, 87, 91–99, 106, 107, 109, 111, 114, 127
  positive
    procedure, 31–32
    therapeutic application
      in neuroses, 38–44
      in psychoses, 35–38
  self, 21
  social, 3, 9–11, 28, 39, 40–41, 43, 49, 50, 67, 114, 138, 195, 201
Reinforcers
  conditioned, 71
  negative, 15, 87–88, 93–97
  positive, 6, 15, 28, 31, 59, 67, 70–71, 77
  token, 27–28, 32–34, 59, 71
Relaxation training, 133–135, 200
Remedial education, 80
Respondent conditioning. *See* Conditioning, classical
Response cost, 81, 97
Response prevention, 152, 199–204
  in animals, 157–163
Rogerian therapy, 12
Role playing, 22, 29, 153, 216

Sadism, 108
Satiation, 68
Schizophrenia, 35–38, 47–48, 67–69, 72, 82, 117, 144, 183. *See also* Anorexia; Autistic children; Delusions; Glass breaking; Hoarding behavior; Mutism
School phobia, 176, 184
Scratching, 48–49
Self-care, 3, 48, 67, 73
Self-control, 21, 90, 113, 119
Self-injurious behavior, 48, 69, 113–116
Self-reinforcement, 21
Senoi culture, 176
Sexual deviance, 88, 95, 104–110, 143. *See also* Exhibitionism; Fetishism; Homosexual behavior; Masochism; Pedophilia; Sadism; Transvestism
Shaping
  in agoraphobia, 9–11
  astasia-abasia, 41
  claustrophobia, 41
  crowd phobia, 42

height phobia, 43
procedure, 15, 31
social interaction, 32–34
vocalization, 35–36
Shock. *See* Aversive stimuli, electrical
Smoking behavior, 111–112
Social reinforcement, 3, 9–11, 28, 39, 40–41, 43, 49, 50, 67, 114, 138, 195, 201
Social withdrawal, 32, 50
Sodium amytal, 167
Spontaneous recovery, 14, 138
Stealing, 117
Stimulus control, 17, 74–75
Stimulus discrimination, 17, 47, 48, 50, 80–81, 116–117
Stimulus generalization, 13
Stimulus satiation, 68–69
Succinylcholine, 101
Sulfereted potash, 113
Symptom removal, 9, 52, 63–64
Systematic desensitization. *See* Desensitization

Tantrums, 50, 113–114, 115
Therapy. See Behavioral therapies; Psychoanalytic psychotherapy; *ind Therapeutic Index*
Time-out technique, 95–96
Token economy
at Anna State Hospital, 72–79
definition, 62
methodological problems, 69–70
preliminary research in, 67–69
procedure, 67–83
use with adults, 82
use with children and adolescents, 79–82
Transfer of training, 13, 29, 32, 36, 37, 90, 119, 128, 138
Transvestism, 106–107

Underachievers, 80

Verbal aversion. *See* Covert sensitization
Verbal conditioning, 38
Vomiting, 39, 49, 115

Work therapy, 75–78

Zen Buddhism, 180–181